Licence to Grow

VU University Press is an imprint of

VU Boekhandel / Uitgeverij bv
De Boelelaan 1105
1081 HV Amsterdam
The Netherlands

info@vu-uitgeverij.nl
www.vuuitgeverij.nl

Design jacket: René van der Vooren, Amsterdam
Type setting: JAPES, Amsterdam (Jaap Prummel)
Cartoons: Lex Dirkse

ISBN 978 90 8659 541 9
NUR 774, 807, 808

Licence to Grow

Innovating Sustainable Development by Connecting Values

An Insight in the
Connected Value Development Approach
for Wicked Problems

Barbara Regeer, Sander Mager, Yvonne van Oorsouw

TransForum & Athena Institute
VU University Press, Amsterdam

This book is a co-production of TransForum and Athena Institute/VU University Amsterdam, under endorsement of Henk van Latesteijn and Joske Bunders.

It is co-developed and co-authored by Barbara Regeer (Athena Institute), Sander Mager (TransForum) and Yvonne van Oorsouw (consultant). This book would not have been possible without the contributions of many people. The authors wish to thank all of them for their enthousiasm, patience and help. The making of this book is financially supported by TransForum, through the project Connected Value Development (KP-119), and VU University Amsterdam.

Text and content contributions
Christine Dedding: Stubborn Reality
Laura Hartman: The Guide (Chapt. 2, 3 and 4), Stubborn Reality, The Bubbles
Janine van der Kraats: Stubborn Reality
Hans Mabelis: Introduction, The Guide, Stubborn Reality, The Bubbles
Prisma & Partners (Theo Groen, Jan Wouter Vasbinder): Introduction and box 1.1, The Guide (Chapt. 2 and box 2.4), The Bubbles

Editors
Hans Mabelis, Zoe Goldstein, Andrew Gebhardt, G. Daniel and Dana Bugel-Shunra

Thanks to
We would like to thank everybody who participated in the projects on which the Connected Value Development approach is based, for sharing their ideas, thoughts, dreams and struggles. We would also like to thank Anne-Claire van Altvorst, Karin Andeweg, Jacqueline Broerse, Rik Eweg, Thijs den Hertog, Anne-Charlotte Hoes, Francien de Jonge, Wanda Konijn, Frank Kupper, Renee Liesveld, Daniel Puente, Lia Spaans, Janine de Zeeuw.

Special thanks to
James M. Bradburne and the Fondazione Palazzo Strozzi

Table of contents

Prologue

Sustainable development, innovation and organisational change are intimately intertwined. All efforts to achieve a more sustainable development will sooner or later discover that improving the way in which we are doing things is not enough. If we look at the agricultural sector, we need to redesign the way in which agricultural production is set up, handled and organised. This calls for innovations, not only of hardware (the mode of production), but also of software (the way agricultural production is handled) and even of 'orgware' (the way in which agricultural production is organised and connected to other spheres). To get this done organisations need to change. This book describes the results of a long journey into the uncharted area of these types of change.

Years of hands on experience with attempts to attain a more sustainable development are the foundation of this book. Within the Athena Institute researchers have had considerable exposure to 'Learning in Action'. So, in these projects research did not hide itself behind the comfortable wall of observation and analysis, but all findings were immediately used to help improve the development process at hand. Within the TransForum programme dozens of practical experiments to redesign agricultural business in the direction of sustainable development revealed that entrepreneurs and other stakeholders have a tough job to overcome normal routines. To help them and others in this process the authors of this book describe an approach that will make a difference. With Connected Value Development the difficult process of innovation, of redesign and eventually of organisational learning becomes much more manageable, within the field of agriculture, but possibly also in other fields such as health care, climate change, or water management.

Next to their own practical experience the authors draw from a vast body of literature that contains little bits and pieces of the approach of Connected Value Development. In this book, however, a more or less complete picture is given. Providing a blueprint for Connected Value Development is not possible. Based on the as yet fragmented experiences with the approach, the authors were able to formulate guiding principles that help in shaping this approach in practice. With Connected Value Development this book opens up new modes of organising processes of innovation and redesign that will bring sustainable development several steps closer. We hope that you will be inspired by what is presented here and step in and start connecting values that together will constitute our common idea of sustainability. Not by dreaming about it, but by stepping out and doing it.

Prof.dr. Joske Bunders – Director Athena Institute
Dr. Henk C. van Latesteijn – CEO TransForum

Introduction

From Limits to Growth to a Licence to Grow

The 1972 Club of Rome report Limits to Growth[1] confronted the world with the consequences of unchecked industrial production: the depletion of natural resources. The impact of the report was huge and for a while some societal groups advocated a "zero growth" policy, effectively denying industry, or at least some types of industry, the right to grow and expand. In hindsight, the report can be seen as the first world-wide plea for *sustainable growth:* if and when economic growth and the creation of more, and more equitably distributed, wealth is to continue, it will have to be in a sustainable way.

One of the results of four decades of hard work by an increasing number of policymakers, societal organisations, entrepreneurs, and scientists on sustainable development is that we have become aware of the magnitude of the challenge. Many environmental and social problems are complex, stemming from multiple activities and interactions across societies and natural systems. In addition, many of the issues concerned are clouded with scientific uncertainty and controversy, both with regard to the causes and their future impact. Proposed solutions may produce unforeseen and unintended effects when implemented, and implementation itself is often – or even usually – fraught with enormous difficulties.

BOX 1.1 "Wicked problems"

Moving toward sustainable development requires concurrent changes at many levels and in different systems (ecological, economic, political, social, scientific), and this is all the more problematic since there is usually no agreement on long term objectives, values, or even facts.[2] It implies that individuals and institutions must make choices and trade-offs, often outside of their 'bubble', thus evoking considerable resistance. For these types of intractable,[2] unstructured,[3] persistent,[4] or 'wicked' problems, new strategies are needed.

In this box we explain the so-called 'wicked problems', a term coined in 1967 by C. West Churchman[5] to describe social planning problems that were complex, difficult to describe, resistant to logical analysis, contradictory, and continuously changing. This notion was later generalised by others,[6] from whom we summarise the following six prime characteristics:

1. You don't understand the problem until you have developed a solution

If we can formulate the problem by tracing it to its source, then we have thereby also formulated a solution. In other words: the problem cannot be defined until a solution has been found. The formulation of a wicked problem *is* the problem.

2. Every wicked problem is essentially novel and unique

Despite long lists of similarities between a current problem and a previous one, there may always be (and usually is) an additional distinguishing property that is of overriding importance. Consequently, every 'solution' will have to be custom designed.

3. A wicked problem has no stopping rule

Since there is no definitive description of 'the problem', there cannot be a state of affairs called 'the solution'. The problem solving process never ends; or rather, it ends when one runs out of resources, not when some pre-defined solution is reached.

4. Solutions to a wicked problem are not right or wrong

They may be 'good enough', 'better', or 'worse' in the eyes of some, but others, equally equipped, interested, and/or entitled to judge, are likely to differ. Each judges from his own societal context and according to his own values, interests, and ideological predilections.

5. Every solution to a wicked problem is a 'one shot operation'

Because every wicked problem is unique and novel, there is no opportunity to learn by trial and error; every attempt is consequential, leaving 'traces' that cannot be undone. Every attempt to correct the undesired consequences poses another set of wicked problems.

6. A wicked problem has no given alternative solutions

There may be no solutions, or there may be a host of potential solutions and probably many other unthought-of solutions. Thus, it is a matter of creativity to devise potential solutions, and a matter of judgement to determine which solutions are viable.

The above six points are not meant to form a definition; rather they are a set of characteristics which wicked problems may possess, ranging from one to all of them. 'Wickedness' is a matter of degree, with many compounded problems comprising wicked as well as solvable (at least in principle) parts. Usually, one cannot tell from the outset whether a problem will prove to be wicked; in fact, recognising the wickedness of a problem is a very important step in itself as it can mean the end of frustratingly unfruitful attempts to tackle it using tried and trusted linear problem solving methods.

In this book we concentrate on possible approaches to tackle this highly complex problem, and other problems carrying the same characteristics of complexity, and propose the Connected Value Development approach as a possible way to lend to economic activity, once more, a "licence to grow".

Complex, persistent problems

Living in a world of seemingly limitless technological means and burgeoning scientific inquiry, we nevertheless discover that some nuts remain hard to crack, and some problems just refuse to go away. Waiting lists in health care aren't getting any shorter, industrialisation continues to be a major source of environmental problems, diseases of a kind we thought under control are popping up again, a longer and increasingly opaque food chain threatens the safety of our most basic needs and finally, the depletion of our natural resources continues, at an ever faster pace even. All these problems are highly complex and thus difficult to analyse and fully understand. They do not fit into any specific scientific discipline, nor into any clearly defined policy domain. Moreover, because they are deeply embedded in our social, technical, and economic systems, this places heavy constraints on possible solutions. Finally, even when a solution presents itself, it doubtless requires the actions of different actors with differing interests, views, and needs. This not only makes any solution difficult to implement and manage, but also offers ample opportunity for endless loops, chicken-and-egg problems, and dead ends. As the need to get some grip on the fast paced changes in our modern society rises, the means to do so seem to become weaker.

For several decades, politicians, entrepreneurs, and academics have made appeals for new approaches to such persistent. They have argued for a more inclusive and responsive culture in science, government, and business, in which knowledge production is user driven, policymaking is interactive, and companies are socially responsible. In the agro business, for example, an increasing number of entrepreneurs have found a way to combine social and environmental responsibility with at least the start of a healthy profit; and universities are increasingly organised into institutes that focus on current and often urgent societal themes, as are funding programmes for scientific research. Besides changes in existing structures and institutions, new arrangements (networks, programmes, intermediaries) emerge in which actors from different domains work together to analyse complex issues and collaboratively implement strategies for change. Integration, participation, innovation, and long term objectives such as sustainability are key concepts in these new initiatives.

The 'Connected Value Development' approach presented in this book is based on practical experience with one of these programmes, TransForum, which has managed to realise innovations towards more sustainable agriculture. The lessons learnt were captured during a five year collaboration with the Athena Institute of VU University Amsterdam. The approach itself draws heavily on all the work done previously by others, their successes and failures. We will expound on it in later chapters, but the essence is easily summarised: the Connected Value Development process aims to create "3-P business propositions", that is: economic activities which, of course, return a Profit but are, at the same time, good for People and respectful of our Planet. In contrast to other approaches, like, for instance, the accumulation of legal restrictions, Connected Value Development seeks to make the 'people' and 'planet' values an *instrinsic part* of the business model.

Since the Club of Rome: a new social space

In fact, a lot has changed since the Club of Rome report. Governments have developed and implemented a host of measures, regulations, and laws to limit the depletion of the earth's resources and restrict or even undo the damage inflicted upon nature by human activity. CFCs are no longer used, waste is increasingly recycled, and unleaded petrol is the norm. Governments work together, ratifying international protocols on emission limits and trading in endangered species. Meanwhile, the number of research programmes into sustainable development has grown rapidly. Today many thousands of scientists work on sustainable solutions to practical problems, ranging from cleaner production methods to the psychology of changing habits engrained in our culture.

Businesses, too, are becoming increasingly aware of the urgency to change production processes and the value of the new venues created by public demand for a more responsible way to run this planet. At the time of the publication of The Limits to Growth, business people looked upon environmentalism as 'a green utopia full of happy tree huggers' and associated 'sustainability' mainly with additional costs. While a few idealists were willing to settle for lower profit in return for reduced environmental damage or social unrest, the vast majority had to be forced by ever stricter government regulations resulting from activist pressure and lobbying. In recent years, however, we have seen a complete turnaround. An increasing number of entrepreneurs are seeing the economic potential of investing in People and Planet values, whereby sustainable development itself becomes an added value, a real asset to their business and the key driver for innovation.

These fledgling developments should not blind us to what is still the global trend: the balance of power in our established institutions is shifting. Business, now organised in multi-national companies of gigantic proportions, finds ways to defy all but the most stringent regulations and profits from newly developed sophisticated methods to influence public opinion. The authority of both government and science has diminished and traditional institutions and mechanisms prove incapable of adequately addressing the new type of highly complex problems we face today. However, as the inadequacies of the old ways become ever more visible to many, new initiatives seem to spontaneously arise to fill the gap, the so-called 'institutional void'.[7] While enthousiasm for traditional voting seems to be in decline, new networks are being formed, enabled by the Internet, and new 'civic' alliances grow surprisingly powerful almost overnight in what has been called a 'third' or 'soft' social space. Traditional hierarchies are increasingly replaced –or rather supplemented– by a multitude of networks focusing on single issues.

Thus, on the one hand we see important policy changes within business, government, NGOs, and science, and on the other hand we witness an upcoming, loosely organised 'network society' where people from all over the world can find each other in order to work towards a common goal. This situation offers unique opportunities for the rise of innovative ways to tackle old problems. A key role here is played by entrepreneurs, eager to turn the dynamics of these changes to their advantage. However, they will need the active support of government, societal groups, and concerned individuals, precisely because an innovative approach often clashes with existing policies, regulations, and societal concerns. Furthermore, both government and business need the support of science, not only to solve practical problems but also to analyse and assist in processes of change.

Connected Value Development: a licence to grow

The institutional void provides opportunities: opportunities for new connections, new dominant values, and new types of business. The traditional dividing lines between business, policy, society, and science become blurred, as do the dividing lines between consumers and citizens, or between making profit and adding value to society. Entrepreneurs that manage to successfully connect a business agenda with a societal challenge have a 'licence to grow'.[8] This is not a literal or tangible licence, and no single individual or institution can award it. Rather, it results from incorporating different societal values into the primary process of a business, which in turn results in new values for society, in terms of the effects of the products and services created on issues such as equity, participation, health, and the environment.

The Connected Value Development approach introduced in this book aims to organise processes that result in added value for business *and* wider society alike. Connected Value Development is an approach that aims to transform perceived trade-offs into complements, by connecting values held by different stakeholders. As the transformation implied by sustainable development pervades all aspects of modern life and its institutions, close collaboration is required between scientists, policy makers, entrepreneurs, NGOs, citizens, and consumers. Connected Value Development is thus a multi-stakeholder process (see fig. 1a and 1b).

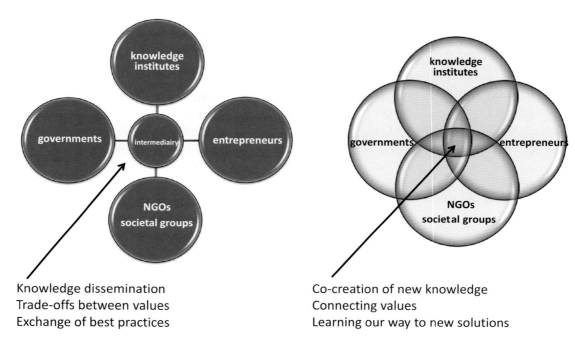

Knowledge dissemination
Trade-offs between values
Exchange of best practices

Co-creation of new knowledge
Connecting values
Learning our way to new solutions

FIGURE 1A *Different parties exchange and negotiate*
FIGURE 1B *Different parties interact and co-create*

A Connected Value Development process is often initiated outside of current, existing institutions in this newly created free space where enterprising actors (albeit from the worlds of business, policy, science, or society) develop and create new values together. The resulting 'value proposition' adds value for each of the participants and the organisations they represent. At a deeper level, this value co-creation process evokes system adaption: the changing of deeply rooted patterns of doing and thinking, and with it the grinding structures that we have built around these patterns.

Connected Value Development thus offers a *licence to grow*. It creates growth in a number of ways. First, it evokes growth by enlarging the perspective from which a problem is viewed: by looking at a problem in its wider context, the problem may vanish, or new types of solutions may emerge. Second, increasing the number of actors involved implies growth of the reservoir of knowledge (scientific and experiential) and values available to co-create innovations. Third, as formal boundaries around organisations (companies, municipalities, universities, etc.) blur, the organisations become larger, because as they become embedded in a wider network of actors these actors in turn become part of the primary processes of these organisations. Fourth, Connected Value Development requires a new type of working, with new competencies, a different view on leadership, mutual reflection, and collective learning. Participating in Connected Value Development processes evokes personal growth. And fifth, by turning trade-offs into complements, Connected Value Development connects economic growth to environmental and social values.

TransForum and Athena

The Connected Value Development approach emerged in the context of a Dutch innovation programme called TransForum. TransForum was established in 2004 to encourage the search for innovative value propositions that would contribute towards more sustainable development in agriculture. This development was needed because the agro-food sector was and is running into ecological and social barriers; and the reasons for this can be found among the same reasons that led to its recent successes. Dutch agriculture and rural areas have changed dramatically over the past century. Productivity soared due to new technologies, mechanisation, the increased use of chemicals, specialisation, and government policies that favoured maximising production. These changes allowed for fewer farmers with reduced labour demands to produce the majority of the agricultural product. This development gave the Netherlands a strong agro-food sector, but also changed the face of the Dutch landscape.

The development of knowledge in the decades after World War II was also directed towards high productivity agriculture. As a result, a knowledge infrastructure developed which focused on new technology development for production maximisation. The implementation was rather linear, science driven, and therefore top-down. Research results were communicated to farmers by means of an extension service telling the farmer how to improve production. While this approach was successful, it led to over-specialisation, environmental pressures, and encroachment on public spaces. It is precisely due to these developments that the social acceptance of an agriculture that operates along these lines has been dramatically eroded.

TransForum chose a bottom up approach by focusing on the development of knowledge, competence, and conditions that stimulate new business models, leading to 'Triple P' (People, Planet, Profit) value chains that others wish to emulate. To make this happen, TransForum was allocated thirty million euros for the period up to and including 2010 under the 'Sustainable System Innovations' budget heading of the BSIK (Knowledge Infrastructure Investment Decree) scheme. Industry, community organisations, and knowledge institutions added a further thirty million euros in project based funding.

TransForum actively looked for possibilities to ensure that the knowledge acquired and lessons learned during their programme would be sustained after its completion. They found a collaborating partner in the Athena Institute of VU University Amsterdam to support learning and knowledge co-creation by means of a monitoring and evaluation approach for system innovation projects in sustainable agriculture. The Athena Institute (founded more than twenty-five years ago, then called the Department of Biology and Society) has a long track record of finding ways to see how science and technology can contribute to the improvement of health and wellbeing in a sustainable and equitable way. Their chief methodology, the Interactive Learning in Action (ILA) approach, introduced and further developed during the 80s and 90s, is a transdisciplinary innovation strategy aimed at organising knowledge exchange between different actors to facilitate a joint searching and learning process. This form of learning leads to insights into both conducive and hampering factors in (system) innovation processes. Furthermore, through the structural inclusion of reflexive monitoring, this type of learning allows participants to understand actions in their context, and in particular reveals underlying assumptions. It provides insight and understanding into patterns, and enables people to adapt working routines.

Thus, this book is based on the experiences drawn from the innovation programme TransForum, combined with scientific research into 'learning in action' conducted by the Athena Institute. Together with insights from other knowledge and entrepreneurial partners, these experiences and insights shape the approach of Connected Value Development.

Readers

This book is meant for change agents who want to put learning into action. All people who find themselves pushing the –often implicit– boundaries of a 'this is how we do (or don't do) things around here' mentality that surrounds them. The context in which they find themselves pushing the boundaries is not necessarily significant, and can be on an individual or organisational level. Some are doing so deliberately, because of their profession; such as programme, process, and project managers, or directors and change intermediaries. Others – we think most of them – can be found in any organisation or as individuals in society. They do not necessarily have the label 'change' or 'process manager' in their job title. However, they are innovative thinkers in technology, committed doers who bridge differences in their neighbourhood, researchers who empower women by developing methods for economic independence in developing countries, visionary museum directors who connect visitors' and curators' views on art, persistent policy makers who consistently speak up when yet another rule for citizens is made up, or simply people who are not being led by opinion makers of either 'side' but think for themselves. Moreover, they can be pioneering entrepreneurs and enterprise builders who take value in all its aspects, not only the monetary or profit side of it.

What makes all of these people change agents is that they have an entrepreneurial spirit and a commitment to bridge what at first glance seem to be contradictions. Change agents find meaning in their efforts to push boundaries. They do not settle for the obvious, and in the process they connect with like minded people and open a dialogue with those who are (still) committed to stay within their perceived boundaries. This book aims to help change agents in their efforts to sharpen their lenses, on a conceptual as well as a practical level. This gives them tools to naturally stretch the boundaries they push.

Reading guide

In Part I, The Guide, we start by explaining the guiding principles of the Connected Value Development approach and build up the theoretical notions, guiding principles, strategies, and action perspectives for starting a Connected Value Development process. The chapters thereafter describe practical approaches to the various phases, or rather aspects, of the process. This is set up with a focus for new business opportunities, perspectives, knowledge, and solutions as the outcome.

Although the Connected Value Development approach is thoroughly grounded in practice, we are all too aware that, despite the wide ranging appeals for meaningful change, despite efforts to put these appeals into practice, and despite the increasing number of practical guidelines and handbooks, nevertheless critical observers have noted that too often rhetoric does not match actual practice and aspirations are not lived up to. 'Interaction with scientists' is often limited to 'presentations with room for questions', mutual learning processes turn out to be regular meetings, sustainable entrepreneurship is in fact mere greenwashing, and public consultation becomes gaining support for decisions which have already been made. In short, there is an apparent discrepancy between theory and practice. To point out these and other pitfalls, and suggest possible ways to avoid them, each chapter is concluded with an intermezzo under the heading of "Stubborn Reality". We trust that anyone familiar with the type of group-processes as here described will be able to recognise some of the examples.

In Part II, The Bubbles, we position the Connected Value Development approach in a wider context of social and political developments. We will describe pleas for new approaches to wicked problems from four different domains: business, science, policy and societal organisations. Key characteristics of these pleas seem to converge toward the kind of participative approach advocated by Connected Value Development. We conclude this part with a discussion of the implications these developments have for Connected Value Development.

Finally, in the epilogue, we take a peek at possible future developments.

In the Appendix, a selection of tools is presented that is particularly suitable to support the challenging endeavour of Connected Value Development.

Pip

Dickens' first line of *A Tale of Two Cities* quoted above this chapter seems as aptly suited for our time as it was for his. While enjoying health and wealth like never before, we find ourselves nevertheless challenged by some horrific problems. Pip, the main character of Dickens' tale, shows the reader the radiance of the ideals of the French Revolution: *liberté, egalité, fraternité,* set against the background of the familiar 'old world'. Let his open attitude in the face of the anxieties which inevitably accompany any step from 'old' into 'new', be our guide when we meet the challenges of our time – truly 'the best of times' when it comes to opportunity.

Part I
The Guide

"There is always an easy solution to every human problem – neat, plausible, and wrong."

Henry Louis Mencken (1880–1956), originally published in the New York Evening Mail, November 16, 1917.

1   Connecting Values

The Connected Value Development approach to sustainable development links societal and environmental challenges to business opportunities. It is a multi-stakeholder approach, bringing actors together from the world of business, policy, science and societal organisations. Turning today's highly complex challenges in the field of sustainable development into 'win-win-win-situations' (good for people, planet, and profit) demands new ways of doing business, of governing and of performing scientific research, which can only come about through collaborative efforts, involving multiple stakeholders willing to learn and build knowledge together in an interactive process. To indicate such partnerships we will use the term KENGi, which stands for Knowledge centres, Entrepreneurs, Non-governmental and Governmental institutions, with the 'i' for their joint objective of innovation.

Connected Value Development requires new innovation spaces where these actors develop innovative solutions for the challenges of sustainable development. It is based on interactivity, dialogue and participation. It connects people on a personal level, while recognising the importance of the values of the institutions they represent. It uses cyclic, reflexive, action-learning methods in which stakeholders interact, any time, anywhere. Eventually, Connected Value Development leads to the co-creation of new values, and at the same time it structurally contributes to system change.

The Connected Value Development approach cannot be described as a neat blueprint, with clear-cut phases, an unequivocal time path and, most of all, predetermined deliverables. Every Connected Value Development process is different, will encounter different obstacles and require different actors collaborating. However, generic features, insights and lessons can be formulated on the basis of a great diversity of experiences with the Connected Value Development approach. Taken together, these lessons provide concrete pointers for action in the form of *guiding principles*. At the same time these lessons point to a process that is allowed to change its short term, and even its longer term objectives if and when warranted by the overall goal. In the chapters to come we will describe a whole range of features of Connected Value Development projects and develop them into guiding principles (clearly visible in the margins of the text).

In the present chapter we will summarise these guiding principles in order to provide a comprehensive overview of the crucial elements of the Connected Value Development approach. The guiding principles comprise both basic assumptions and pointers for action. We will also distinguish three phases of the process of Connected Value Development.

Tangible and intangible outcomes of the Connected Value Development approach

The Connected Value Development approach supports the development of new economically viable solutions to wicked or highly complex problems. Whereas many efforts for addressing wicked problems associated with sustainable development (e.g. those initiated in the realm of policy) remain in the public domain, the Connected Value Development approach aims to bring the problems also into the private domain in order to support the development of socially robust solutions. It is based on the premise that giving entrepreneurs a prominent role in the process will lead to the actual realisation of solutions in the form of (new) sustainable business development. It is crucial that these businesses are not 'business as usual', but that they connect a diverse set of values. Therefore a so-called '3P value proposition' is developed in the process, to build a solid business case that can resolve complex problems through innovation and multi-stakeholder cooperation.

> **BOX 1.1   Elements of Connected Value Development in practice**
>
> Two examples of guiding ideas and 3P value propositions with their associated network of actors that were developed in the context of TransForum are the following:
>
> **Challenge**: creating new and structural linkages between the city and its surroundings
> **Alliance**: health care institutions, municipal services (spatial planning, welfare), agricultural entrepreneurs, and scientists
> **Guiding idea**: medical and social recognition of the farm as a therapeutic environment
> **3P value proposition:** Landzijde as professional broker for care farming
>
> **Challenge**: using the remainders and by-products of one agricultural production unit as input for another unit: closing the loop
> **Alliance**: three different (agricultural) entrepreneurs, an interdisciplinary team of scientists, municipal governments and local community
> **Guiding idea**: combining different agricultural business activities (poultry, pig farm) with each other and with a bio-power plant and a recycling factory
> **3P value proposition**: New Mixed Farm

To emphasise the role of entrepreneurs, we talk about 3P value propositions as the outcome of the process of Connected Value Development, rather than about socially robust knowledge, or credible solutions (which in fact may for other stakeholders refer to the same outcomes). A 3P value proposition is a description of the reciprocal benefits, in terms of people, planet and profit, of a product, service or solution (see Chapter 2 for further elaboration). However, the process does not start with the goal of formulating a 3P value proposition; this would give the impression that the process of Connected Value Development is only instrumental to the business needs. Rather, Connected Value Development starts from the recognition that there is an opportunity in connecting the values of different stakeholders, seen from the perspective of each of the stakeholders involved. An example is the notion that the activity of care farming can lead not only to economical value creation for farmers, but also to a higher governmental and citizens appreciation and thus social-political drivers to conserve the agricultural green landscape around cities (see box 1.1).

Thus, eventually, the Connected Value Development approach leads to viable business propositions for entrepreneurs that may result in such tangibles as a new type of greenhouse, an innovative husbandry system, or a new business linking city needs to surrounding farms. At the same time, the intangible outcomes of the process are indispensable. The lessons learned in the course of the process, and the change in mindset it may have produced will continue to have an effect. Moreover, as obstacles that are encountered in the wider system are addressed, system changes are instigated. In all, output and outcome of the new sustainable practices developed through the process of Connected Value Development result in structural contributions to sustainable development. This leads to the following guiding principles (see also Chapter 2).

Guiding principles on balancing the tangible & intangible
- Actively search for diverse value perspectives to create added value on 3P dimensions
- Pay ample attention to intangible values as these are indispensable for tangible output and structural change

Basic assumptions of the approach

Putting sustainable development in the heart of innovation requires much more than renewing a product or process. These kinds of innovations are the most complex forms of innovations since they involve rethinking value propositions by all relevant stakeholders, generating different revenue streams, changing delivery mechanisms, creating a corporate innovation culture, coping with intercultural differences, adapting governmental regulations, transforming mental models and so on.

It also requires specific methods relatively new to business development, such as dialogue with previously ignored stakeholders and methods to facilitate mutual articulation and learning processes. Furthermore, it is not just about new methods. Ultimately, it is about starting to think about approaches from new frames of reference. Frames that are able to encompass a holistic view on relevant issues, where the focal organisation is only a part of a network of interrelated actors and processes of production and consumption. This is something that should not be conducted in isolation; involving stakeholders from all parts of the supply chains and stakeholders from governments and societal groups is essential.

Traditional project management approaches are not suited to deal with this complexity. We need a more encompassing approach that will lead to re-valuation, re-design and re-positioning of business activities. And we know that just focusing on the business element is not enough, because we need to simultaneously give attention to obstacles in amongst others the socio-cultural, financial, and regulatory domain. Many of these obstacles we cannot define at the start, but we will tumble upon along the way. The design of the transformative approach towards a solution is therefore more a process than a clearly defined project. It is not just a business development model, but it is an approach to manage the inherent complexity that the business and its extended network partners face.

Getting a grip on complexity is not done by cutting big problems into little pieces and giving ownership of each particular piece to a small group. Rather getting a grip on complexity implies seeing the parts as part of a whole. To this end an innovation space is created in which participants start trusting the iterative process and letting the answers emerge through networking and reflection instead of trying to implement a development model, formulating a mission statement and executing subsequent steps to a final goal. This would be missing out on the added value of the creative innovative process in which new ideas and answers can emerge which can eventually lead to 3P value propositions for entrepreneurs, to a new kind of knowledge for scientists and to a situated standpoint on a much broader issue for political and societal organisations.

Guiding principles **on balancing between the parts & the whole:**
- Zoom out to get a better grip on complexity
  - See your project as snapshot in a wider transition (instead of an isolated result-driven process)
  - Don't start from scratch – there is always a 'before the beginning' and an 'after the end'
- Zoom in to create focus and direction
  - Unite different value perspectives around a guiding idea

Employing an emergent strategy means giving room to variation. This may be contra intuitive and is even risky. Indeed just looking at the whole without a clear direction may lead to an aimless endeavour. This classical management dilemma (let the process emerge versus determine before hand) leads to the second set of guiding principles:

Guiding principles **on balancing between openness & direction:**
- Use a strategy that is both emergent and deliberate
  - Start by co-developing a guiding idea, rather than rolling out a project plan
  - Find a balance between letting ideas develop freely and developing them deliberately
  - Do not separate idea development from implementation

Hence, the process characteristics of Connected Value Development are both exploratory and focused. The intricate relation between the parts & the whole, and between openness & direction is ever more apparent in the relation between people & the content of innovation: they are like two sides of the same coin. Ideas can only be developed by connecting people: a broad variety of people may substantially enrich good ideas. Vice versa, appealing ideas have the power to mobilise people, an essential requisite for the survival of good ideas and their ability to turn into innovations.

Guiding principles **on balancing between people & content of innovation:**
- Develop ideas by connecting people and connect people around developing ideas
- Develop a new sustainable practice around and for value creation
  - Create new knowledge and give meaning to knowledge in a shared practice

Thus, direction is provided by the guiding idea that is able to unite various perspectives. The importance of the emergent character of the process can be found in the room this creates for learning: "Purely deliberate strategy precludes learning once the strategy is formulated; emergent strategy fosters it".[1] Learning feeds action and action feeds learning. This does not happen automatically, leading to the fourth set of guiding principles:

Guiding principles **on balancing between action & learning:**
- Organise reflection to stimulate learning by doing
  - Appoint a dedicated 'reflection monitor' to support learning
  - Identify the tough questions: those issues that are normally 'swept under the rug'
  - Develop strategies and generate action to resolve tough issues in practice

Thus, the Connected Value Development approach has a number of principles that can be considered basic assumptions of the approach (see Chapter 3). In any approach, whether for business development, scientific research or policy making, tensions exist between focusing on the parts or on the whole, keeping things open for exploration or giving direction, connecting people or generating content, mobilising action or stimulating reflection. Often this balancing act is rather implicit and automatic in incumbent practices. When realising a *new* practice one cannot rely on existing approaches and their underlying assumptions. Connected Value Development involves developing a new approach and redefining underlying assumptions. To this end, it is helpful to make the aforementioned balancing act explicit. Reflection monitoring can focus specifically on these tensions (they are tough issues in themselves). Thus, what seem to be contradictions at first glance are in fact productive steps in a learning expedition. Leading to the overall guiding principle:

Guiding principle **on dealing with contradictions:**
- Use any change or dilemma as a source for value creation

Phases of Connected Value Development

The Connected Value Development approach has an emergent character and its action strategies are tailor made. The iterative and cyclical character of the process should not only be stressed, but also shown in practice. One of the intangible benefits of this process is the development of a sensitivity of the participants to the fuzzy and cyclical character of Connected Value Development. Even though the idea of slicing up a project in specific phases does not sit well with the network approach advocated here, it is possible to distinguish three different phases that we will describe below and are further elaborated on in Chapter 4 to 6.

Phase 1: Exploration & alliance building

Different stakeholders explore the possibilities of linking a specific societal or environmental issue to business opportunities; they share a challenge or a thematic concern. It results in a coalition of unlikely allies around a shared innovative 3P guiding idea: e.g. care farming or a new type of stable for chickens.

In this first phase (exploration & alliance building) this notion is explored, to identify if there really are mutual/reciprocal benefits (and not just a single bottom line of business development, or a scientific idea without any market value). Along the way, stakeholders that are crucial for the successful development and implementation of the idea are identified and actively involved in the process. The collective exploration of the 3P idea is really about reflexive learning that takes participants away from their formal positions (on which it is often difficult to create meaningful connections) and organises learning on the deeper level of the values that drive the different stakeholders. Out of this exploration emerges a broadening and deepening of the idea, something that is often crucial to foster commitment among all the stakeholders. In this phase, the emerging multi-stakeholder alliance learns to use inclusive language ('yes and' instead of 'yes but'), and to hold differences in a container of respect. They are encouraged to practical actions among unlikely allies, and often participants end up agreeing more than they thought they ever would.

Guiding principles on the involvement of participants:
- Organise active participation and commitment of all relevant stakeholders to realise the innovation
  - Build an alliance of unlikely allies, by taking all concerns seriously
  - Stimulate the internalisation of the guiding idea to give direction to all actions
  - Create a shared responsibility for the process, and individual commitment to actions
- Do not involve everybody at the same time
  - Take care that equal input can be realised by stimulating preparatory activities, e.g. to empower less dominant stakeholders
- Prevent debates around fixed positions and stimulate dialogue
  - Focus on personal involvement to facilitate the shift from representative to participant

Phase 2: Co-creation & experimentation

Only after the reciprocal benefit has been identified and acknowledged by the different stakeholders is it possible, in the second phase (co-creation & experimentation), to talk about how to really create these benefits and start talking about this elaborated notion as a 3P value proposition. The 3P value proposition is thus not instrumentally constructed, but it emerges from the process, because the right conditions (for learning, reflection, co-design) have been set in place. And of course, no guarantee is given that it will (always) lead to a predictable result. Implications for actual implementation are explored, for instance through the development of prototypes and experimentation. Necessary knowledge is co-created or brought in and given meaning in the projects context.

In the further development of the 3P value propositions, the team will also meet the obstacles in the wider system that prevent optimal 3P value creation. The reflexive learning approach not only leads to identifying the obstacles, but also to formulating ways around the obstacles, or approaches that eliminate the obstacle. This is possible because the stakeholder(s) that have the capacity to act in the domain in which the obstacle originates are also involved in and committed to making the 3P value proposition come true. The activities of co-creation & experimentation are done in the context of the new sustainable practice that is developed. This new practice has the characteristics of a Community of Practice.

Guiding principles **on developing an identity:**
- Collectively create your own set of rules instead of working according to the default set of rules of one or each of the supporting organisations
- Find a balance between shared ownership and individual leadership to stimulate agency
  - Different management roles do not necessarily have to be engaged by different people
- Create small tangibles; they feed the process of co-creation
- Use a transdisciplinary approach for a joint process of knowledge creation and problem solving
  - Combine tacit and explicit knowledge of all stakeholders

Phase 3: Embedding & alignment

The third phase (embedding & alignment) is about further developing the idea in such a way that it will sustain over time; that it is anchored in new businesses and supporting structures, cultures or solutions. To guarantee the optimal reciprocal connection between the economic, ecological and social values created, developing a 3P value proposition into a 3P-business case also is a co-creation process between the different stakeholders. Often the realisation of the 3P value proposition requires not only investments of commercial parties, but also investments of other stakeholders (e.g. public campaigns by NGOs, government adaptation of regulations). The business case that is built on the basis of the 3P-value proposition (and one could say that even this business case emerges from the process) often consists of a consortium (which can still be informal) in which commercial and non-commercial parties are brought together.

Through collective coordination, each of the stakeholders takes responsibility to actively support the 3P value proposition from their own world. Entrepreneurs turn the 3P value proposition into a business case. Policy makers and politicians align the initiative with policy regulations. NGOs support the initiative and the newly created knowledge is aligned with the scientific community to give further credibility to the innovation. This leads to systemic change.

Guiding principles on realising Value Creation:
- Use any change or dilemma as a source for value creation
- Include a go/no-go moment; it will demonstrate true intentions
  - Moving into the phase of realisation requires the initiators to let go
- To embed a 3P value proposition, it should be developed into business, but also linked to the broader discourse
  - Make transparant and accountable how value is added to the different domains

Guiding principles on dealing with institutions & change:
- Temporarily ignore the home base, so as to stimulate openness and creativity
- Give meaning to the Connected Value Development process in the respective home bases to increase support

- Involve institutional actors in the Connected Value Development process
- Instigate structural changes in the respective home-bases to accommodate Connected Value Development (change frames of reference)

In the chapters to come, we will describe the Connected Value Development approach in more detail. We will show how the strategy unfolds in the innovation space where participants actually have room to experiment. And how this is done in such a way that it leads to value creation in multiple ways, emphasising people, planet *and* profit. Different steering strategies can offer guidance and help build an alliance of unlikely allies in such a manner that there is deep reflection on one's actions, while at the same time things are getting done. But first we will explore what we mean by values, by value creation and by connecting values.

2.   The Two Faces of Value

When asked what people associate with the word 'value' they can answer this question from many levels, being personal, relational, economical, moral or societal and global in general. The answers they give also depend on where they work, what they do, and what they find important in life. For instance, businesses are easily consumed by the need to chase quarterly numbers and cut costs. Over the long haul, however, successful businesses are often those that do long-term accounting of a range of costs and benefits, including costs and benefits to the people and places touched by their business networks. These costs and benefits reflect output related values that can be measured, or assessed. But often people also refer to values as those things motivating them, inspiring them or uniting them. To sum up all these different outlooks, or ways of filling one word with meaning, the Oxford Dictionary distinguishes between:
- Value as the material or monetary worth of something for someone;
- Value as the regard that something is held to deserve; the importance or; usefulness of something for someone.

In Connected Value Development, we see the first definition as output related costs and benefits, and the second as outcome related motivating factors.

Value as (monetary) worth

A company's ability to create value is put to test in the market continuously. That value is not only determined by the buyers, but also by the company's innovation skills, the performance of other companies in the network and by the company's competitors. Creating value is a joint effort of actors ranging from customers to suppliers.

Sustainable development is increasingly seen as a business opportunity. Companies can lessen resource use and lower their costs, and generate additional revenues by producing goods that will perform better on the market because they better meet the needs and values of consumers. By involving a wider network of actors than in the traditional value chain, in the value creation process, added value is co-created, and companies achieve a licence to grow. While other licences are obtained by meeting certain minimum rules, a licence to grow is achieved through maximum 'connectedness' (of people and values in the process and beyond).

BOX 2.1   New values in food system

Hal Hamilton of the Sustainable Food Laboratory[3]: Large food-service companies are dependent upon volume discounts, and retail chains frequently charge stocking fees. The reason that incremental improvements don't cascade through the industry at a sufficient rate is that the very structure of our economy resists systemic change. All publicly traded companies must increase their quarterly numbers in stock value. These structures reward mass production and ensure that companies chase short-term goals. Sustainability is about creating long-term value, but many structured incentives reward short-term measures that might even sacrifice long-term value. Global commodity markets reward mass efficiencies and penalise any initiatives that increase costs. Companies only make changes that are cost neutral or that gain consumer support. They cannot add costs, in isolation, that make them less competitive. They would not survive. Some of the costs of sustainability thus require co-investment by other sectors.

The Connected Value Development approach introduced in this book builds on the notion of value as worth, by using it in the broader sense of creating value (worth) in terms of people, planet and profit. Connected

Value Development aims to develop and implement innovative ideas in such a way that different value perspectives are united. This process will lead to added value not only from the perspective of the single bottom line of monetary profit, but it adds value to the so called triple bottom line.[2] The triple bottom line incorporates the dimensions of profit, planet and people, in which profit refers to economic prosperity, planet to environmental quality, and people to social justice.

BOX 2.2   3P value proposition

Value Proposition: an offer that, based on a quantified analysis, describes the benefits, costs and resulting value that an organisation can deliver to its customers, prospective customers, and other stakeholders within and outside the organisation.

3P Value Proposition: an offer that describes the multiple and reciprocal benefits, in terms of profit (economic), people (social) and planet (ecological) values created, of a product or service offered by an organisation, alliance or other collaborative network to a broad set of stakeholders, inside and outside the traditional value chain.

In Connected Value Development we refer to a 3P value proposition as the centre that unites various value perspectives. Often in businesses, a value proposition is a statement about a product or service that very clearly describes why a customer would chose that product or service over another. It describes the benefits (value) offered by the product or service to customers (see box 2.2). The development of a value proposition is a key part of the design of a business model.[4] It is used internally to guide the development of partnership strategies, marketing strategies, product development, etc. A 3P value proposition connects benefits in terms of people, planet and profit, not by the 'addition' of values from different worlds (e.g. profit from business, people from government, planet from societal organisations), but by co-creating new value in which the people, planet and profit dimensions complement each other.

Instead of envisioning the three elements of a 3P value proposition as mutually exclusive or in competition with one another, we approach them as a collective dynamic, and treat them equally (see box 2.2). A 3P value proposition, in this sense, is the outcome of a process of value co-creation, which started off with an (unquantified) guiding idea.

3P value creation is based on innovative collaborations between knowledge institutes, entrepreneurs, NGOs / societal organisations and governments. Bringing all these people together and creating change through the actual realisation of the business opportunities that grow out of these collaborations is the core challenge of the Connected Value Development approach. These people often come from profoundly different backgrounds with different ideas about value and about sustainable development. The multi-stakeholder characteristics of the process as such requires us to focus not only on the tangible outcomes of the process (added value), but also on the values that each of these stakeholders bring into the process in terms of what they consider of importance; the second description of the meaning of the word value in the Oxford Dictionary.

Guiding principle
Actively search for diverse value perspectives to create added value on 3P dimensions

---

BOX 2.3   3P and the economic crisis[5]

The economic crisis does not come as a threat to sustainable development. Quite the contrary: in the US as well as in Europe, companies that are strong in 3P thinking have proven to perform financially above average over the last two years, whereas laggards perform below average. This indicates that for the top performers there is a direct link between integrated 3P thinking and the ability to perform well in times of crisis.

Value as usefulness and importance

All stakeholder parties must cooperate and invest to get a good idea developed into an interesting 3P value proposition and implemented in practice. Here, the second way in which we generally use the word 'value' comes in. Next to (monetary) worth, we use the term 'value' to refer to what is useful or important to us; in short, it refers to what is valuable, or of value. Values in this sense encompass our personal beliefs and ideals, preferences and ethics, ambitions and a general outlook on life. They range from almost universally accepted values to more personal values. Individual people and communities value all these tangibles and intangibles, because they are there (or because they are not) or can be experienced.

Ethicists make a distinction between moral values and values. Where values denote what is of importance to us, what is valuable, moral values denote issues that are of great importance to us, for what we consider important for living well and doing right. There is no agreed set of such values; they range from a few general values to dozens more differentiated values. Typical examples are loyalty, responsibility, compassion, and fairness. These values are deeply embedded in our world view and are often not consciously articulated. If you have to consciously deliberate whether you are going to kill that annoying neighbour or let her live, there is something seriously wrong with you. It is self-evident that you do not kill another person. Other values are more culturally sensitive or change over time. And finally different values can be conflicting in one person. If your best friend tells you she has cheated and her husband asks you subsequently if his wife has been faithful, you may experience a moral dilemma between the values honesty and loyalty.

Guiding principle
Pay ample attention to intangible values as these are indispensable for sustainable tangible output and structural change

In recent years, we have seen an increasing emphasis on intangible values in professional life and organisational development, particularly as the urgency for sustainable development becomes more apparent. Many companies feel the need to articulate a set of core values as guiding principles for their strategy. Employees are invited to articulate their own personal values and to connect these values to those of the company. Managers are trained in 'authentic leadership' through expressing their own identity and personal values. At the same time, individual values often differ from those adhered to in their professional community. Many people in business prefer not to pollute, or frown on power hungry practices; many civil servants prefer to be in personal contact with citizens, rather than through bureaucracy.

Under the right conditions, personal values can drive change. If one's personal values are in line with the vision behind an innovative idea, or a 3P value proposition, the commitment to the endeavour is personal and lasting. At the same time, participants of Connected Value Development processes bring in their professional knowledge and experience that they derive from their professional affiliation. As they are also expected to represent their organisation, this may bring different, potentially clashing, values into the process. For instance, within academia the main incentive is the number of peer-reviewed articles a scientist produces and a scientist is not automatically celebrated in his field for contributing to reducing hunger, unless he publishes about it. These kinds of cultural or institutional values also play a role in the process, since they motivate people to undertake certain actions or restrain from them. Bringing diverse groups of people together, all with different value-frames and interests, in such a way that they really start co-creating together and trade-offs can be turned into complements, is an important challenge of the Connected Value Development approach.

Values in the sense of what is valuable, or of value, are often very implicit and not articulated. But, just like values in the sense of worth, they provide much of the drive behind human actions and motivations and as such play an important role in any development process. In fact, it seems like they are two sides of the same coin. Let us have a look at this dynamic relation between (both types of) values and human behaviour.

How values guide our actions

Values inform and judge people's actions, choices and decisions. Values generate and influence behaviour, both at the individual level and in groups, as the backbones of their opinions and judgements. They give guidance to people's decisions in their private, social, spiritual and professional lives. They play a role in the choice of products consumers buy, in the way people develop their careers, in the way entrepreneurs give focus to their organisation and its employees, and in the way governments create and execute policies. Understanding the basic distinction between actions and underlying value-frames is very helpful in forging alliances and establishing shared goals. Collaboration between people with different belief systems, world views and value-frames is at the core of the Connected Value Development approach.

Thus, values guide our behaviour, whether at the level of the broader professional systems we are part of, the many subcultures or communities that we are members of, or as individuals in 21st century society. Each of the worlds of the KENGi partners has its own set of values. The decisions and choices made by individuals within each world are shaped by, and reinforced within, the communities they are part of. For instance, in business, the decisions of any employee will be made against the background of a set of values shaped by environments including the society at large, the business community, those specific to a particular company and of course also those of the individual. Likewise, the decisions and actions of a scientist should be seen against the background of the set of values held by the institution the scientist works for, by his or her specific discipline and by what is valued by science in general.

Thus, the way professionals act, their choices and decisions, are always the expression of both their personal values and the institutional or cultural values of their communities. At the same time their decisions and actions reinforce the core institutional values of those very systems. Political actions, for example, are taken against the background of the core institutional value of credibility, which in turn stabilises the political system itself.

Thus, in this meaning of the word, 'values' form the basis of the continuity of any entity or system. In fact, these institutional values are so fundamental and inherent to the functioning of the systems that they are rarely made explicit. One hardly finds mission statements of companies claiming their aim is to make money, or of knowledge institutes proudly advertising that they aim to increase the knowledge base. On the other hand, many of these implicit institutional values can be quantified by very tangible measures of success, such as the number of donors of an NGO, the impact factor of publications or rankings of universities.

What this boils down to is that there is a dynamic and recursive relationship between the social system and the individual, between values and behaviour. Our society is a Complex Adaptive System, an interactive system governed by patterns (e.g. culture, values, rules, resources, discourse) and agents (e.g. people, natural resources, technology) (see box 2.4). Through continuous interaction over time, a configuration of agents forms certain patterns. These patterns in return influence the individual behaviour and interactions of the agents. In a similar way, personal and institutional values guide our behaviour, and specific (mixes of) values are constituted through interaction in our subcultures, communities and professional social systems. More generally put: the interaction of agents form system-wide patterns and in turn, these patterns govern the actions of agents. Acknowledging the fact that our society is a Complex Adaptive System brings implications for Connected Value Development approach. This means that the Connected Value Development approach plays out at different levels; solely focussing on building collaborations of unlikely allies without considering the structures in which they are embedded is a futile enterprise. And, the top down implementation of new policies or change of culture is hardly ever successful for wicked problems if relevant societal actors are not involved.

BOX 2.4 **Complex adaptive systems**

Sociologist Anthony Giddens[6] introduced the distinction between 'agency' and 'structure' and contends that 'agency' and 'structure' create and reinforce each other. Thus, human action is always performed in the context of a social structure (culture, community) which is governed by a set of rules, resources and/ or norms. At the same time, human action (and interaction) sustains, but also modifies, these rules, resources and norms. There is a dualistic relationship between structure and agency, between social system and individual, between cultural values and behaviour. Structure and action exist and change as a result of each other.

To visualise this intricate relationship, we turn to the theory of Complex Adaptive Systems. Hollands theory of Complex Adaptive Systems[7] also recognises two distinct levels which constantly interact; patterns (structure) and agents (agency). Through continuous interaction over time a configuration of agents forms certain patterns. These patterns in return influence the individual behaviour and interactions of the agents (see fig. 2.1).

A system, in general, is a collection of elements that interact with each other. Each element may be different and shows 'behaviour' in its interactions with other elements. Seen from a distance, the system as a whole also shows behaviour. The higher the number of elements and their interactions, and the higher the diversity of the elements and their interactions, the more complex is the system.

A complex adaptive system (CAS) is a complex system that can change in response to external or internal changes. Typical properties of a CAS are:

- The elements (usually called: *agents*) are capable of changing their behaviour: they have an *internal model* that determines their behaviour and that model can change with time;
- Agents are involved in *transactions* with other agents. Transactions cause *flows* (e.g. of materials, information, money and energy) in the system. Agents also have *tags*: labels that make clear to other agents what their nature is. Tags help to accelerate transactions;
- In a CAS more or less stable patterns develop: groups of agents that share transactions with each other and, as a group, are successful in the system. Such patterns of transactions, called *building blocks*, can be copied, as a clone or with variations. Building blocks and the internal model of agents are the 'memory' of the CAS. This memory is the basis for the system's capacity to develop and adapt, but at the same time for its stability against changes;
- Agents can *aggregate* to form *subsystems* with their own building blocks; aggregates interact with other aggregates or with the environment of the CAS. Such aggregates may develop to more of less isolated subsystems that have *boundaries* with other parts of the CAS;

- A CAS as a whole is *non-linear* by nature: its future behaviour cannot be calculated from its actual status and its reaction to changes (internal or from its environment) is unpredictable;
- A CAS shows *diversity*: there are different types of agents, flows and building blocks;
- A CAS is evolutionary: unsuccessful agents, building blocks and subsystems will loose 'influence' in favour of those who are successful, or they may even disappear.

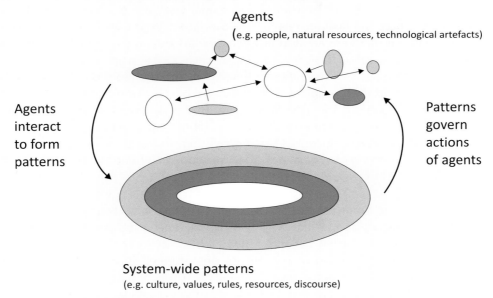

Agents
(e.g. people, natural resources, technological artefacts)

Agents interact to form patterns

Patterns govern actions of agents

System-wide patterns
(e.g. culture, values, rules, resources, discourse)

FIGURE 2.1 Complex Adaptive System

System changes occur with two different speeds. The faster speed is that of the transactions and flows between agents. The slower speed is that of changing internal models (the 'learning' of agents), changing aggregations and the evolution of building blocks. The study of CAS is a new and interdisciplinary scientific field that aims to find general rules and patterns in a variety of complex adaptive systems, ranging from ecosystems and the global economy to cities and the human brain.

In conclusion

Connected Value Development is about linking environmental and societal challenges to business opportunities by bringing different people together in a process of value co-creation. This poses challenges. Actors will differ in the way they frame the problem which the project aims to address, based on their value frame. They will have different perceptions of what constitutes the guiding idea of the project and they all are members of different communities and organisations that provide them with different value frames. Forming alliances can stir up tensions between the collectively developed value frame of the project team discussing a new idea and the modes of operation and background culture of each of the participants. This is shown in figure 2.2, where the innovative idea pulls an individual towards the new collaborative practice while the requirements of the institutional setting pull him in the opposite direction. The forces pushing outwards are often very powerful and threaten to dilute or abandon the innovative idea.

The tendency exists to search and account for people and planet aspects of value, in a similar way in which we anchor (making a) profit. This is to be expected. We live in a time in which reality seems to be stipulated only by what is measurable and can be described in words and in which desired behaviour must be supported by inspecting codes, which indicate that a product we buy or a service we desire meets certain measurable criteria.

Like a community, a value chain, or a society and its individuals, the global economy is a complex adaptive system. In this system, the players themselves are independent learning entities, and continuously adapt to new circumstances, search for new connections with other independent entities and adapt the strength and meaning of old connections to new circumstances. Fixing certain working methods within the context of such a system damages the nature of it, i.e. the capacity to adapt dynamically to changing circumstances. So, measuring people and planet values similar to profit, would not be the same as anchoring these values. Therefore the Connected Value Development approach needs an experimental space for tinkering and social learning while developing a 3P value proposition. It is not just an analytical exercise combining 3P values, but also a process of internalising 3P values in personal behaviour and embodying change in one's being.

To support such a process it is important to have room to experiment; to create an innovation space that is free from the rules of each supporting organisation, so that creativity and cooperation can be stimulated fully. In the next chapter we describe how to get a grip on the dynamic reality of Connected Value Development.

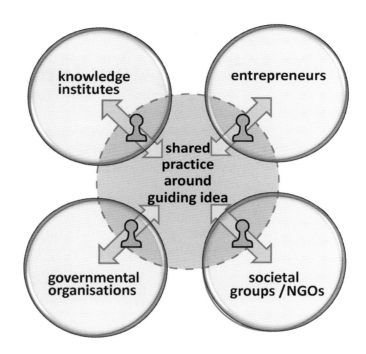

FIGURE 2.2 Innovative ideas pull towards new practice. Institutional requirements pull in the opposite direction

3 Creating Innovation Space

Combining people, planet, and profit values in a manner that simultaneously creates business opportunities and addresses environmental and social challenges sounds great. But what does this mean in practice, in this institutional void, outside the boundaries of each of the organisations involved? What characterises this 'open space' and what quality does it bring to the process of Connected Value Development? What do these characteristics require you to take into account, before you start as well as when Connected Value Development is up and running? To answer these questions we must explore the context of Connected Value Development and with it, we will formulate guiding principles for getting a grip on this open space where innovations seem to thrive.

Crossing institutional boundaries

When working in an organisational framework, the required contribution to the organisation is generally clear: there is a job description, the incentives are clear, and so are the targets. Mostly, you work in a department that is responsible for a segment of the value creation process of an organisation and there is a certain hierarchy when it comes to decision making, with all the plans, planning, and meetings that go with it. These are not usually disputed, and because nowadays organisations are mostly output- or result-driven there is a sense of direction. In terms of social rules, both written and unwritten rules exist, either few or many. The very fact that you behave professionally when in the office seems to suggest that there is only a partial overlap of your 'personal' and 'professional' aspects. Still there are also casual Fridays, informal get-togethers, annual trips to an amusement park, and strategic retreats, which combine business with pleasure. Thus, due to the boundaries of the organisation, you often have an idea of 'what business you are in' and you work according to al the implicit and explicit values that your organisation has built up over the years and in this context they create a sense of purpose and meaning within these boundaries.

As in any other organisation, in Connected Value Development there is a sense of purpose and direction: addressing wicked problems in such a manner that 3P value propositions are developed for new businesses that are ready to market and up for competition. Since Connected Value Development brings together different stakeholders in a space between organisations, there are no set rules or procedures that make it obvious what it is one has to do, which road to follow, and how to behave. Different stakeholders may have differing perceptions of what the problem, the outcome, and the output are or should be. Most importantly, though, the set of rules of your own organisation cannot be applied one-on-one in this open space. Boundaries of Connected Value Development are not clear, neither are consecutive process steps, and decision making moments are not to be outlined in advance. Even the question of who is in and who is out during the process cannot be clear from the outset, nor can deliverables and outcomes be described precisely upfront. This makes Connected Value Development fuzzy and its process emergent. Planning, decision-making, content, and involving other actors intertwine in multiple ways.

Guiding principle
Collectively create your own set of rules instead of working according to the default set of rules of one or each of the supporting organisations

To create a sense of direction within Connected Value Development, it is important to acknowledge our default tendency to define initially what is inside and what is not in a project, and what must be delivered. In singular problem solving the first objectives are defining project boundaries and output. Doing the same when starting Connected Value Development is failing to realise that one automatically creates a single direction and a path, and with it fences and destinations instead of making the emerging context an integral part of the process. Starting to see the difference between this default tendency of defining a project in advance and simply dealing with what is there, is an example of what Scharmer pinpoints in Theory U as "[w]hen we stop the habit of downloading, we move into the state of seeing", "[w]ithout a direct link to the context of a situation, [...] we cannot learn to see. But it is only in the suspension of judgement that we can open ourselves up to wonder. Wonder is about noticing that there is a world beyond our patterns of downloading."[8] Therefore, by simultaneously acknowledging our default mode and accepting that the open space is not structured in a manner similar to what our default mode is set to expect, we can open up to the fuzziness and create an innovation space for the process of Connected Value Development.

BOX 3.1   TransForum as an innovation space

TransForum was founded by several KENGi-partners, that aimed to provide a more sustainable perspective for the Dutch agro-sector by searching for and experimenting with sustainable value propositions. To organise room for experimentation, TransForum acted in between the different institutional partners. By doing that, a space was created where innovation could be stimulated, not hindered by the rules of each of its founding partners.
To ignite creativity TransForum did not work with a strict set of criteria. Instead it used a set of guiding principles which provide a framework that is used to shape all action-learning projects it supported. The following guiding principles were used[9]:

1. Sustainable development is a dynamic process.
No closed form definition exists for the concept. It must be given realisable meaning in a multiple of valued dimensions that evolve across time.

2. Sustainable development needs system innovation.
More of the same is simply not enough. The hardware, software, and orgware of agriculture must be innovated if movement toward sustainability is to be achieved.

3. System innovation is a non-linear learning process.
The normal science approach of problem-solution-application must give way to a messier process of consensus goal setting-joint knowledge creation-reflexive learning.

4. System innovation requires a multi-stakeholder approach.
All stakeholders bring existing knowledge and concern to the process, and their collective presence is needed for legitimacy and productive creativity.

5. Multi-stakeholder approaches imply trans-disciplinary knowledge creation.
Complex, messy problems do not know disciplinary bounds. All relevant skills and knowledge must be combined and extended to create the new knowledge that will evolve the system.

6. New business models based on new knowledge lead to better 3P performance of agriculture
The essential elements in these new business models are the inclusion of people and planet aspects next to the regular profit aspects in a transparent and accountable way. So, from the business model it must be clear what the contribution to these three domains will be. And by presenting them in a transparent and accountable way, the implementation of the innovation can be truly assessed on its performance.

The character of fuzziness

In the actual practice of Connected Value Development, the project moves from one event into the next. Unexpected events happen, opportunities arise, people decide to step out, national policy changes, there is a critical story in the press, etc. In the mean time, meetings take place, knowledge is co-created, lessons are learned, decisions are taken, and documents are written. We usually forget about this fuzzy history, especially when the process has resulted in concrete products or innovations. The messy development process is often easily reconstructed as a neat linear process of idea generation, concept development, testing, implementation, marketing and distribution. People closely involved in a process, any process, are aware of all the details, the discussions, the uncertainties, the possible alternatives. People less closely involved necessarily skip such details and see a neatly and logically structured outline, created after the fact. To compare, many people will be able to relate to the experience of starting to work in an organisation, when the whole structure turns out to be a lot more fluid than it appeared from the neat organisational chart presented in the brochure. The same goes for any planning process within organisational boundaries. The process often appears to be more certain, linear, and deliberate when one is more distant (in space, time and in social sense) from the locus of the process: distance lends enchantment to the view (see box 3.2).

BOX 3.2   **Distance lends enchantment to the view**

Sociologist of science Harry Collins has used the expression 'distance lends enchantment' after studying the construction of scientific facts from nearby.[10] He concluded that the closer one is to the practice of knowledge construction, the more uncertainties are apparent, even if from a distance, e.g. in the media, controversies seem to have been concluded and uncertainties resolved.

The more distant one is (in space, time, and in a social sense) from the locus of a process, the more certain, linear, deliberate and neat the process will appear. This neat image of a linear process is supported further by efforts to model innovation processes to improve management of innovation. Modelling efforts started off with typical linear innovation models of the type:

FIGURE 3.1   *Linear innovation model*

The problem with linear models of this type is the assumption that one stage can be brought to completion before a transition to a next phase takes place. In reality, changes in the environment (market or otherwise) require a return to previous phases or to execution of different phases concurrently. The discoveries made within the course of the innovative development itself can be just as important as such outside developments.

As it became obvious that linear methods are rarely applicable even to simple problems, new models were developed which all incorporate, in one stage or at various levels, the idea of *feedback,* thus making the process essentially circular or *iterative* (analogous to the mathematical procedure where the result of a formula is fed back into the formula itself).

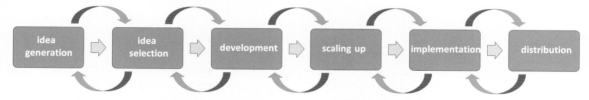

FIGURE 3.2 *Innovation model with feedback loops*

One can easily imagine more advanced and sophisticated models with even more feedback loops and iterations, making the models more closely resemble actual practice. Moreover, the sophisticated models have been complemented with 'cookbook' methodologies, including step-by-step plans, lists of standard solutions, transformation rules and inventive principles.

Over the past few decades the distant, neat and orderly view of innovation processes has been dropped; the trend has been towards the opposite of the cookbook formula: a loosely coupled set of rules of thumb rather than a well defined strategy. Methodologies like Radical or Extreme Project Management stress an "open, elastic, undeterministic" approach as precondition for success as well as a truly cyclical development path where feedback is used, not just to adjust some details, but, if need be, to completely overhaul the premises.[11]

This, however, has consequences for the way we think about managing processes. We start to believe that proper project management is clear-cut and neat, demarcating necessary project activities from external influencing factors, leading to success via a number of well-defined stages. From this perspective, a project may start with a so called 'fuzzy front end', in which many different and disparate ideas are generated; it is soon to be funnelled down to a small number of the most feasible concepts, which can then be developed into business cases. The idea is that after a 'fuzzy' phase, a regular, well-planned and well-managed product development phase commences, as exemplified by figure 3.3.

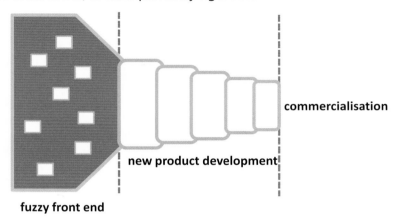

commercialisation

new product development

fuzzy front end

FIGURE 3.3 *The typical place of 'fuzziness' is at the front end of an innovation process*

However, the Connected Value Development projects show that creative, and thus necessarily fuzzy aspects play an important role throughout the whole process and not just in the 'Pre-Project-Activities' as this fuzzy phase is often called. Comparing Connected Value Development with existing literature on new product development, it becomes obvious that a description as depicted here may well be useful within the context of new product development within a company, but is inadequate for more complex propositions involving multiple stakeholders from different organisations, each with their own value frame.

From a corporate perspective, government policy, environmental regulations, science, technology, and other companies are all largely uncontrollable by the corporation and thus belong to the influencing factors of the outside world which, nevertheless, constantly influence people's thoughts and actions. The Connected Value Development process, on the other hand, aims to involve business, government, science, and NGOs from the very start, and this implies that confining the fuzzy part to the front end is not an effective avenue.

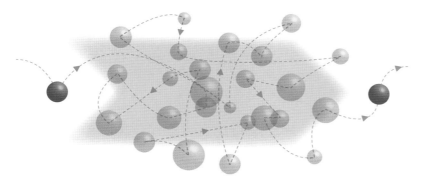

FIGURE 3.4   *Fuzzy throughout*

Box 3.3, the natural history of innovation, shows the patterns that are important to innovation space. The fuzziness of the open space that surrounds and is worked from in Connected Value Development creates an innovative environment that optimally supports the basic principles of the Connected Value Development approach (knowledge co-creation, joint problem solving, mutual learning, etc.) and is thus able to stimulate creative thinking from start to finish (see fig. 3.4). As stated before, the surroundings for this environment lie in the fact that in an institutional void there are no upfront set rules and routines like those that already exist in the context of regular organisations. These natural qualities of the open space, where nothing is quite set yet, make it the right environment in which ideas develop and new connections are made. This makes fuzziness a fertile basis to work from. However, since we are so used to working within boundaries, the creation and enhancement of such an environment – the innovation space – is a continuous task and constitutes part of the process itself.

Guiding principle
Use any change or dilemma as a source for value creation

BOX 3.3 **Conditions that provide a rich soil for development**

Where good ideas come from–the natural history of innovation
From a historical study of innovation, Steven Berlin Johnson[12] identified seven patterns that are important to successful innovation spaces:

The adjacent possible
Make combinations based on what you have. New ideas are often combinations of existing parts of another domain. The adjacent possible expands as you explore.

Liquid networks
Ideas are not isolated: they are more like a swarm, exemplifying movement and the possibility of making new connections. Especially the information exchanged at casual water-cooler conversations stimulates creative thinking.

The slow hunch
Innovations often emerge when an idea that has been kicked around for years is combined with other ideas. Hunches need space and time to evolve: A real 'eureka moment' does not often occur.

Serendipity
Ideas need to be able to bump into each other; this is how we make new connections that spark. New ideas often arise from information not intentionally sought.

Error
Being right keeps you in place, being wrong forces you to explore. You may be wrong on why something is working, but still come to a working system.

Exaptation
Take something that emerges from one use, and repurpose it for another.

Platforms
Platform-building is about emergent behaviour: beavers do not set out to create an ecosystem to support kingfishers and dragonflies when they build their dams, but they do create one.

A space for handling fuzziness

In the past decades, the importance of the economic-political-social-cultural environment, of local factors and trajectories, of global developments, and last but not least, of sustainability issues, has gained widespread acceptance. At the same time, developments in psychology and management theory not only clarify the role of psychological factors but also provide handles to influence them. Books with titles like 'Positive Thinking' and 'The Colours of your Mind' abound in the management domain. Within management theory, the cookbook formula has been replaced by an entirely opposite approach: a loosely coupled series of rules of thumb rather than a strategy. The "inherent sloppiness of innovation"[13] becomes a near-paradigm. Terms like Creative Chaos, Cross-Functional Groups, Loose-Tight Management, and Adaptive Organisation have become an integral part of every manager's vocabulary (which is not to say that they have actually been integrated into every manager's practice) – whether in business, science or government. The influential work of Peter Senge portrays the future company as a learning organisation, where "people continually expand their capacity to create the results they truly desire, where new and expansive patterns of thinking are nurtured, where collective aspiration is set free, and where people are continually learning to see the bigger picture together".[14]

This is not to say that guide books with clear rules and procedures have lost their attractiveness, but that the practice of innovation is necessarily much more complicated than can be represented by a three-phase model, and that any guidebook will have to incorporate that in order to be useful. Moreover, a growing number of examples of old and new businesses that have been able to transform pressures into challenges over the past decade and which proved successful by a complete overhaul of their business model – or rather, of *the* business model – clearly demonstrates two things: first, that the successes did not come from a recipe book; and second, that the traditional 'closed' innovation process, where a 'new product' is secretly developed within a company, protected as much as possible by patents and copyright law, is not the only successful game in town; it is increasingly replaced by the idea of 'open innovation',[15] which uses the efforts, knowledge and creativity from within the organisation as well as from outside of it, in order to create value.

Back to the challenge of handling Connected Value Development in its fuzzy context; where, in practice it is difficult to distinguish the usually demarcated phases and even harder to actually manage it as a *project* with successive stages, for several reasons:

- Connected Value Development projects do not start from scratch; they are part of a larger movement starting well before the project and going on well afterwards. Thus, realising the project is not a goal in its own right;
- due to its complexity, a blueprint does not suffice. Next steps and possible interventions emerge along the way and learning is an integral part of the process design;
- in Connected Value Development, relevant actors are not involved successively. Instead, actors that are normally at the end of the value chain are brought forward in the process to ensure inclusive development.

The strategy employed in the innovation space needs to accommodate these characteristics. Below we will refine these characteristics and draw up guiding principles that should be considered when choosing a Connected Value Development approach.

A space for an expedition

A project never starts from scratch. The kick-off meeting, the approval of funding, or the starting date in the project plan may seem like starting points, but they are not. Neither plans nor problem descriptions arise from thin air: many fuzzy processes have been going on before anything takes the form of a written report or proposal. A 'new' process necessarily builds on the soil already laid down by certain key figures, a regional culture, ongoing projects, identified problems, and vague wishes. For the TransForum project Streamlining Greenport Venlo, for instance, not only were certain existing projects and platforms relevant to the start of the project, but so were the problems in the region (high unemployment rate, youth moving away), policy decisions (e.g. assigning the Greenport Venlo label to the region's agricultural development) and an informal network of people that shared their concerns about the future of the region. From this fertile soil it was possible to streamline different developments, build up a network, and create a vision for the region, which in turn provided a fertile ground for inclusive and integral regional and logistic planning and for the implementation of Cradle to Cradle principles in large building projects.

In fact, in most innovative processes one can never really pinpoint a specific starting point of the process: ideas and visions may have been brewing in the heads of the key persons for years, but, being innovative, they tend to remained confined there. Some initiatives may already have been taken, which can be seen as precursors, but only after the process is underway. At some point however, the brewing ideas and ongoing events turn into a project – usually because someone has been able to find funding to develop the idea. With funding come requirements like project plans and deliverables, in cases of external funding as well as in cases of internal investment. Simultaneously, projects of the type that would use the Connected Value Development approach have high ambitions, usually beyond the scope of regular project timelines and possible effects. In terms of Complex Adaptive Systems, Connected Value Development aims to create new configurations of actors who form new patterns and structures through regular interaction, and who may change existing structures so 3P value creation will be accommodated even after the officially-designated project comes to an end.

What is considered to be the role for the project in the larger transition makes a big difference in terms of managing the project. As one participant remembers: "When I was trained in project management in the beginning of my career, I was told to demarcate my project from external affairs right from the beginning: to make a sharp distinction between the intended effect and the activities that may lead to this intended effect.

Guiding principle
See your project as snapshot in a wider transition

The idea is that you are only accountable for the activities that you agree upon in the contract with your financer, not for their effect. Of course this is true; you cannot be accountable for changes taking place in the behaviour of other people or institutions. You cannot control them. However, merely delivering the deliverables as promised (e.g. poster campaign, 6 network meetings, a scientific article, a business plan) will not change the world."

Seeing the project as a means to an end rather than as an end in itself creates a different mindset, a different platform from which to make choices. It makes it much easier to see opportunities and change course where necessary. It also makes it easier to skip project activities that do not, in retrospect, seem to contribute to the intended transition. Leadership flows not from the planned project activities but from the vision of the future; it is the dream that drives people. The end of the project might come just as unexpectedly as its start. For most participants in this phase of the process, the end of a project does not bring much change to their focus and activities: their expedition continues.

Guiding principle
Don't start from scratch – there is always a 'before the beginning' and an 'after the end'

A Connected Value Development approach can thus be seen as an expedition that starts off with a notion that will develop into a guiding idea, during which different opportunities occur. In this specific guiding idea a link is made between environmental and societal challenges and a business opportunity. An expedition is not organised like a project with a clear beginning and end, but rather like a series of projects growing out of each other over time. The project is then a link in an extended network of activities that were already ongoing before the project started and that will go on after the project ends. Project definitions must reflect this expedition character. Projects that are too strictly defined in terms of traditional project management will certainly have difficulties in dealing with the emergent design of Connected Value Development. Projects that do not have a clear guiding idea that is either developed or recognised and acknowledged as attractive to all stakeholders will tend to default to business as usual. Choosing an approach for managing and guiding a process is an important and explicit decision, one that will highly influence the outcome of a project. This also applies to project selection.[16]

A space shaped around an idea

For the Connected Value Development approach to have direction, it is crucial to have a guiding idea accompanied by an entrepreneurial mindset. Like a lighthouse these two guarantee focus and direction and they also aim at creating a tangible outcome and impact.

Mintzberg and Waters[17] identify this as the Entrepreneurial Strategy which is one of eight described strategies; or "patterns in streams of actions", as they define strategy. Their Entrepreneurial Strategy is driven by the vision of the individual leading the organisation. The vision provides only a general sense of direction. Within it, there is room for adaptation. Because the leader's vision is personal, it can quickly adapt to changes in the environment. In several cases it was observed that "when important aspects of the environment changed, strong new visions emerged rather quickly."[18] Also, the details of the vision emerge *en route*, which is only possible because the person who formulates the vision is the same person who – simultaneously – implements it. The Entrepreneurial Strategy is deliberate and emergent at the same time; it is deliberate, because of the clear sense of direction and the intentional actions that follow; and it is emergent, because of the possibility to change the vision completely and because of the ability to adapt actions along the way.

Mintzberg & Waters' description of the Entrepreneurial Strategy is very close to the practice of Connected Value Development in several ways. First, Connected Value Development is also both a deliberate and an emergent approach; a promising guiding idea provides a clear sense of direction, which is simultaneously adaptable. For managing wicked or complex problems, such as the ones addressed by Connected Value Development, the problem cannot be divided into clear-cut pieces which can then be solved individually, because of its high dynamic complexity (see box 3.4).

Guiding principle
Start by co-developing a guiding idea, rather than rolling out project plan

---

BOX 3.4   Solving tough problems according to Adam Kahane

After 25 years of working professionally on tough questions, Kahane[19] reached the conclusion that solving tough or wicked problems requires approaches which are simultaneously systemic, participative and emergent. "Find a way of working systemically, working participatively and learning as we go. These are new muscles that we need to develop."[20] This conclusion is based on the observation that in highly complex problems, three types of complexity converge: that is dynamic, social and generative complexity.

dynamic complexity
cause and effect separated in time and place
systemic approach

generative complexity
the problem fundamentally new and unfamiliar: we have to learn our way towards a solution
Connected Value Development

social complexity
actors have different views, value frames and interests
multi-stakeholder approach

FIGURE 3.5   Dealing with highly complex problems

A problem has a low dynamic complexity if cause and effect are close together in space and time. These problems can be dealt with piece by piece, dismantled into easily resolvable components. By contrast, a problem has high dynamic complexity when cause and effect are far apart in space and time, requiring a systemic approach.

Social complexity involves the understandings and the mental models of the people involved. A problem has a low social complexity if people share common assumptions, values and objectives regarding the problem. Problems with a low social complexity can be resolved by authority and expertise.

In contrast, in problems with a high social complexity, the people involved look at things very differently. Therefore, with socially complex problems, issues can only be addressed by involving all the relevant stakeholders themselves.

In addition, generative complexity concerns the unpredictability and unfamiliarity of the problem. A problem has a low generative complexity if its future is familiar and predictable. Wicked problems, however, often have a high generative complexity, implying that they are fundamentally new and unpredictable. Therefore it is not possible simply to apply past best practices; people need to learn their way as they try to resolve the problem.

TABLE 3.1   Different approaches for different types of complexity

Complexity	Low	High
Dynamic	Piece by piece	Systemic
Social	Authority	Participative
Generative	Best practices	Emergent

Moreover, due to the social complexity of wicked problems, the people involved often have different understandings and mental models, wherefore problems cannot be resolved using an authoritative approach. Instead, a participatory approach is required, where all relevant stakeholders take part in resolving the problem. Next to the dynamic and social complexity, a wicked problem also has a high generative complexity, meaning that its future is often unfamiliar and unpredictable. To attempt this unpredictability and to be able to adapt to changing dynamics, an emergent approach should be adopted. The approach unfolds while it is being executed, see figure 3.5.

The second way in which Connected Value Development adheres to the Entrepreneurial Strategy of Mintzberg & Waters is that the formulation of the vision and the implementation of the vision in actions are part of the same process, with overlapping actors and activities (developing the vision and concept continues throughout the process). The actual context in which Connected Value Development is employed is, however, much more challenging than in the original meaning of Entrepreneurial Strategy (their research was done in single organisations, in the 80s of the last century). Particularly because in Connected Value Development there is usually not one single leader, but rather a multi-stakeholder collective, an alliance.

Guiding principle
Use a strategy that is both emergent *and* deliberate

We use the two main characteristics of the original Entrepreneurial Strategy to describe experiences in Connected Value Development projects: i.e. the strategy is both deliberate *and* emergent and in the strategy vision formation *and* implementation are intertwined. Employing a strategy which is both deliberate (the ambition being very clear to everyone) and emergent (the actual implementation being open for discussion) proves key for Connected Value Development. The innovation space supports this deliberate and emergent design of the process because it is formed around a guiding idea.

A space for action learning

Guiding principle
Organise reflection to stimulate learning by doing

How does one organise an emergent design? How does one know what to do when? The action learning spiral may be helpful for envisaging an emergent design process (see figure 3.6). Action learning approaches have provided evidence that following a cyclical interventions strategy, where tailor-made interventions follow observation of and reflection on previous interventions, is particularly suitable for the types of problems associated with sustainable development.

The process involves an ongoing reconsideration and redefinition of the problem at hand on the basis of new experiences and observations. In the Rondeel project (a project aimed at designing a radical innovative poultry-stable), in a first learning cycle an inventory was made of issues surrounding a new hen husbandry system. After that, a second learning cycle commenced in which new actors were involved and reflected on new issues that arose from the process. Because of the different types of complexity involved, it is not sufficient to start with an exercise to structure and define the problem with a small group of participants, and subsequently roll out the project. Subsequent events will throw a different light on the problem, requiring different actions. Moreover, involving other actors at later stages has consequences for the perception of the problem, as they contribute different values, views and knowledge. But before new actors can be invited to offer their perspectives, the problem must be 'opened' to them. Only if the problem is salient to them, if they have an interest in the outcome of the process, they will commit to it. In other words, whatever the inner circle of participants understands the problem to be may well be revised, adjusted, or complemented in a subsequent phase.

Indeed in some projects it was found that the introduction of new actors often implies the need to revisit discussions: "I realise that they have to go through the same learning process that we have already gone through." This is not a problem at all if it is seen as an essential part of the iterative process. However, to some it may seem that 'we are back at square one', which may be somewhat disheartening. One option to address this is to prepare the participants for this new, cyclical and iterative approach, by means of a start-up workshop explaining the nature and purpose of the new approach. However, we have experienced that soon after the start of a project participants are often more eager to start executing part of the project plan than to reflect upon underlying assumptions about the approach. Positioning this type of reflection between the first and second learning cycle makes it much easier to connect participants' experiences to the reflection on the approach. Bringing in an outside expert on new approaches to complex problems is also very useful at this stage, as long as this expert is able to relate to the inherent intransigence of changing routines. Even if informed by theoretical considerations, adequate strategies for sustainable development can only be developed in action; participants cannot be

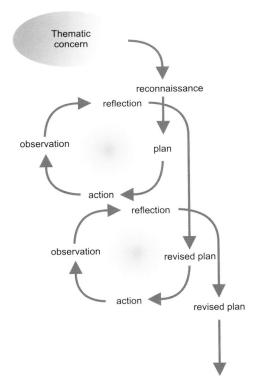

FIGURE 3.6 *Action-learning spiral*

expected to have all the necessary competences from the start. A second way to address the feeling of being back at square one is to keep track of developments in the learning cycles meticulously, in order to show how learning questions have deepened, broadened and sometimes even appropriated by other relevant actors. Showing what knowledge has already been gained helps to point out that 'we are *not* back at square one'.

An action learning approach, as the phrase implies, is not just about reflection, but also about action. It is "a continuous process of learning and reflection [...] with the intention of getting things done."[21] Action, observation, reflection, and the revision of ideas, insights, and plans continuously alternate, or even take place at the same time. This may happen at different speeds and at different levels. At one particular moment a small observation-reflection-plan-action cycle may take place (a reflection on what happens and an immediate response). An action may also take place after a meeting, and be reflected upon one month later, in the next meeting. But it is also possible to distinguish three large learning cycles in a two-year project. The action-learning spiral will then support the iteration between exploration, development and implementation.

A space where stakeholders innovate together

Increasingly we see pleas for involving so called end-users – the people at the very end of the value chain. Involving end-users and other stakeholders from the beginning of the creation process results in products, services and solutions that are socially robust, credible and incorporate a broader set of values. In the Connected Value Development approach, this multi-stakeholder approach is referred to as KENGi collaboration.

This has consequences in terms of how we usually envision the order and role of actor involvement in innovation processes. In the Entrepreneurial Strategy employed in Connected Value Development, vision formation (or idea generation) and implementation are intertwined. In Rondeel, for instance, in the exploration phase, consumers, NGOs and industry were all able to bring in their views, knowledge and ideas on husbandry systems for hens. The idea of a new sustainable type of hen house was further developed into a preliminary design, involving different stakeholders from the entire chain of the poultry industry and NGOs advocating animal welfare and environmental efficiency. This technological design of Rondeel, however, existed merely on paper. The transition to the actual implementation phase required the involvement of investors, support from local governmental agencies, and from businesses who believe in the concept. In the mean time, the development of the design continued; adjustments were made to the design on the basis of new input or unexpected developments.

Guiding principle
Do not separate idea development from implementation.

A successful market introduction of a sustainably produced egg required the development of a 3P-value proposition with active involvement of investors, local governmental agencies, and businesses (farmers to retailers) who believe in the concept and are committed to bringing it to reality. This meant finding common ground between animal welfare, environmental efficiency, consumer appreciation and market viability. During the process many adjustments were made to the initial design of the husbandry on the basis of new input, the choices made in the business model and stakeholders joining or stepping out of the process.

So, if we just zoom in on these two phases of the development process: idea development (developing concepts and designs) and implementation (bringing ideas into practice, realisation of concepts, successful application of ideas in practice), we see that in the case of Rondeel, 'implementation' is brought forward in the process and at the same time 'idea development' is stretched out over a longer period of time and all actors are involved in the whole innovation process.

This phenomenon (moving implementation forward and idea development backward) is typical of the Connected Value Development approach. A common criticism on participatory methods in which end-users are involved from the very beginning of the process in group discussions, focus groups, design workshop etc., is that they cost a lot of time and money.

However, by incorporating the traditional outsiders early in the innovation phase and by taking their ideas very seriously, there is an increased likelihood that the resulting innovation will be socially robust and commercially viable. Or, as design critic John Thackara said: "We need to design from the edge, to learn from the world, and to stop designing *for*, but rather: design *with*."

A space for change

Connected Value Development is a fuzzy, if not messy, process that requires continuous reflection on what happens along the way and responsiveness to those events and the underlying obstacles. Departing from a multi-stakeholder environment, it aims to achieve tangible results, but recognises that in order to achieve these, a number of intangible results have to be established as well. These may range from establishing a stimulating environment, through 'stepping out of your bubble' (e.g. 'frame reflection') to accepting a shift in paradigm, the kind of new thinking which sheds a new light on all established knowledge. It also recognises that the values created may be very different for the various stakeholders taking part and that for some, a short term objective may be the reason to participate, while for others the long term benefits are decisive.

The Connected Value Development approach accommodates the challenges that derive from the aforementioned notions and develops responses to them. Through the Connected Value Development approach, a guiding idea is developed into a 3P value proposition that links societal and environmental challenges to a business opportunity. Different stakeholders are connected around this guiding idea in an innovation space; an environment conducive to the development of ideas and the creation of new connections without the need to be accountable on a day-to-day basis to the rules and regulations of the associated institutions. The innovation space offers room for experimentation. In this innovation space, methods and tools are applied for connecting the value frames of the involved participants and for co-creation of knowledge, as are solutions and business opportunities.

It is an essential characteristic of approaches for the management of wicked problems, such as Connected Value Development, that the necessary conditions (a good idea to start from, the competence of the participants, support from institutions) will never all be present from the start.[22] In the Connected Value Development approach creating these necessary conditions is an integrated part of the project. The whole design of the Connected Value Development approach is focused at organising learning in action between the participants. Through action and reflection the skills and capabilities, the awareness and sensibilities, and the attitudes and beliefs[23] of each of the participants are deepened and participants become better capable of dealing with the uncertainties involved in developing sustainable innovations.

In conclusion

In this chapter we have emphasised the non-linear and emergent character of Connected Value Development processes: First, by looking at a Connected Value Development project as a link in an extended network of activities, that were already going on before the project started and will go on after the project ends. Second, by perceiving the innovation process not as a linear plan-action model, but as a cyclical and iterative process of action and reflection. Third, by considering the involvement of actors not as a consecutive but as a parallel, and at times intertwined, involvement. And fourth, as a process in which a guiding idea and an entrepreneurial mindset of all the stakeholders makes the process not only emergent but also deliberate.

Crucial for the creative and innovative character of Connected Value Development is a sensitivity to the intangible aspects of the process. Many Connected Value Development processes are about creating a connected vision, a shared vocabulary and trust in each other in unusual forms of collaboration. Therefore, every Connected Value Development process is different, will encounter different obstacles, and requires different actors to collaborate. One just cannot extrapolate a successful trajectory and implement it in another region or on another case. To the contrary, it is "highly dependent on resources which are location specific" and "impossible to reproduce elsewhere."[24] The participants have to go through the same process, overcome obstacles together, and develop a shared vocabulary suited to the subject at hand.

It may be clear by now that guiding a Connected Value Development process is quite a challenge and that creating an innovation space is crucial to this approach. It is an environment conducive to the development of ideas and to the making of new connections. The innovation space offers a room to experiment, without having to be accountable on a day-to-day basis to the rules and regulations of associated institutions. But it is this very nature of the innovation space that can pose tensions that might frustrate participants. In the coming intermezzo we therefore describe situations that illustrate the stubborn reality when working with Connected Value Development. To deal with the stubborn reality of an innovation space, we present common situations and possible strategies to cope with them or avoid them.[25]

The Stubborn Reality of the Innovation Space

1 Pressure to operate via traditional project management rules

When a project participant arrived at her office she talked very enthousiastically about her inno-vative project, but when her boss asked her: "what are the concrete results; what are you going to do tomorrow?" she started to stutter. Because there was no specific project outline planned, it was difficult for her to get the message across. This was not only a problem at the beginning of the project, but throughout the whole first year.

The character of an innovation space, in which the development of a guiding idea rather than specific output is part of the process, often creates tensions between the enthusiastic participant and the demands of the organisation which forms the home base of the participant. This is especially true for employees of project-based organisations such as governmental bodies and funding parties, who usually require a concrete project outline. In this type of organisation, a person or a company are considered professional if the consequences of a certain action are precisely known in advance.

Within these organisations, the deliberately flexible process of Connected Value Development time and again leads to difficulties in the participant's own organisation. Interestingly, the projects demonstrate that it does not matter very much in which kind of organisation one works; whether it is an environmental NGO, a knowledge institute, a governmental body, or a multinational company: in all of these, a number of hours is allotted to the project and a specific set of project outputs is expected. While such a mode of operation makes sense when the only objective of the organisation is to run as efficiently as possible, it is detrimental to the whole concept of innovation.

Usually, the need to innovate is amply recognised by the highest levels of the organisation, but that does not imply that individual executives and managers are judged by anything other than the scrupulousness with which they stay within their budget and the timeliness of their deliveries.

As emphasised in Chapter 3, Connected Value Development has the structure of an emergent design. This means starting out with a shared vision in which the participants discover the relevant subsequent steps, as part of the process. The vision is the guiding idea. If the solution were known up front, it would be possible and desirable to develop a concrete plan, submit it to whatever body decides on funding, and subsequently move into the implementation phase. This approach does not work well for complex problems, a feature of which is precisely that the solution is not known in advance but has to emerge from the cooperative process in which many different parties bring their knowledge and experience to the table. Thus, trying to formulate concrete and practical goals too early in the process hampers creativity and can prematurely kill off a brilliant idea or reduce it to a business as usual or a heavily subsidised showcase of good intentions.

Moreover, the pressure to come up with a concrete plan with concrete deliverables within a predetermined timeframe completely denies the value of the collaborative process itself. Even in the extreme case that nothing tangible can be pointed out as a result of the process, there is still the process itself, which may well turn out to be valuable, as it brings together professionals from different spheres of life: businessmen gain an understanding of what it entails to draw up workable regulations; civil servants get first-hand experience of the way in which procedures and regulations work out for well-meaning citizens and entrepreneurs; scientists observe how distant and theoretical their models seem in the eyes of people who are supposed to profit from them; community organisations are confronted with realities which are an inevitable part of sharing responsibility.

Connected Value Development is about keeping options open and being able to modify the concrete objectives within the frame of the overall guiding idea. As one representative of an NGO remarked: "We have a toolbox of methods and a vision of the direction in which we want to go with a process, but then it becomes custom work which gains shape as we go along. You cannot determine in advance what results you are going to achieve, only what the efforts will be and what quality conditions you will place on the process. Then you just have to trust that it will generate meaningful results. This also means that you should not drive it towards something which will be 'scalable' – the experiment is worthwhile in itself."

Some practical tips

Acquire a clear mandate for the innovation space
Requests for a concrete project outline often come from the standard project orientation of your institution. It represents a denial of the emergent learning character of the process of Connected Value Development. The best way to prevent tension between the process in the innovation space and your own institution is to acquire a clear mandate for this new approach from the start. It is important to create understanding for this kind of processes and to make oneself accountable for the outcome of the whole process, rather than on a day-to-day basis for every activity in the process.

Reflexive monitoring instead of evaluation
Evaluation, as it usually understood, asks for a comparison between goals and the progress made. This is not the most adequate way to determine the progress, let alone the value, of a Connected Value Development process. It would be a good idea to make this clear from the outset, and propose reflexive monitoring as alternative means of assessing progress. Process monitoring and reflection was one of the two core strategies of TransForum[26]. When a project team was asked to write a midterm review for a funding party, they realised they could not refer to their original proposal, as this was not what they had pursued in practice. Instead of reporting on what they had done, they decided to report on how things were done and why this was different from what they had planned. This way, they were able to shift the focus from pre-perceived deliverables to the dynamics of the process itself, the learning around the challenges at hand and thus to inspire confidence in future results.

Reconnect with the other participants to regain motivation
When returning from an inspiring meeting, it can be demoralising to meet with the incomprehension and resistance of your colleagues at work. Reconnecting with the other project participants can help to regain motivation. It can also strengthen the argument in defence of pursuing a moving target rather than a well defined goal. As one participant puts it: "When I was asked, time and again, for a concrete project outline, I just did not know how to answer that anymore, so it took me a few days before I started calling around; and that's what is so nice about a group like this, that you can fall back on the others, and you notice that you share the same feelings and that you can help each other."

2 Losing sight of the big picture

In an international project dealing with complex issues touching on several different areas of policy, a great deal of effort was invested in a shared and integrated formulation of the knowledge questions. At the end of the meeting, the project manager decided to break down the complex challenge into more manageable packages and made sure that everyone was enthousiastic about their assignment and knew how to continue. However, after the participants returned to their own departments they lost sight of each other, and when they met again after three months of work, it proved very difficult to find a common denominator again.

This example illustrates the difficulty of not only achieving but also maintaining an integrated perspective. The very complexity of the issues for which the heterogeneous collaboration from different participants is an asset makes it challenging to keep an integrated perspective during the process. There is a tendency to reduce complex problems to several parts and to assign the participants a specific part of the problem based on their expertise. In this example, this resulted in losing sight of each other and in difficulties in finding a common denominator again.

For Connecting Value Development, the tendency to reduce problems to several parts is hazardous, since a lasting integrated view of the problem and solution requires several 'learning loops'. The approach is not focused on exchanging the already existing viewpoints of the different parties, but on jointly developing, formulating and inquiring as yet unarticulated ideas, value conflicts and uncertainties. For this creative, interactive and iterative process to work, meeting once or twice is not enough.

Some practical tips

Tackling crucial issues is everyone's responsibility
A normal workgroup meeting concludes with the assignment of tasks or action points according to the functions and expertise of the participants. In a Connected Value Development process, however, it is precisely the exchange of knowledge and roles, the 'looking over the fence', which is essential. This requires from the project manager and from all participants to go against ingrained habits and keep working together, especially on crucial issues. For example, when it comes to formulating a profitable business proposition, this is not something that can be left to the entrepreneurs; instead, the whole group should be thinking business at that crucial phase of the process. Only then can the entrepreneurs rest assured that their problems are really understood.

Invest in face-to-face meetings and (virtual) network building

Resist the tendency to send people home with just their own piece of the puzzle; rather, they must also invest in face to face meetings and network building. A (virtual) platform and network of different actors from the institutional settings can ensure balance and adequate support and resources to maintain the project and to ensure its implementation. It is also important to demonstrate to actors outside the project what the process is expected to produce, in order to facilitate participants to spend enough time on the project. Experience shows that commitment easily fades, when work on the project is seen as additional to ordinary work activities. With the next meeting still months away, it can easily be postponed or delayed. To avoid this, it is important to constantly maintain contact. Virtual networking (Skype-meetings, email, private forums, groupware) can be very helpful. Yet, it also offers ample opportunity for postponing work and reactions to emails, so never do without face-to-face meetings.

Work in small subgroups

If necessary, for example due to travel distances, one can decide to work in small subgroups. Appoint a facilitator who supervises the process of communication, co-operating, and learning and is responsible for building and maintaining a network between the different subgroups.

3   To adapt to new ideas or not

A scientist was involved in the development of an innovative business idea that would shorten the supply chain between farmers and supermarkets. His task was to generate data on sales and logistics. A few weeks after he started his analysis, an entrepreneur participating in the project told him enthousiastically that he had met an interesting new partner last week, who had offered him the means to scale up his business. He told the scientist: "as you will understand, this offer is one I cannot refuse." While listening to the entrepreneur's enthousiastic stories, the scientist realised that this move implied yet another change from the original idea and that he would once again have to adjust his research design.

The entrepreneur in this case is easily enthousiastic about new ideas and activities and when he sees an opportunity to expand his business or make it more financially robust, he will jump at it. He admitted: "I am quite an impulsive person and quickly enthousiastic for new adventures." However, when confronted with these new business ideas the scientist was not only frustrated by the fact that he could throw away his work, but also because it would once more shift the focus of the project to a much more traditional business model, instead of the sustainable business idea the team had committed to at the outset. His original enthousiasm was dampened by the many changes and he started wondering whether they would ever reach their goal when participants kept on changing direction.

An innovative process needs people who can think outside the box, who are creative, able to adapt to new circumstances and quick to see opportunities that arise along the way. Yet it also requires the participants to reflect on the way their personal choices affect the other participants and the process as such. This reflection is of great importance for gaining insight in what has been achieved and what the consequences are of individual decisions and actions for the project. Adjustments can be painful, due to investments in time already made, but nevertheless judged worthwhile. However, such decisions should always be taken in close consultation with all stakeholders. For the entrepreneur, reflection was not at all a natural habit, but at the end of the process he commented: "I learned that I need to take some time every now and then in order to rethink my choices and examine the consequences, to avoid being pushed around by whatever the illusion of the day may be."

Some practical tips

Create fixed moments for reflection

A policy advisor involved in a project remarked: "Routine becomes obsolete if one does not engage in reflection. But reflection is tiring. There is little time for it. All day long one is busy with other things. It is a matter of setting priorities." Since reflection is easily undervalued or forgotten, it is best to create fixed moments for it, for example every last 10 minutes of each meeting. At fixed times, e.g. twice a year, a longer session can be organised. A process manager could be given the responsibility to set these times so the team can collectively check whether the process and (individual) decisions taken still further the goals and vision of the project. Ideally reflection is done individually as well as in the project group or small subgroups. In some cases, subgroups can be more effective, due to organisational constraints or a perceived imbalance of power between the stakeholders.

Dynamic Learning Agenda

The Dynamic Learning Agenda (see Appendix, Tool III) can be used as a tool to enhance learning in the course of the process and to make such learning explicit. In the Dynamic Learning Agenda, problems faced by participants in the development and implementation of a project are formulated as questions, and listed explicitly. It allows participants to explicitly articulate the challenges as they perceive them and helps to address specific questions about the process. Also, it shows changes over time, and the actions taken.

4 Exploration and Alliance Building

Connected Value Development is about developing a new practice amidst existing practices. It is about connecting ideas, connecting values and connecting people. Thus it is about bringing different people together – creating new alliances – that together instigate, enable and embody change. First, change is instigated by developing innovative 3P value propositions that exemplify profit, people and planet values. Second, change is enabled by bringing these propositions one step further, beyond the drawing table and beyond assessments and analyses. Third, because innovations are by definition deviations from the existing routines, knowledge, or practices, innovations will challenge existing interests and set ways; and learning and reflection are essential to embody the envisaged change.

As was shown in the previous chapter, the innovation space can be seen as a rich soil from which ideas emerge. The first phase of the Connected Value Development process – exploration and alliance building – is about taking the next step: sowing seeds. Sowing seeds is about *developing ideas* and *connecting people.* People who (are invited to) articulate their concerns and their dreams, and people who see opportunities to turn ideas into robust value propositions. As one project participant commented: "The process starts there, where energy is and where people feel their shared sense of urgency." In this chapter we will describe how ideas develop and how people get connected. From these starting points we will formulate guiding principles that are supportive to the design and management of this first phase of the Connected Value Development process.

Guiding principle
Develop ideas by connecting people and connect people around developing ideas

Developing ideas

Guiding principle

As with all good ideas, 3P ideas are not manufactured: they emerge. In the previous chapter we have seen that there is always a 'before the beginning'. Connected Value Development processes do not start from scratch, and each of them starts in a different way. An innovative idea may have been brewing in someone's head, waiting for an opportunity to be shared, after which the Connected Value Development process starts and a group of different stakeholders deliberately get together, in order to turn this idea into development. Alternatively, a group of people is brought together because a great sense of urgency is felt by different community groups around a certain issue, such as the husbandry of egg-laying hens, the use of pesticides in field cropping, or energy consumption by the greenhouse sector. In this network, the sense of urgency for change is reinforced, a new discourse is developed, and new ideas are generated. These ideas are subsequently taken into new networks and practices, they settle in the heads of individuals and wait for a window of opportunity. Thus, 3P ideas usually result from serendipity, a pinch of chaos, vague notions, previous experiments, and especially from actively building on the ideas of others and recognising and acknowledging the complementary opportunities the multi-stakeholder environment offers. Thus, *developing ideas* is meant in the active sense of developing ideas but also, perhaps even more so, in an emergent sense: ideas develop.

Connected Value Development provides a way to approach increasingly complex and interrelated challenges that do not adhere to traditional geographic, disciplinary, and sectoral boundaries. In short: wicked problems. These types of problems cannot be divided up easily into resolvable pieces. On the contrary, dividing up the problem into pieces and resolving them separately by different actors will not lead to the desired change. Zooming out and taking a broader perspective really helps getting a grip on wicked problems. Questioning the premises of the original problem is often very productive. The example of Rondeel shows how involving multiple stakeholders with different problem perceptions helps with zooming out and moving beyond the original premises. The usual approach would

Guiding principle
Find a balance between letting ideas develop freely and developing them deliberately

Guiding principle
Zoom out to get a better grip on complexity

be to start from the interests of the farmer and from veterinary and human health risks (a major community concern in the Netherlands). Instead, in Rondeel the wellbeing of the hens as well as the associations of the public with animal welfare is integrated into the design challenge from the start. Rather than choosing which values take precedence (e.g., by making a trade-off between health risks and outdoor areas for hens), the project team has taken a design approach. The making of trade-offs leads to incremental innovations in which the existing systems are merely adjusted. A design approach leads to new designs (and eventually to value propositions), incorporating concerns and the underlying values of a range of actors. So instead of taking the current husbandry systems as a starting point, the starting point in this case was to listen carefully to and interact with all involved parties: what does the public actually mean when it wants more natural food, or more natural growing conditions? What are the essential elements of a "natural" life style of hens? We see here that through incorporating other actors, such as citizens and an animal welfare NGO, new perspectives and ideas emerge that can eventually lead to a co-created design that can connect values that seem contradictory at first sight, and in this way resolve a network of problems without breaking them up into pieces. Thus, instead of the familiar outlook where environmental and social measures were regarded as extra costs that threaten the profit margins, the approach advocated here stresses the opportunities for new ways of doing business where these three elements reinforce each other and create added value. Conducting a causal analysis in a focus group with all participants in the exploration phase helps by widening, deepening, and connecting the different perspectives (see Appendix, Tool VI and IV). This example shows that instead of cutting big problems into little pieces and giving ownership of each particular piece to a small group, zooming out and uniting different value perspectives is more helpful.

Guiding principle
Unite different value perspectives around a guiding idea

The guiding idea provides direction amidst uncertainty

A guiding idea provides a great sense of direction. A vision of the future can be created using various techniques, such as visioning or scenario planning, but if there is no deeply felt conviction about the idea, it will not function as a *guiding* idea, pulling the process forward. A guiding idea provides direction. Naturally, diversions or detours may occur when they are necessary, but the guiding idea keeps the process heading in the same general direction. A guiding idea is not carved in stone but rather, it is loosely defined. It is redefined again and again when new actors come in, by connecting the idea to their preferred discourse.

Changes in the environment (market or otherwise) may give reason to develop an idea in a different direction. To give a simple example: in the 1960's, innovative designs to recycle cans from domestic waste were caught by surprise by the staggering rise in the use of aluminium cans (used for beverages). As these cans are non-magnetic, in contrast with the cans used until then, this required a complete re-thinking of the design, from which the innovative eddy current separator resulted, which can cope with magnetic as well as non-magnetic metals. In the TransForum cases we see that involving outside actors and really listening to their concerns, with the intention of addressing them, often leads to adjustments in the design. Community concerns are then translated into design criteria for a solution that complements the dimensions of people, planet and profit. In the New Mixed Farm for instance, concerns raised about animal welfare led to a rejection of pig castration practices on the new farm.[27]

But as important as such outside developments can be, the discoveries made within the course of the innovative development itself require or cause changes to the idea. The case of Closed Greenhouses discussed in box 4.1 is a case in point. The actual idea (a closed greenhouse that stores summer heat underground and uses this heat to warm itself in winter) manifested itself in different forms when it was brought into practice. Local development appeared to be crucial, resulting in different heat exchangers, new climate management, and different crop production

Guiding principle
Stimulate the *internalisation* of the guiding idea to give direction to all actions

Guiding principle
Actively search for diverse value perspectives to create added value on 3P dimensions

BOX 4.1　Adoption of the closed greenhouse

Within the Synergy project, one of over thirty innovative TransForum projects, the adoption of the 'closed greenhouse' concept was stimulated. A closed greenhouse is a sustainable invention that uses summer heat to warm the greenhouse in winter.

Since the closed greenhouse was at that time a novel, innovative technology, only limited experiential knowledge about the use and functioning of the system was available. Therefore, a learning network was initiated in which a platform for growers was generated to share experiences and to develop the closed greenhouse further.

In their analysis of the wider adoption of the concept of Closed Greenhouses by growers, Hoes et al. [28] show that concept development continues well after the formal closure of this phase. After the Closed Greenhouse pilot, a phase of implementation would have been expected in which different growers would have adopted and implemented the concept, but instead each of the growers turned the Closed Greenhouse into a new design, another innovation. They reconstructed the design and adapted the closed greenhouse to their own contexts and business needs. The picture below illustrates the reconstruction process and how it resulted in multiple closed greenhouse designs.

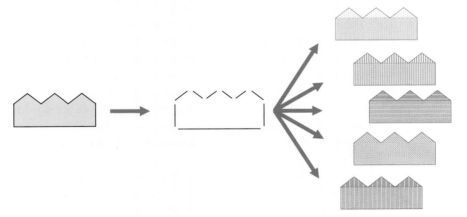

FIGURE 4.1　*Closed Greenhouse*

This example shows that the adoption of novel system innovations should not be perceived as implementation, but rather as learning trajectories which include experimentation.

methods. Thus, the development of the idea, the design, remains open to change throughout the process. This is only possible if initiators that remain involved do this with the mindset of achieving change (e.g. reducing energy use of greenhouses), not if their mind is set on realising a specific design (copies of the first pilot Closed Greenhouse). The Closed Greenhouse is a concept that provides direction; it is not a closed and detailed design. How to move in this appealing direction remains open for discussion and experimentation.

Connecting people

In Connected Value Development, alliances are forged between entrepreneurs, knowledge institutes, governments, NGOs and community organisations around the development of an innovative idea that links societal and environmental challenges to a business opportunity. The idea is that involving such a wide range of actors from the start of the creation process results in products, services, or solutions that are socially robust, credible, and that incorporate a broad set of values. It takes the concerted effort of farmers, scientists, and government bodies, along with the active participation of local community groups, to achieve the desired change through co-creation.

Guiding principle
Build an alliance of unlikely allies, by taking all concerns seriously

Involving KENGi actors is a very general concept. It is a guideline that helps broadening the perspective on whom to involve. Conducting a stakeholder or actor analysis at some point during the first phase will provide a significantly better understanding of the actors that should be invited (see Appendix, Tool V). Thinking about the different processes involved in Connected Value Development in relation to actor involvement may be helpful as well. Rather than organising relevant actors per phase (e.g. scientists in the exploration phase, entrepreneurs in the investment phase, and civil servants in the implementation phase) processes are initiated to involve each of these groups from the start. Box 4.3 describes the idea of three inseparable, but distinguishable process lines: the generation of ideas, the

Guiding principle
Organise active participation and commitment of all relevant stakeholders to realise the innovation

organisation of support, and implementation. These processes do not occur successively, but in parallel, or even simultaneously.

BOX 4.3   Three inseparable process lines

Based on their experiences with regional dialogues in the Netherlands, Van Mansfeld et al.[29] describe multistakeholder innovation processes not as three successive phases of 'generating ideas', 'organising support' and 'implementation', but rather as three process lines that are inseparable in practice, but can nevertheless be distinguished.

Each of these processes plays a role in all these phases, but in each phase the emphasis and type of involvement is different. Each of these lines represents the involvement of different actors:

- generating ideas: actors that have knowledge of and ideas about the issue at hand;
- organising support: opinion leaders, politicians, representatives of the institutional settings of participants;
- implementation: entrepreneurs, civil servants, NGOs, etc.

Actors from the scientific and business communities, from governmental organisations, and from NGOs all play a part in each of these process lines, albeit in different ways. In the previous chapter we stated the importance of the intertwinement of the generation of ideas and their implementation. A great idea that is developed separately from the context(s) in which it is implemented will remain isolated and not grow into a business opportunity or a 3P solution. Involving the representatives of the poultry industry in the exploratory phase of Rondeel is a way of including their insights, knowledge, and ideas. When it came to implementation, the role of the poultry industry was very different: it demonstrated commitment by making investments. Likewise, in the implementation phase, animal welfare NGO demonstrated their commitment by publicly showing their support.

As Connected Value Development is used for complex issues that require not only new 3P solutions but also systemic change (change in culture, institutional structures, and discourse), another essential actor group that needs to be involved is the group that can give support to the new development: "project ambassadors" such as opinion leaders, politicians, and representatives of the institutions of the participants.[30] Again, it helps to create a support network early in the process. In Streamlining Greenport Venlo, for instance, this was done explicitly during a four-day creative session at the beginning of the process. Civil servants, scientists, lecturers, and entrepreneurs worked together to develop a vision of the future of the Venlo region. In the evening of the third day, opinion leaders and politicians were invited for a presentation. This not only put a healthy pressure on the group, it also gave the invited leaders a feel of the creative and collaborative process that was going on, and made them part of it.[31]

Thus, in all three processes – the generation of ideas, the organisation of support, and the implementation – KENGI parties play a role, but in each of the processes the emphasis, the actual person, and the kind of involvement is different.

Guiding principle
Do not involve everybody at the same time

Guiding principle
Take care that equal input can be realised be stimulating preparatory activities, e.g. to empower less dominant stakeholders

Until now, we have discussed the creation of a shared vision by bringing together people from various domains, in order to generate diversity and bring in all relevant perspectives. Only then, the thought is, can inclusive and robust ideas be developed. However, we have experienced that it is an illusion to think that bringing all these people together and creating heterogeneous networks is always productive, even if interactions are professionally prepared and facilitated. A phase of single actor-group processes (e.g. entrepreneurs developing a shared vision together, or tenants articulating their needs) in which the under-articulated needs of specific actor groups are formulated, have appeared to aid the overall process of multi-stakeholder collaboration (see box 4.4).[32] Earlier, in experiments with patient participation, it was also found that only after organising separate focus groups with patients and with biomedical scientists it was possible to bring these actor-groups together in dialogue workshops.[33]

Congruency is sought, rather than complete intertwinement. What is needed is interactional expertise: the expertise to create a constructive interaction between multiple stakeholders.[34]

FIGURE 4.2 *Action learning for system change*

BOX 4.4   Single actor-group processes

Solving highly complex problems requires close collaboration between actors from different disciplines. Traditionally, scientists, entrepreneurs, policymakers, end users, and other entities do not work together, and each has its own working culture, expressed by specific identities, languages, values, and routines. The differences in the interests and cultures of the various participants, which result from their different institutional backgrounds, stand in the way of effective interaction and processes of mutual and joined learning. How can these barriers be overcome?

Interestingly, even though most projects set out to develop heterogeneous collaboration, Hoes et al. (2008)[35] observed that some TransForum cases chose to develop activities for the separate, homogenous trajectories as well. For example, in New Mixed Farm and Synergy, action learning trajectories for entrepreneurs were developed, and in New Mixed Farm, also an interdisciplinary team of scientists was built. Considering that the initial goal within the TransForum projects was to build heterogeneous learning groups, the development of homogeneous learning groups may be understood as a kind of letdown.

However, we have seen that in some cases of heterogeneous collaboration it is useful or even necessary to start the articulation processes within the different disciplines, in order to deploy the full potential of the participants' knowledge. A process of successful articulation, initiated within a homogeneous setting, enables, rather than disables, a productive dialogue when heterogeneous collaboration is sought. With both New Mixed Farm and Synergy, the interaction between the scientists and the entrepreneurs was most productive in terms of mutual contributions to solving each other's problems and increasing each other's insights. It seems that the points of interaction between the homogeneous spirals can be considered the focus of the heterogeneous collaboration, see figure 4.2.

Personal commitment

The core challenge of the Connected Value Development approach is bringing together all these people with their profoundly different backgrounds, and creating change through the actual realisation of the business opportunities that grow out of these collaborations. Each participating individual is subject to a certain amount of tension arising from the value frame difference between the new innovative idea on the one hand and the modes of operation and judgement of success in their institutions on the other. While the requirements of the institutional setting may pull the person away from collaboration, the guiding idea may pull the person towards the new collaborative practice. The chances that this happens are higher if the values that drive the participating individuals are in line with the values embedded in the innovative idea.

As values are fundamental to a person's being and identity, acting in accordance with one's values is a very powerful driver for change. The Connected Value Development approach therefore involves bringing *people* together, not just stakeholder entities. It is only with personal involvement that there can be a shift from being a negotiating representative to a participant in value creation, and this shift is necessary for the process to be successful. Participants in processes of co-creation "speak as individuals, from their own unique experience. People chosen to participate are not necessarily outspoken leaders. Whoever they are, [...] their behaviour is likely to vary—to some degree and along some dimensions—from stereotypic images others may hold of them."[36] Bringing together a diverse group of people, each person with their own value frames and interests, is not a matter of an analytical alignment of the various interests of the participants. Rather, it is a matter of connecting people to each other and to the challenges that lie ahead. The approach relies on experiencing, acting, reflecting, and personal commitment.

Note, for example, the difference between the commitments of the following two project managers. In an introductory meeting a project manager was asked about his personal dreams with respect to the project. He answered: "I have no personal dreams, this is just one of the projects I do in my nine-to-five job, that's all. I just want to make sure all deliverables are delivered according to the plan." In stark contrast, another project manager had a long term vision for his project, even though his own involvement was limited to just a few years. Even so, he acted as if the project was a lifelong commitment. "We were not doing a project, we were contributing to a development, a transition," he said.

Evidently, when an innovative idea that connects social and environmental challenges to business opportunities is created in an enthousiastic and competent mind, and if the person gets an opportunity to develop this idea further, in the context of an innovation programme such as TransForum, the necessary connection between personal drives and values on the one hand and the project's ambition on the other is there from the outset. Best practice examples from social responsible entrepreneurship underline the importance of personal commitment.

Such a personal commitment may flow naturally from the people who came up with the innovative idea in the first place, but the process manager may also inspire enthousiasm and personal commitment in other participants. We have experienced that a personal and experiential approach to a subject matter often sparks personal commitment, which is very necessary when dealing with wicked problems. It is essential that commitment be seen as more than a mere procedural step in the process (e.g. signatures of heads of departments on project plan), but as the involvement of people at their value level. This implies that people are approached personally, rather than as representatives of their institutions or by their group affiliation. In the three-process-line approach to system innovation (see box 4.3), it is emphasised that generating ideas requires open-minded people who are free from agendas, interests, and institutional incentives.[37] To address the views and interests of their institution, people are invited to put their strategic agenda on the table. This requires trust and an open dialogue.

A process manager can start an open dialogue about people's personal ambitions within the project from the outset. Even if the personal interest

Guiding principle
Focus on personal involvement to facilitate the shift from representative to participant

is not yet very clear, at least such inquiry can stimulate thinking about this and articulating under-articulated dreams and aspirations. The mode of talking becomes "I" instead of "we" or "in my discipline", or "in my department". This movement from institutional interest to personal commitment may take some time to develop in all participants. The extent to which it needs to be supported by the project manager depends on the individual, on the organisation he is representing and on his role or rank within that organisation. The head of a small company may find it easier to say "I want…" than the employee of a large corporation, whereas civil servants of whatever rank may have difficulty expressing their personal ambition. From this position it is possible to start working towards generative dialogue in the group. The dialogue that is organised between the stakeholders requires a 'yes, and' state of mind, instead of 'yes, but'.

The way we behave in conversations, the way we talk, and how we listen are vital for the outcome of the conversation. On a company level it can even be essential for the way a company is able to innovate. Creating the right type of dialogue is also crucial for the process of Connected Value Development. Although it is so very important, most people are not aware of their way of talking and listening. Usually, when we talk, what we really do is 'telling': we tell what *should be* rather than exploring other truths or possibilities. And when we listen, we usually listen to ourselves rather than to others. This might be effective when simple problems are discussed, but not when we try to deal with more complex issues. In his book *Solving tough problems: an open way of talking, listening and creating new realities*, Adam Kahane described four ways of talking and listening.

Guiding principle
Prevent debates around fixed positions and stimulate dialogue

Downloading

When we download, nothing new is explored. We say what is expected to be said, and we do not really listen to the other person. Downloading is driven by politeness and socially acceptable conversation. This way of talking and listening is sufficient in a day-to-day context. However, it is ineffective when we are dealing with serious complex issues.

Debating

When we debate, we are actively trying to find out different perspectives and options. We challenge others by saying what we really think, or even by giving strong dissenting arguments. This often exposes contradictions, where opposing arguments are objectively judged by the other party.

In debating as well as in downloading, we stick to our own opinions without looking at them from the perspective of the other person. We do not create anything new, nor do we reach agreement. Instead, our belief of what is 'right' and what the other thinks is 'wrong' is being confirmed. To create solutions for the complex problems that we are dealing with in Connected Value Development, we must explore new options. Therefore, debating and downloading are inefficient communication modes. We need new ways of talking and listening: dialoguing has proven to me most successful.

Reflective Dialoguing

When we engage in reflective dialogue, we try to imagine ourselves in the way the other person sees us. We try to move outside ourselves and see the world through the eyes of others. In the same way, we try to listen to ourselves through the ears of others. When we talk and listen this way, we are much more open for the ideas and opinions of others, and we create mutual respect. This is the first step in creating change. Because we try to listen subjectively rather than objectively, we see the things that are possible.

Generative Dialoguing

When we engage in generative dialogue, the separation between people in a group is removed, and a 'collective I' is created. Individual goals disappear and a common purpose is realised. Together we can see what really matters, and what can be done together to achieve our common goals. This type of talking and listening is described, among others, by Otto Scharmer[38].

It is clear that in order to make a change in complex situations, dialoguing is much more effective than downloading or debating. Dialoguing is a way of communication that expands our capacity to hear and see what is needed. These four ways of talking and listening provide us with a framework to reflect upon the type of conversation that is taking place in our project (see fig. 4.3). Sharing this framework with the project participants will help us recognise and address situations in which conversation reverts to debating and downloading.

In this way, the grounds for creativity are developed and new venues opened, unhindered by existing structures and institutional values. People will connect on a personal level to the project and to each other. Through personal commitment 3P ideas are developed that are strongly felt by people, ideas that are connected to their core values, so that they can act as a marker of direction, a beacon in the distance.

Frame reflection; the start of learning

Personal commitment to the endeavour helps generating energy around the innovative idea in the middle, it is however not enough. It would be to render the power of the institutional settings irrelevant. Our personal values can be said to consist of everything we believe in, of what we find important. They provide much of the drive behind human actions and motivations: it is 'what makes us tick'. Our values are constituted through interaction with our subcultures and communities. To a large degree, we share our values with others in the communities that we are part of: our families, our friends, our political party, but also our colleagues and professional peers, our broader professional system, and broadly speaking, other members of our 21st century Western society. Our value-frame is thus made out of mixed sets of values, which are reinforced time and again by our actions and interactions in these communities. They guide

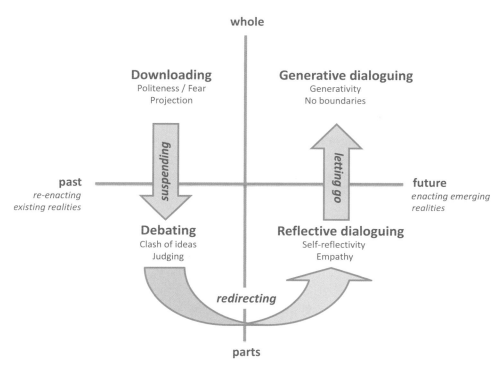

FIGURE 4.3 A Framework for talking and listening (Kahane 2010, after Scharmer 2007) [39]

our actions and decisions in our private, social, spiritual, and professional lives.

Not only as citizens or consumers, but also as professionals, our actions are guided by the values shared with other members of the communities we belong to. This has consequences for participating in Connected Value Development processes, as the new approach proposed in this book differs substantially from more traditional courses of action. This newly proposed approach is referred to as a new paradigm: a new set of routines, working methods, vocabularies, perceptions of relevant outcomes and underlying assumptions, beliefs, and values. To change such perceptions and common practices requires first and foremost that participants become aware of their current 'value frame', that is: of their values, assumptions, perceptions, and practices. This involves reflecting on one's own actions, and on the underlying beliefs, assumptions, and values. This is not easy, precisely because the usual perceptions and practices constitute the default mode of functioning. Values are deeply embedded in our world view, and often they are not consciously articulated. Compare this with the parable of the two young fish swimming about their business when they meet an older fish, who nods at them and says, "Good morning, boys, how's the water?" The two young fish swim on for a bit, and then eventually one of them looks at the other and wonders, "what is this 'water' thing he's talking about?"[40]

Usually, underlying value-frames only get questioned when something is 'off', when a person becomes uneasy about aspects of his or her environment. One becomes conscious of one's body when it loses function; of the values of one's circle of friends when disagreements continue to rise; of the air when it starts smelling bad. The relevant question for Connected Value Development is: how can we support people in becoming aware of their default mode, of their underlying value frame. The next questions then are how to challenge, how to change it. This involves what Bateson[41] has referred to as second-order learning. He describes learning as a Russian-dolls set of feedback loops. The general assumption of learning in the loops is that all forms denote change, and that every level is the basis for the context of the following, in a nested manner. Three levels of loops are illustrated in figure 4.4.

Learning in the first feedback loop is represented by the question: "are we doing things right?". This means that individuals receive feedback about performed actions, and then correct their actions based on this information. In the second loop, the values, assumptions, objectives, and policies that prompted the action in the first place are questioned. This is represented by the question: "are we doing the right things?".[42] In a third loop, an even deeper question is addressed: "How do we decide what is right?" This requires a distance from the situational context and reflection on the prejudices, and underlying assumptions concerning this context. This has previously been described by others as 'reflection on reflection-in-action'[43] and as 'knowledge about the preconditions of reflexive knowledge'.[44]

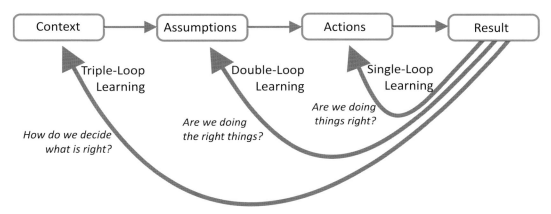

FIGURE 4.4 Single-, double-, and triple-loop learning

In the context of TransForum projects, participants have recognised the importance of these deeper levels of learning: "Every now and then I just think about why we do the things we do and about what the real problem is, and whether it is necessary for me to act on it immediately. I think this is necessary, especially in a dynamic network, where all kinds of ideas come up and people are reinforcing each other's enthusiasm. That's the whole point, of course, but it means I have to take a step back sometimes."

The Connected Value Development approach stimulates reflection by bringing together a great variety of people around a certain issue, challenge, or idea. These people will be confronted with different ways of doing things, with different assumptions and different values, just by participating. In addition to that, specific methods are employed to stimulate reflection. Appointing a dedicated person in the team to observe and

Guiding principle
Appointing a dedicated 'reflection monitor' to support learning

BOX 4.5   Interactive learning and action approach

The ILA is a transdisciplinary innovation strategy that was developed in the 1980s and 1990s.[46,47] Its aim was to increase the sustainability of agricultural innovations in developing countries towards the needs and interests of small-scale farmers. Since it was first introduced in the late nineteen-eighties, it has been applied in Zimbabwe, South Africa, Bangladesh and in the Netherlands, among others.

The approach is structured around a number of principles:

- End-users have a prominent role in decision making processes. Active participation during the innovation process is the best guarantee that the development of technologies meet their needs;
- One specific vision forms the basis of the innovation process; the innovation has a positive effect on the living conditions of the end user. Commitment to this vision creates a greater willingness to collaborate, to solve problems, and to deal with uncertainties and risks;
- Building a relationship of trust is crucial. The ILA methodology involves mechanisms to create circumstances that contribute to the building of trust;
- The ability to interact and communicate mutual learning effectively is essential;
- ILA promotes coalition building;
- Different types of knowledge are integrated;
- An interdisciplinary team of intermediaries guides the process of communication, teamwork, learning, and coalition building between the participants of the process.

The ILA has many similarities to the Connected Value Development approach. Although it was originally conducted in a transdisciplinary, scientific research setting, this approach also acknowledges the active participation of end users in the decision making process. The effect of the ILA, however, is originally formulated around the enhancement of the (poor) living conditions of end-users (in developing countries). Connected Value Development aims for knowledge co-creation in the light of 3P value propositions and (new) business development that comes from there.

facilitate learning is an effective means to this end. Based on years of experience with the Interactive Learning and Action approach, the Athena Institute of VU University Amsterdam developed the ILA monitoring approach. It is an interactive and participatory evaluation approach (see box 4.5), where a reflection monitor stimulates system thinking, reflection, and learning.[45] This dedicated person participates in the project team, meticulously observes the process, and conducts interviews with participants and other actors. Observations and results of analyses are fed back into the process through informal conversations, contributions to meetings, and by facilitating specific sessions for reflection. In this way, an iterative process of action and reflection takes place.

One of the project leaders described the added value of the reflection monitor as follows: "We work with technical experts who are absolutely indispensable in the process. However, with all due respect, the technical experts as well as the entrepreneurs tend to think in terms of technical solutions. As a project leader, I also tend to focus on how to get the whole thing implemented. The reflection monitor really helps us to take a step back and reflect upon what we are doing. The entrepreneurs really appreciate the feedback and the new insights they gain from the reflection monitor too."

In conclusion

Building new alliances of actors around a guiding idea does not automatically lead to a well-functioning collaborative practice. Personal commitment and frame-reflection are necessary, but not sufficient conditions. Actors will differ in the way they frame the problem, the guiding idea, the preferred mode of operation, and the desired outcomes. Participating individuals are members of different communities and organisational cultures that may clash. With such a variety of actors involved, even if the guiding idea motivating the process has the potential of connecting the visible and outwardly professed values, the unarticulated and unconsciously applied value frame may prove to be a major obstacle for mutual understanding and fruitful collaboration. Realising a groundbreaking idea then requires regular interaction between the stakeholders involved. We will discuss this in the next chapter, on co-creation. First we will take a short detour to the intermezzo of the stubborn reality of alliance building and idea exploration. There we present common situations, and possible strategies to cope with them or avoid them.

INTERMEZZO 2
The Stubborn Reality of Exploration and Alliance Building

1   Lack of cooperation between entrepreneurs and scientists

In an agricultural innovation project, a lot of research money and time was invested in the development of a computer model for the logistics of potted plants. When the scientist finally presented their results, the entrepreneurs reacted with frustration and exclaimed: "What is this?", "How can we possibly make use of this model?" "What does it imply? While the scientists had mapped what exactly the current situation was, the entrepreneurs were looking for concrete directions for solutions. "This may be nice to know, but we should focus on what we need to know", one of the entrepreneurs concluded.

Taking time for an in depth analysis of the current situation, and relating questions to the relevant theoretical background and literature is a normal way of working for scientists. For practitioners outside the world of science, this time-consuming process can be highly frustrating. Entrepreneurs look for quick and applicable knowledge and do not care that much about what sometimes mockingly is called "nice clean reports" and "the larger scientific picture". Theoretical position papers may have proven valuable for conferences only to wind up in a drawer after the conference because they had no practical value.

Though a time discrepancy is often first mentioned, it is not the only problem in the cooperation between scientists and entrepreneurs. In many cases, the actual problem was the framing of the question, which was often too specific and narrow for scientists to develop a proper research framework, as a researcher experienced: "The questions that were asked were entirely legitimate and sensible, but not easy to respond to through research. So we had to give it a theoretical framework. In essence, we had to translate the challenges of the project into sound research questions. It is crucial to check such a translation with the other stakeholders."

In another project, the discrepancy between the practical challenge and the research question suitable for scientific inquiry was noticed at an early stage; the necessary 'translation' was done by the scientist and discussed with the other participants. In Connected Value Development, the most useful contribution of participating scientists is often not so much their subject knowledge, but their ability to structure problems and distil relevant questions. Every stakeholder has their own unique contribution to this process, but it is crucial to give meaning collectively to the knowledge and experience brought in by each and any stakeholder.

Some practical tips

Change your perspective via learning journeys
To be able to get fully acquainted with all the issues around a challenge, it is important to remove one's own biases, whether one is a scientist or an entrepreneur. A good way of changing one's perspective is by going on location, on a learning journey. A learning journey is a physical trip around the "system" in which multiple stakeholders travel together in order to immerse themselves in the issue that they are trying to address. This allows them to see the issue with fresh eyes through the experiences and perspectives of others. If people stay where they are and survey their system from a fixed angle, they will never gain the deeper understanding that is necessary in order to effect transformational and sustainable change. One of the best ways to build that understanding is to go out into the world and change one's frame of reference. Shifting between seeing a problem from 'the inside looking out', to 'the outside looking in' makes it possible for valuable insights to emerge.

Formulate the knowledge questions together
Make sure that all stakeholders are equally involved in the first formulation of the challenges and the knowledge questions ("what do we need to know?") associated with the guiding idea. This does not necessarily mean that the formulation of research questions that will give scientific input to answering the knowledge question, is done in a multi-stakeholder group. Sometimes it is useful or even necessary to start articulation processes within separate groups, in order to utilise the full

potential of the participants' knowledge.[48] A process of successful articulation, initiated within a setting of only entrepreneurs or only scientists, might enable rather than disable, a fruitful dialogue[49]. But it is crucial to keep a focus on what the project needs to know, instead of on what a scientist just feels is interesting to inquire.

In the dialogue between different groups the task of a process manager should be to verify that in the final articulation of the research question, all aspects that are perceived as valuable by the different participants (and their institutes) are addressed. The Dynamic Learning Agenda (DLA) is a tool to record the essence of the fuzzy learning trajectories of innovative projects. The Dynamic Learning Agenda tool especially attends to make visible the tough issues that are 'swept under the rug'. Because this avoidance phenomenon hinders effective learning, the monitor steers towards making these under articulated topics tangible. The monitor does this by delicately addressing the issue and opening it up for discussion.

Give meaning to knowledge and experiences together

Even more important than formulating the knowledge questions together is giving meaning to the results of research or scientific data. It is not a matter of implementing these results, but of interpreting these results from the frame of reference of the participants. What do the scientific results mean for this project? Giving meaning to results requires a dialogue between the scientist and the other sta-

keholders; merely giving a presentation or handing out a report will definitely not do. But the same goes for experiences that the group has as a whole, or for anecdotes that a stakeholder might be able to tell about something that went wrong with another company that tried to develop a more sustainable product. Reflecting on each other's knowledge and collectively giving meaning to it is the key activity in the innovation space.

Deviate from standard role division

In a project where collaboration between scientists and entrepreneurs proved difficult, the breakthrough came when a meeting was arranged in which the entrepreneurs took the lead. While in previous meetings the scientists had dominated the agenda, this time the scientists were asked to wait with their input and theories until after the break. Entrepreneurs were asked to share their ambitions and future vision. The researchers listened carefully and then asked questions. When the scientists reflected on the stories of the entrepreneurs, they started to realise and truly understand why entrepreneurs saw some parts of the process as needing either more or less attention.[50] It is important to keep in mind that Connected Value Development is not about doing research or about designing new concepts. The output of the process needs to be a 3P value proposition that is well-aligned with the needs of the different stakeholders and therefore, to the needs in which all these stakeholders are committed to invest.

2. Nobody is perfect (but a team can be)

Based on her experience as executive, a senior civil servant is appointed as project manager of a Connected Value Development project. She has a coaching management style, which functions very well within her own department but, as it turns out, her style is far less effective in this project. She gets frustrated that the entrepreneurs in the project do not listen to her in the way she is used to and apparently pay more attention to another team member; to someone who just point blank tells them: "Guys, this is not possible; it has to be done like this…"

There are different management styles, each with their own value and limitations. So it is important to recognise what works best under the circumstances, without taking it personally and getting dragged into some kind of competition. In the course of the project, the project manager learned to appreciate the outspoken team member; his input was needed to ensure that the participants, and especially the entrepreneurs with a strong focus on action, stayed inspired and motivated.

In setting up group processes, it is often underlined that basic functions, like that of a project manager, monitor, and secretary, must be fulfilled by capable and experienced people. Such a function-based approach has the advantage of making it clear what role in the process is to be expected from each of these functionaries. Yet precisely this clarity, this well-defined set of roles, is also a weakness, as it may limit the possibility to use optimally the personal talents of each of the participants and, by its rigidity, it does not do justice to the obvious fact that different phases of the project ask for different styles of leadership.

But in fact, this consideration does not apply only to leadership, but to any formal or otherwise established function. In amateur theatre, when each of the players is cast in a certain role, he or she goes about learning the lines for that role. Professional actors, on the other hand, often learn and play all the parts. Too rigid a reliance on the function each of the participants is supposed to have diminishes the shared responsibility for the progress of the project, leading to people unduly waiting for each other to carry out certain tasks and to tasks being carried out in a less than optimal way by the designated person instead of the person most able or most eager.

The Connected Value Development approach asks all participants to take responsibility for the whole of the process and, if necessary, to fulfil any function. It is crucial to acknowledge that a project manager cannot be solely responsible for all aspects of the process.

Some practical tips

Do not try to combine all roles in one project manager

It was noted in the TransForum projects that projects perform well if there are three different roles identified: the project manager, responsible for the progress of the project, the process manager or facilitator, responsible for the characteristics of the process, and the 'owner' of the project idea, who has seen the potential of connecting social and environmental challenges to a business opportunity and are responsible for keeping direction and a focus on impact. These roles are hardly ever combined in one person, since they really require different skills and capabilities. Alongside that, it is important to make use of each team member's unique strengths and capabilities.

Delegate roles according to personal capabilities

Delegating tasks is the hallmark of a good manager. In a multi-stakeholder setting, it is tempting simply to delegate according to function; that is, according to what the participants represent, rather than to what they can do best. Yet, the idea behind Connected Value Development is that it is about a group of people, not a group of institutions. Making use of individual talents can be one way of blurring the traditional distinctions and undermining preconceptions. It is also important to reflect on one's own abilities and on what the project needs at specific phases of the project

3 It is not my problem

A team member shrugged and told her colleague, another participant in the project "Why should I address these questions and be the first to show my cards? Besides, I have other things to do." The project leader looked at her while she rapidly walked away. Every time he tried to discuss the core issue in this project nobody was home. To his dismay, not one of them seemed willing to take on responsibility for the project.

This team member does not feel responsible for the whole project, but only for the part she is involved in and many others felt the same way. In fact, the group was avoiding a number of tough questions that were never properly discussed, notably about openness and trust: with a number of comparable businesses round the table, openly sharing business figures and discussing plans and expectations is not at all evident. Most participants were hiding their information and, instead, asked for more scientific papers and research. Although intellectually interesting, these papers were obviously not going to solve the underlying issue: a lack of trust.

For Connected Value Development, it is important that participants are willing to take responsibility for the whole project. Inviting someone to participate only at a certain stage of the project because of his or her expertise on a specific subject is obviously an option, but we caution: it can sometimes disrupt a collective learning process.

Some practical tips

Building a team

It is always preferable to invite participants as individuals rather than as representatives of stakeholder parties. However, in many projects there simply is not much choice. In those cases, a lot of explicit attention should be given to turn a gathering of stakeholders into a project team, consisting of individuals who are personally and collectively committed to the guiding idea of the project. Several of the possible techniques to use have been discussed earlier; they all come down to devoting enough time, at the very beginning, to creating a generative dialogue, not just about the objectives and needs of the stakeholder parties but also about personal goals, commitments and expectations. These can be listed explicitly and later, when necessary, brought to the table again to reconnect with the ideas which brought the participants round the table in the first place.

Building trust

The abovementioned group dialogue may go a long way to build trust among the participants, but more is needed when there are concerns about what will happen with the information provided. The first and most important way to meet those concerns is to get them openly on the table and discuss them. This, by itself, can make it clear to all that the project is not going anywhere if the attitude does not change. Apart from this, there are several tried and tested ways to ensure a certain amount of confidentiality, such as non-disclosure and non competition agreements. Such explicitly formulated documents can certainly help clarify expectations.

Skilled process management

In order for the strategies mentioned here to work, a competent process manager is indispensable; this would preferably be an intermediary who does not have an institutional stake in the project. As one process manager and intermediary put it: "The team has to build up faith in the process and trust the intermediary. This takes a lot of time. The participants must trust that whatever is laid on the table is the whole truth and nothing but the truth. People must not think that you might have a hidden agenda or a connection to one of the stakeholder groups, because then you will never get anywhere." The process manager should therefore be chosen on personal merit, not on the authority of the organisation which he or she represents.

The situation every process manager or intermediary should be working towards is one where the group as a whole feels responsible for the project. This is called taking collective ownership. It can be enhanced by any of the strategies mentioned before, and in particular, during meetings, by giving ample attention to questions, and certainly to proposals, from an unexpected side. This is the kind of atmosphere where people dare speak up about matters they know little about. All this can help to get the participants to think outside their particular box and start feeling responsible for the project as a whole.

4 Participants leaving and joining

The meeting with all stakeholders of the project started very well, but halfway through it became clear that the expectations of the manufacturer of the packaging materials differed fundamentally from those of the other stakeholders. The project manager had tried several ways to bring them together, but was unable to come up with a plan both parties could agree on. Later that day, the manufacturer called to say he had decided to step out of the project. The project manager was upset, they all had invested a lot of time and energy in this relationship, and she worried about where she would find another manufacturer willing to step in on such short notice.

After some initial panic, the project manager in this case realised that it might not be so bad that this manufacturer had stepped out of the project, as his ideas did not fit in well with the original guiding idea. Moreover, the manufacturer was especially wary of the possibility that others would hesitate too much and too long, thus creating exorbitant delays in time. In this, he plainly showed no confidence in the other participants. One of the pitfalls for process managers in such situations is the wish to keep everybody on board and satisfied, instead of keeping an eye on what is best for the process. If there is too much difference of opinion about the guiding idea, and too little confidence in the commitment of each of the participants to the creation of a viable business case, it is sometimes better just to look out for an alternative. As it happened, another manufacturer of packaging materials was found and a new packaging was created which was much more in line with the ideas behind the project.

In the course of a Connected Value Development process, different participants can be involved, depending on the phase of the process. Also, the role and function may vary in the course of the process. For example, a scientist contributing fundamental knowledge can play an important role at the start of the process, while in a later phase his expertise is less relevant. The phasing in and phasing out of stakeholders is a normal part of the Connected Value Development process.

Some practical tips

Analyse and discuss why someone is leaving

Sometimes the reason for leaving can be a clear signal that insufficient attention had been given to the goals of that participant. Without remedying this shortcoming, any new participant taking his place would be likely to end up in a similar predicament. However, there are a host of other reasons why a stakeholder might quit which may have little or nothing to do with the process or with a failure on the part of the project manager. Although it is painful to say goodbye when one has been making plans together and invested much time and energy in the collaboration, it may be the right choice for an individual stakeholder, and his departure might even benefit the process, as it creates room for change and may lead to new opportunities.

Re-evaluate the composition of the group

Someone stepping out of the process may lead to a re-evaluation of the composition of the group. This is something which should be done regularly but is often forgotten as, after many meetings and shared experiencing, the composition of the project group tends to go unquestioned unless there is some particular reason to bring it up. In the above example, the manufacturer left of his own accord, but of course it could also have been the process manager asking him to step out for the sake of the project.

The spiralling progress of a Connected Value Development process is full of evolving objectives and changing attitudes, but these tend to be slow and almost imperceptible. Therefore, it is advisable, at least for the project manager but in fact for the whole group, to regularly bring up the question whether the composition of the group is still optimally suited to get on with the guiding idea in the form it has taken. It may be time to turn to the list of objectives and motives drawn up during the initial phase and put two crucial questions on the table: "Why are we still in this?" and "Are there others we should invite to join?"

5   Debating instead of co-creating

A process manager concluded that, in spite of an enthousiastic start and a large number of meetings, no shared community developed in the project. He remarked: "Actually, there were two parties during this phase. On the one hand there were people from the local community, and on the other side a project team, a housing corporation, a real estate developer, an architect, and a environmental adviser–on the other side." Each group had their own goals: the local community wanted to have their houses and living environments improved; the project team wanted to meet the challenge of achieving a sustainable real estate renovation project. Alignment between the objectives and expectations of these two groups proved difficult, since each party seemed to represent a different problem and solution.

An important characteristic of Connected Value Development is that meaning is created in a collaborative process. Meetings are not, or at least should not be, merely interchanges of information; instead, they should contribute to a dynamic process in which new knowledge and insights arise.

Some practical tips

Do not start with a design, but start by exploring the challenge

Spend sufficient time at the beginning of the process to get familiar with each other's worlds, ideas, dreams, and expectations. Starting with a multi-day expedition or learning journey, by literally visiting each other's worlds, proves to be very valuable to create an atmosphere of openness, togetherness and trust, provides a strong basis for a successful process and helps avoid quarrels, conflicts and competition. It often lays a foundation for a generative dialogue leading to co-created solutions. Placing the dialogue in the future will help to minimise the impact of the participants' current interests. It also means that one works with 'problem definition in motion'–continuously establishing what is at stake–instead of a clear-cut definition.

Experts: start by listening, not by explaining

For the real estate project, a general urban development plan was already drawn up. Yet the process manager decided to start from scratch, as the whole idea of a Connected Value Development project is that all plans are made in collaboration from the start. Presenting ready-made ideas is a sure way of creating a division between parties. As a project leader for the housing corporation explained: "We started the discussion with what people believed to be the problems in this residential area." That is the type of question that creates a level playing field for each of the participants. In fact, especially for the 'experts', in this case the participants in the design team, it is a good idea to start by listening, and listening well. This may demand some effort. As one of the environmental advisers stressed: "The main thing is that you listen. For example, there was a man in our project who was very difficult to deal with, but if you really listened to him, you could pick up his points."

Make the tensions in different demands explicit

For an individual participant, it is important to actively and consciously challenge the methods, knowledge, and values of his own organisation. One can ask questions such as "this is the way I normally work, but is this constructive in this setting?" This can be done individually, with the help of a log book, or through reflective meetings in small groups, in which participants use each other as a sounding board and get feedback on their own everyday actions. Making the tensions between different demands explicit helps to prioritise and find a balance. At the same time, as one executive of a large company remarked, "You have to be completely clear about your goals. You can say: 'I want a particular focus in the process because eventually for me these goals have to be met.' If some of the actors then say: 'Well, we have a problem with that', then you will obviously talk about it. But you have to be clear about where your paths might diverge."

Make use of informal moments

Informal moments, e.g. while making coffee and at lunch, can be helpful in getting to know each other, but also in sharing and resolving tensions, as a local administrator explained. "When I say openly and clearly in a meeting: 'I am sorry but I cannot guarantee it will be there in time', of course they are not that happy with my answer at that moment. But at least it is honest and it is the reality we have to face. I always use the so called 'after meeting' at the coffee machine to explain why I cannot make certain promises. Usually they get my point and next time round they accept the limitation I raise more easily." For process managers, this implies that the schedule of a meeting should not be too tight; it is important to leave room for informal chats. These chats can prove very valuable as a social lubricant, to get to know each other, to get things done, or to smooth uneasiness between participants or organisations.

Transformational leadership

When the process gets stuck in a division between parties who are debating each other from their own unmovable points of view, a different style of leadership is required. In the words of one participant, a representative of a governmental institution: "What is most difficult is to get people to be prepared to relinquish their own interests or those of their environment, and to participate in thinking about, and searching for, a solution. You have to take the time for this, but it is also a matter of creating collective inspiration." A divided community is often a signal that the wrong type of dialogue between the stakeholders is being organised. As another experienced process manager remarked: "You have to be able to see things from the point of view of the other person; you have to be a bridge-builder by nature, rather than someone who likes polarisation and conflict; you have to be a good chairperson to be able to get to the essence of things and then take things a step further. I do not think that these are skills you can teach everyone. You have to look for people who have it in them, and then give them the opportunity to develop their skills. You have to look for people showing transformational leadership."

6 Low valuation of intangible benefits

When a participant reported enthousiastically to his superior about the progress of the Connected Value Development process he was involved in, he was asked for the minutes of the meetings: his boss wanted to get a better understanding of what was going on. Only at that moment did he realise that the minutes did not describe 'what was going on'; in fact they did not do justice to the process at all: there were many intangible benefits which could hardly be described in formal minutes of team meetings.

The aims of Connected Value Development go beyond delivering tangible outcomes. In Connected Value Development, elements like discussing with new people with different perspectives and knowledge, defining a shared vision, creating a 'community of learning', connecting with the process, and staying motivated are all valued. Many participants are surprised to realise that such aspects are valuable. As one participant put it in the evaluation: "We now know that, apart from the Three P's there is a fourth P which is essential too: the Process. Our shared vision has been alive throughout the project. Together we felt responsible for developing and implementing next steps." And "The most important impact this project had was getting the companies to discover each other's frame."

While these achievements may be apparent, and evidently useful, in the eyes of the participants, they will not sound very convincing to outsiders, especially superiors worrying about budgets, time delays, and 'moving targets'. Furthermore, when the intangible benefits stay as intangible as described above, they cannot very well benefit others, who did not take part in the process. Clearly, then, it is of great importance to invest in ways to make the intangibles as concrete and visible as possible. This demands an explicit effort on the part of the participants in the process, who may experience this as superfluous on the one hand, and very difficult or even impossible on the other.

Some practical tips

Make intangible outcomes visible

A process manager concluded: "Too little attention is paid to establishing the results of interactive processes, both in terms of form and of content". This means that knowledge and experience are lost. What is most important is to obtain the knowledge acquired in the process. To do this, one could organise a research process by formulating research questions with regard to the process, such as: 'Which actors are relevant for a certain issue to involve in an interactive process?' 'Can parties change their existing behaviour?' 'Is the composition of the group important if one wants to break through firmly established institutional barriers?' I see this as an important step."

This approach proved a way to make intangible outcomes visible by explicating what they are about and why they are important. This can be done by organising a research process or by other means, like, for instance, in-depth interviews with participants at the end of a project which are gathered into a book. This way, the individual experiences of the participants may become useful learning material for others.

5 Co-creation and Experimentation

Connected Value Development brings people together from different domains to generate diversity and bring in relevant perspectives. KENGi actors bring in the professional knowledge and experience that they derive from their professional affiliation; that is, scientists bring in specialised knowledge, entrepreneurs bring in expertise on effective business strategies, policy makers bring in knowledge on current regulations and policies, and NGOs and other societal groups bring in their understanding of societal concerns and needs. At the same time, the close cooperation that is sought for in Connected Value Development can converge to an 'experience of one'.[51] When this happens it is no longer possible to distinguish the separate roles of the participants; when consumer and producer, scientist and entrepreneur, or policy maker and local citizens become 'equal problem solvers'.[52] In the current chapter we describe this phase in which a new sustainable practice around a guiding idea is developed. The initial idea is developed into a 3P value proposition and mutual benefits are further explored. After this phase there should be commitment on the part of the business partners to make the financial investments needed and commitment on the part of the governmental and societal groups to support this business proposal by investing in the creation of the necessary conditions at home base. But before that, it is necessary to start the process of co-creation that will eventually lead to viable business propositions that meet the needs of our contemporary society.

We start this chapter by exploring what type of knowledge is needed to create viable solutions to wicked problems. It is argued that new knowledge needs to be created in which tacit and explicit knowledge of all stakeholders is combined. This then leads to the question how the *creation of new knowledge* for the development of sustainable products, services and solutions is best facilitated. We will introduce the concept of a *Community*

Guiding principle
Combine tacit and explicit knowledge of all stakeholders

of *Practice* as a conducive environment for experimentation and co-creation of the new knowledge needed for the development of solutions to wicked problems. The next question becomes how in a Connected Value Development process such a Community of Practice is managed. It appears that it is not so much a leading project manager steering the process of Connected Value Development, but rather it is a matter of *creating shared ownership and stimulating adaptive leadership*. Finally, we will reflect on the question of how to realise a high quality process that will lead to the ambitious outcomes envisaged at the outset. To this end the concept of *reflection monitoring* introduced in the previous chapter is further elaborated.

The creation of new knowledge for 3P value creation

3P value creation requires an approach of knowledge co-creation applied within a broad stakeholder network (see Box 5.1). Such an approach has by some scholars been called a transdisciplinary approach.[53] It is a different form of knowledge development, in which the perspectives of different actors are integrated in the identification, formulation and resolution of problems. Issues are therefore not formulated from the viewpoint of a scientific discipline, and assessed by other researchers ('peer review') using scientific criteria which are relevant within the discipline. In transdisciplinary knowledge creation, the issues, and therefore the required expertise, are formulated from the context of the problem. Different societal actors, including scientists, search in a joint deliberative process to clarify the problem and find possible solutions. In this process, through mutual exchange new knowledge is generated. It is not a matter of 'knowledge transfer' or of applying (or making applicable) scientific knowledge in a specific problem context. The different perspectives on the issue are integrated in a collective learning process, whereby in the course of the interaction new knowledge is construed, shared and tested. In this kind of process, 'socially robust knowledge' can be generated, which Nowotny et al.[54] indicate is not only scientifically reliable, but is also accepted and applicable in the contexts of the issue at hand.

Guiding principle

Use a transdisciplinary approach for a joint process of knowledge creation and problem solving

BOX 5.1 Developing new knowledge

Peterson[55] argues that including sustainability as an attribute of products and services is challenging due to its nature as a wicked problem. With these types of problems many different perspectives exist that all define and structure the problem in different ways; the view that one has of the problem and the knowledge which is relevant for it will be different for the various stakeholders involved. Creating sustainable products involves bringing these actors together in a process of knowledge co-creation. According to Peterson, the new knowledge that is developed in this process has high strategic value, especially compared to explicit knowledge, which despite its most frequent use, has limited strategic value, and tacit knowledge, which has moderate strategic value.

TABLE 5.1 The knowledge continuum based on strategic value[56]

Dimensions	Explicit Knowledge	Tacit Knowledge	New Knowledge
Accessibility	Easy (codified; internalization; unless isolating mechanism, e.g. patent)	Moderate (socialization)	Difficult (creation precedes access)
Relevance to innovation	Technical innovation (application to new settings)	Adaptive innovation (adoption with enhancements in new settings)	Transformational innovation (breakthrough or new-to-the-world)
Application Risk	Relatively certain, highly predictable	Moderately certain, predictable	Uncertain, unpredictable
Dynamics	All knowledge "decays" to explicit or becomes obsolete	Becomes explicit through externalization (theory/science)	Becomes tacit through practice or explicit through theory/science
Strategic Value	Low/limited (unless an isolating mechanism, e.g. patents) "Commodity"	Moderate (causal ambiguity) "Differentiated"	High (first mover advantage) "Unique"

A strategy for approaching wicked problems in this manner is one based on a de facto interweaving of domains (see figure 1b). Knowledge creation and problem-solving are not clearly distinguishable from each other and the primacy for solving wicked problems does not therefore lie clearly with one of the domains. This notion of co-production fits with the idea that it is not only scientific knowledge that is relevant for the resolution of unstructured, social problems but also societal or experiential knowledge. The knowledge that scientists contribute to this process is integrated with the knowledge that other participants contribute on the basis of their experience. This has consequences for the perceived role of scientists; both by the scientists themselves and by the other participants. Scientists do not have the sole right to contributing knowledge and knowledge production does not take place in the way this is normally done within the scientific community. As one of the project leaders states: "I often hear people say: Let's go and get some knowledge from the university, but then you'll only get part of what you need. You need to mobilise knowledge and expertise, from entrepreneurs, but also from scientists. You should include scientists with an entrepreneurial mindset who are open to designing and thinking about the best solutions together with you. We are aiming for the highest input of these scientists and this is only possible when they are directly involved in the project and feel what is at stake. Otherwise I will receive a spreadsheet and that is not what I need: I need a solution." Thus, rather than receiving ready-made knowledge from scientists, all participating actors co-create knowledge in the Connected Value Development process. This approach is based on a set of assumptions of what knowledge is.

Two perspectives on knowledge can be distinguished. From one perspective knowledge is considered to be a static entity, 'contained' in people or reified in procedures, books, scientific articles, legislation, etc. Knowledge can be stored, and as such exist independently from the knower. In this way it can be transmitted to others as explicit knowledge, remaining unchanged. This view of knowledge is referred to as the cognitive, possession, or stock approach.[57]

The second perspective on knowledge starts from the premise that knowledge development is essentially a communicative process, and that our claims to knowledge are grounded in actual practice, rather than in objective reality. Scholars of organisational learning and knowledge co-creation have referred to philosophers like Dewey and Wittgenstein, and to the concept of Communities of Practice as developed by Wenger and Lave to support this view.[58] Interestingly, knowledge creation in a Community of Practice is not so different from scientific knowledge development. Sociologists of science too have found that scientific knowledge production is a social activity taking place in so called epistemic cultures. Epistemic cultures refer to the particular communities of scientific practice in which scientists share their perception on what valid knowledge is and how it is created. Thus, whereas it is often thought that *real* knowledge is produced in a specific, scientific, way, these studies show that all knowledge (also scientific) derives from social practices.

This means that existing explicit knowledge can have benefits in the process of Connected Value Development when it is adopted and given meaning in the shared practice of the participants. By developing a shared practice through intensive interactions, tacit knowledge of participants may be shared too. Tacit knowledge is shared, not by translating it or converting it into explicit knowledge. This is misunderstanding the nature of tacit knowledge, which is inherently embedded in action. Rather, tacit knowledge can be "displayed and manifested in what we do".[59] Thus, a shared practice is where we give meaning to explicit knowledge, where we share tacit knowledge through practise, and where we create new knowledge through the integration of explicit and tacit knowledge of all participants. It follows that creating a Community of Practice with the participating KENGi actors is a fruitful strategy for Connected Value Development. It also underlines that a process of Connected Value Development is not just aimed at generating new knowledge, but is aimed at creating an innovative practice in which viable business propositions are developed. If we assume that we acquire knowledge, and ascribe meaning to this knowledge, through participation in societal practices, and co-creation of new knowledge for the development of 3P value propositions is required in

Guiding principle
Create new knowledge and give meaning to knowledge in a shared practice

Connected Value Development, than interaction between the different KENGi actors should be set-up according to the principles of Communities of Practice.

Facilitating co-creation by means of a Community of Practice

Guiding principle
Develop a new sustainable practice around and for value creation

A Community of Practice is characterised by the mutual commitment of the participants, by sharing a common goal, which is determined by all the participants together (see Box 5.2). The Community of Practice also has a shared repertory of resources which become available in due course to ascribe meaning and to create knowledge, such as routines, words, instruments, working methods, stories, symbols and gestures. In this way, the members of a Community of Practice develop their own organisational culture, guiding "the way things get done around here." Whilst originally Communities of Practice were formed of members of the same profession or interest, in Connected Value Development members of the alliance are people from diverse backgrounds and stakeholder groups.

BOX 5.2   Communities of Practice

Cognitive anthropologists Jean Lave and Etienne Wenger[60] introduced the concept of 'Community of Practice' in 1991 to increase our understanding of acting and learning by professionals. According to Lave and Wenger, groups of professionals are bound by a shared practice and a shared repertoire of resources that are developed over time, such as routines, words, stories, symbols, gestures, working methods and instruments. Through participation in a community, members build collaborative relationships and establish norms.

Communities of Practice evolve naturally all around the world, wherever practitioners of skill-based activities meet regularly over time to share experiences and insights and mutually engage in a common practice. Their emergence can also be supported specifically, making the concept of Communities of Practice particularly relevant for Connected Value Development.

Each of us is part of multiple communities of practice, and as such guided by multiple sets of values, conceptions and preconceptions. Wherever people are in regular contact with others in the same line of work, they share practices, assumptions, values, preconceptions and habits. They share the way they judge duties should be performed, what is acceptable behaviour and how people should interact with each other and with people outside the organisation. Not only as professionals, but also as citizens or consumers our actions are guided by the values and norms shared with other members of the social groups we belong to.

Bringing together KENGi partners in a Connected Value Development thus poses challenges. Actors will differ in the way they frame the problem which the project aims to address, based on their value frame. They will have different perceptions of what constitutes the guiding idea of the project and they all are members of different communities of practice which provide them with different cultural value frames.

In one of TransForum's projects, greenhouse farmers experimented with the implementation of the 'closed greenhouse'; a greenhouse that produces rather than consumes energy. A collaborative practice was formed with greenhouse farmers, scientists, and administrators. For each of these actors, the closed greenhouse as 'innovative idea' was framed differently. For the administrators, it was a way to reduce CO_2 emissions and comply with international environmental agreements. For the scientists it was a way to learn more about plant growth and for each of the farmers it was different again: for some the closed greenhouse was primarily a way to reduce production costs, for others it was a way to better working conditions, and for still others it was a way to increase crop production.

In this case the different value frames of the participating actors are complementary, or congruent; they do not conflict with each other. In other cases, or at different moments in the collaborative process, value frames may conflict. With such a variety of actors involved, even if the guiding idea motivating the process has the potential of connecting the visible and outwardly professed values, the unarticulated and unconsciously

Guiding principle
Create a shared responsibility for the process, and individual commitment to actions

applied value frames may prove to be a major obstacle for mutual understanding and fruitful collaboration. That is why, in Connected Value Development, interaction between stakeholders is organised, not as standard project team meetings with agenda's, minutes and action plans, but as co-creative processes with regular, intensive interactions and reflection sessions aimed at furthering the development and implementation of the 3P value proposition. In Connected Value Development the emergence of a new Community of Practice is supported, which not only focuses on developing 3P solutions, but also on the underlying values and world views of the different participant. In this way, possible complementarity or congruence between the value frames of the actors can be sought.

Realising a groundbreaking idea requires that the different stakeholders are willing to invest and cooperate. They need not just bring in their knowledge and expertise, they are also expected to act. Supporting agency implies that people need to appropriate the process themselves, they need to become owners. A Community of Practice, in which a shared identity is developed in a growing network, is a way to develop a strong sense of ownership. Personal membership to a community of practice is very different from being delegated to a project team as part of your job (see box 5.3).

In each case, supporting the emergence of a Community of Practice requires a different method. It may involve collaboratively developing the idea through joint fact finding, collectively analysing potential opportunities and barriers, adjusting project activities based on experiences and many other commonly undertaken activities. Whatever the shape and content of the interactions, through regularly working together, a shared practice will develop, with new routines, a different language, shared jokes and specific ways of valuing policy options, knowledge and business opportunities. In short, a community of practice will be formed, with emerging patterns, values, norms, and a shared meaning.

In order to really develop a Community of Practice, meeting 'in the flesh' is essential. Senge[62] describes a team of mechanics who fix copy machines of

---

BOX 5.3   **Communities of Practice compared to a project team**

According to McDermott and Douglas[61] a project team differs from a community of practice in several significant ways.

A project team:

- is driven by deliverables with shared goals, milestones and results;
- meets to share and exchange information and experiences, but team membership is defined by task;
- typically has roles designated to members that remain consistent during the project;
- is dissolved once its mission is accomplished.

By contrast, a community of practice:

- is driven by mutual commitment of the participants to a shared goal (guiding idea), but develops organically;
- meet to exchange knowledge just as the project team does, but community membership is defined by the knowledge of the members;
- consist of members who may take on new roles within the community when required. Moreover, membership may change as interests and needs arise;
- can exist as long as the members believe they have something to contribute to it, or gain from it.

---

a certain brand in various offices. Every Friday they come together in a bar to drink beers and celebrate the start of the weekend. According to Senge, the importance of these informal meetings cannot be overestimated. In these gatherings the previous week was an important topic of conversation: the different machines were discussed as well as the management. Meanwhile, new mechanics picked up some essential secrets of their trade they would never otherwise have learned. An important characteristic of a Community of Practice is that meaning is created in the process together and is confirmed time and again. It is a dynamic process in which new knowledge and insights arise, instead of a static event where new knowledge may or may not gain acceptance.

In Streamlining Greenport Venlo this process was initiated by bringing together all relevant actors from the domains of education, policy, research and business for four days and nights, to develop a shared dream, a shared vision. By spending so much time together, and away from the normal work place, real connections were made and an enormous amount of positive energy was generated. The time was also long enough to actually meet obstacles of different interests and value frames, that in a normal project team meeting would have been 'swept under the rug'. "People hardly knew each other. Therefore, we focused on getting to know each other before starting to work on the content. (…) This personal contact and getting to know each other is very much needed to bring the process up to speed. Because, apart from the topics you are talking about, it is about what you have in common: What is it really about?".

Thus, to develop a community, an essential prerequisite for Connected Value Development, it is very important to come together physically for dialogues and spend lots of time together. The next question becomes, how such a Community of Practice is managed? What are the consequences of the Connected Value Development approach for our ideas about leadership? Below we will see that an important characteristic of Communities of Practice is that the traditional distinction between leaders and followers fades. In stead shared ownership of the process develops.

Shared ownership through adaptive leadership

When asked to define leadership, it is difficult not to think of a single individual providing direction and inspiration to a group of followers. Leadership is indeed most often studied in terms of the person. In reality, however, leadership is rarely exercised just at the individual level. Rather, it is a complex and dynamic process in which leadership is taken up by multiple individuals and exchanged across people in the network: leadership is distributed.[63] Moreover, leadership is not to be seen just as a property of a person, or a role, but also as a property of a process. "Using the concept of complex adaptive systems (CAS), we propose that leadership should be seen not only as position and authority but also as an emergent interactive dynamic – a complex interplay from which a collective impetus for action and change emerges when heterogeneous agents interact in networks in ways that produce new patterns of behaviour or new modes of operating".[64] In 'Complexity Leadership Theory',[65] three kinds of leadership are distinguished, of which adaptive leadership is most relevant to the practice of Connected Value Development. Adaptive leadership emerges in the interaction (or overlap) between actors and results in ideas, coalitions of people, and movement. Adaptive leadership is recognised as the 'significance' (the potential value) and the 'impact' (the extent of acceptance by third parties) of the ideas. A societal direction, surfaced from the interaction between actors, can show adaptive leadership.

In Streamlining Greenport Venlo, the notions of distributed and adaptive leadership were employed through its network strategy. Streamlining Greenport Venlo experiments with new ways of 'steering' complex societal processes by organising a learning process between a variety of stakeholders involved in that specific region. Greenport Venlo. Greenport Venlo is one of the five 'Greenports' designated by the Dutch government as growing regions for greenhouse agriculture and horticulture. In the region around the city of Venlo, the name 'Greenport' has become a regional 'brand name' that encompasses 'Cradle to Cradle' (C2C) developments. The TransForum project facilitates the co-development of the many local initiatives: hence the project name *Streamlining* Greenport Venlo. It starts from the assumption that Greenport Venlo has a different meaning for different stakeholders, but that the overall interest in the economic and ecological development of the wider region is shared. This TransForum project supports the regional process by stimulating network building, problem articulation and competence development on network management in a Community of Practice.[66]

Guiding principle
Find a balance between shared ownership and individual leadership to stimulate agency

Central to the network approach of Greenport Venlo is the shared ownership of the concept and its meaning by all those involved (professionally and otherwise) in the development of the region, of which the team members of the TransForum project (*Streamlining* Greenport Venlo) only form a very small part (with a core team consisting of five members of which only two are living and/or working in the region). One of the challenges was to develop shared ownership for challenges of developing the region into the future and make it an effort *by* rather than *about* the region.

In contrast to other Dutch Greenports, in Greenport Venlo the development of an identity was not done by a core group writing up a vision document (a strong default tendency), but by cocreating meaning within a growing network of professionals in the region. In this way, the development of shared ownership was supported. The question 'What is Greenport Venlo?' became leading in interactions with actors concerned; they generated energy and aided the development of agency. Thus, through an interactive process of deliberation and dialogue, new understandings of sustainable development, or Greenport Venlo in our example, can be developed and aligned with the local contexts of participants. We have found that these new understandings contain *sensitising concepts*. Through these sensitising concepts people perceive more clearly the aspects that are or seem relevant to the issue at hand. Moreover, the local articulation of these issues stimulates further development through discursive activity. Similarly in the context of systems inquiry and evaluation it is observed that "deeper meaning-making is more likely to promote valuable action than better data".[67] Thus, mutual sense-making stimulates the development of agency; the capacity of an individual to act.

At the same time, enthousiastic initiators have appeared essential to starting up the process of Connected Value Development in the beginning. People that share their enthousiasm, ideas and visions with others are crucial in the pioneering phase of Connected Value Development. What does distributed leadership mean to these visionary leaders? One of them explains how it was for himself to transit from the role of informal leader to being just one of the players in the network. "I am so committed and involved in the process that I really felt, especially in the beginning, that I actually directed it, which of course I didn't say. On the contrary, I always said this was a collaborative process with no leader or boss. But, I knew what was going on and this was confirmed by everybody coming up to me 'you have the overview, what's going on?'. I felt very comfortable in that role. But the process became bigger and bigger and things started to take place without me. And the most surprising thing was that I really did not like this, even though I had always said that this needed to happen. So I really had to learn to let go. It took several years before I really made the move, also internally, from being the initiator to being just one of the many players in the field. Only now can I talk enthousiastically about initiatives I read about in the newspaper. So my learning was perhaps the most important, and now I can easily see that initiatives are very successful while I'm not involved myself. Now, I realise that I have stood at the beginning of creating a climate, an environment, and the conditions for these initiatives to happen. Thus, what surprised me most in this process is myself, and I thought I knew myself pretty well."

Supporting agency – the ability to act - implies that people need to appropriate the process themselves, they need to become owners. One of the strategies employed to create shared ownership and to make the network self-supportive, is to give away credits in a smart way. In this way, initiators can move to the background. The embedding of change also implies that activities and developments are initiated as much as possible by people of the network instead of by members of a core team. As we saw in the previous chapter this may give tensions with the need to show concrete deliverables to commissioners and financers at the end of the day.

Although the process of innovation and knowledge co-creation thrives with adaptivity and an emerging design, it is very important in this phase to also start with deliberately transforming knowledge into concrete outcome. In other words, we turn back to the entrepreneurial mindset as described in chapter two of the guide, that is focused at developing the guiding idea into something tangible. As the Rondeel case shows, producing tangibles was not a linear trajectory of implementing drawings,

Guiding principle
Create small tangibles; they feed the process of co-creation

sketches and design proposals. It was an intertwinement of the development of the idea and of the 3P value proposition via prototyping. It is deliberate, because of the clear sense of direction and the intentional actions that follows prototyping, showing what can be done, instead of talking about what can be done, and at the same time feeding the knowledge co-creation process with actual work and artefacts. In the spirit of Connected Value Development, we found in different projects that it is not only the entrepreneurs that have a entrepreneurial mindset. First, "you have to be decisive to act immediately. Someone comes with a question, and the best thing you can do is not only respond to it, but keep it moving, act. As a result, the work is off your desk and the other party is happy." But it is also an attitude: "It is the entrepreneurial attitude you need, the attitude of 'if it doesn't work this way, I'll try it another way.' This entrepreneurial thinking is crucial. I assume that not every farmer has this entrepreneurial attitude and I certainly don't believe that every civil servant or scientist already thinks and act as an entrepreneur." Indicating that not all entrepreneurs (farmers) are entrepreneurial, but also that entrepreneurial civil servants and entrepreneurial researchers are crucial too. We saw this already with respect to the NGO involved in the Rondeel; they were entrepreneurial, doing new things, taking risks, finding solutions to obstacles

As stated before in Connected Value Development the focus on value creation demands an entrepreneurial attitude of all participants. Apart from this attitude also four complementary roles can be distinguished. Firstly the role of 'owner' of the idea. The owner is the one that is strongly committed to the realisation of the dream (the guiding idea), who feels personally 'hurt' when the process takes a long time, because realisation of the dream is important for his/her own future or company. The 'owner' makes sure that the focus of the process is on the aimed for outcome, but may have relatively little attention for the steps needed to realise the dream.

Secondly, there is the role of 'process manager'. The process manager monitors a careful process in which justice is done to the interests of all involved stakeholders. Although the 'owner' may perceive the new business as the ultimate aim, for many other stakeholders this new business may only be a means to realise their envisioned value creation. This requires a process in which all stakeholders participate on an equal footing and in which their knowledge is considered equally important. However, the process manager may be inclined to put too much emphasis on the value of the process. There are always new challenges that require attention, but which entail the risk of going astray. Therefore the third role of 'project manager' is also important. The project manager safeguards the progress of the project within the given conditions of time, people and resources.

Last, but certainly not least, there is the fourth role of 'reflective monitor'. The reflective monitor organises reflection sessions to enhance second order learning in participants. Thereby he/she is focussed on both content and process, keeping a close eye on the realisation of both the guiding idea and the principles of the project.

A good interaction between the roles of owner, process manager, project manager and reflective monitor is the key to a successful co-creation process. These different roles do not necessarily have to be engaged by four different people. A good co-creation process is characterised by a mutual responsibility of all stakeholders to the process and individual commitment to actions in the process.

Guiding principle
Different management roles do not necessarily have to be engaged by different people

Warranting quality through reflection monitoring

In this phase of the Connected Value Development process, obstacles may be signalled in the wider system; certain regulations, a specific point of high risk, or even an incommensurability of value frames of the different participants. Reflection is a necessary condition to deal with these obstacles and warrant the quality of the process. Being aware of one's own value frame, one's own assumptions, sub-cultural habits, policies and practices makes it possible to meet with the diverging value frames of others in an understanding and respectful manner. In addition, collective reflection enhances the process of Connected Value Development. As described in Chapter 4, ILA monitoring supports Connected Value Development as a process of individual, organisational, institutional and societal change. Learning and reflection is stimulated along these different dimensions. An effective tool to this end is the Dynamic Learning Agenda (see Appendix, Tool III).

Learning starts with articulating questions. The learning agenda contains the issues (formulated as questions) a Connected Value Development project team struggles with, in the development and implementation of the strategy for realising sustainable development, at a specific moment in time. It does not only focus on technological questions (hardware), but also on issues with respect to attitudes, believes and competences (software), as well as 'orgware' questions (mode of cooperation, power relations, institutional obstacles). By constructing a sequence of learning agendas, the agenda becomes dynamic. Dynamic Learning Agendas can be constructed in different ways. Often, the first learning agenda is constructed by explicating the challenges, as they are implicitly discussed in a meeting on the progress of the project. The learning agenda then forms input for the next meeting and after some meetings may become a device to structure the meeting and discussions about progress. Learning agendas can also be constructed in interactive working sessions, using interactive group methods such as focus groups, open space, etc. Furthermore, specific working sessions are organised addressing specific questions that remain on the agenda for a considerable amount of time. Reflection monitors take different roles in these activities and need corresponding skills; ranging from analytical capacities to facilitation skills.[68]

Dynamic Learning Agendas start from the specific and situational, and are constructed in a participative way. They should be "judged by the quality of the conversation they provoke".[69] As such they are intended to contribute to the *sensitisation* of participants to the issues that emerge as relevant. By including perspectives of a wide range of participants (initiators, followers and opponents of the sustainable development at stake) no one perspective on sustainable development is excluded in advance.

Guiding principle
Identify the tough questions: those issues that are normally 'swept under the rug'

Furthermore, the Dynamic Learning Agenda is devised not as an end in itself but rather as a means towards learning and mutual sense making, and is thus inextricably linked to the intervention process. The intervention process is a continuous and ongoing flow of decisions, observations, actions, thoughts, reflections, interactions, adjustments, etc. The Dynamic Learning Agenda strengthens the intervention strategy by articulating and generating feedback loops that enable actors to learn. Finally, Dynamic Learning Agendas are particularly aimed at bringing to light the difficult, tough issues, that are normally "swept under the rug".[70] In a similar vein humanistic philosopher Kunneman noted in his account of the existential state of contemporary societies,[71] that although tough questions may be shoved away under the table, from this subordinate position they will continue to give importunate signals. According to Kunneman, these signals can become visible when there is room for exploration and even acceptation of differences between people and positions. Reflecting on the Dynamic Learning Agenda in the safe environment of the innovation space in the Connected Value Development process aims at exactly that.[72]

Preliminary analysis of Dynamic Learning Agendas shows that some issues remain on learning agendas for a considerably longer time than others. As the resolution of single loop learning questions lies within the capacities of the practitioners (single loop learning involves doing things better through incremental improvements of existing routines), they disappear from the agenda relatively easily. Double loop learning questions however are particularly persistent (they involve change in underlying beliefs, norms and assumptions), and exceptionally relevant to the challenges of sustainable development. These tough question appear in two forms: they are either about the difference between the intended strategy and actual practice within the Connected Value Development process (i.e. intransigence of the internal dynamics: about the role, strategy and competence of the project team it self), or they are about the difference between prevailing modes of operation and judgement of success of the institutional settings compared to those of the Connected Value Development process (i.e. intransigence of the boundary dynamics).[73]

Guiding principle
Develop strategies and generate action to resolve tough issues in practice

In conclusion

Building an alliance of unlikely allies with diverse value frames around a guiding idea may be the start of a new Complex Adaptive System; a system that over time will influence the experiences and behaviour of new actors engaging in the practices of these new communities. The structural patterns emerging from the process may be a mixed bag, consisting of "software" (the cultural and discourse aspects emerging from creating a shared practice), "orgware" (institutionalised collaborations: e.g. long term contracts between farmers and care institutions) or "hardware" (new production techniques or new infrastructure).

The robustness of these new structures will depend on their ability to link the new practices instigated by the co-created 3P value proposition and prototyping or experimenting to existing practices and structures. It may be that the new practice lends itself to being copied – and thereby, no doubt, adapted – by others, eventually leading to a system change. Or it may be that it inspires a comparable but somewhat different idea. In the next chapter we will elaborate on strategies for embedding and aligning. But first we present in the following intermezzo common situations and possible strategies to cope with every day stubborn reality of co-creation and experimentation.

INTERMEZZO 3
The Stubborn Reality of Co-creation and Experimentation

1 Experts undervalue tacit knowledge

In the project it was decided that four ideas had to be further developed. As the project was set up as an experiment in network management, the process manager felt that this should be done in close collaboration with all the relevant stakeholders from the region. However, one civil servant had already made a draft text on one of the ideas, 'quality of life', and wanted the network to proceed with his concrete ideas.

Thinking for people instead of working together with them is still the rule rather than the exception. Even when the contributory expertise of all participants is acknowledged and there is the willingness to act on it, it can still go wrong when there is not enough of what Collins and Evans call 'interactional' expertise:[74] the expertise to create a constructive interaction between different stakeholders. That is what Connected Value Development is all about: providing the structure and the expertise to enable a fruitful dialogue between all participants; between scientists and businessmen, between government officials and citizens. As one environmental adviser concluded: "As a result of the contribution of the residents, the design became significantly different from that which the architect would have designed sitting at his drawing board." In order to be able to make a contribution to resolving complex problems, different types of knowledge have to be integrated.

Since Connected Value Development specifically aims to connect business opportunities with social and environmental challenges, one of the basic principles of Connected Value Development is to involve implementers and end-users, or entrepreneurs and their customers from the start, to bring the demand for knowledge and the supply of knowledge in line with one another in a process of co-creation. However, underneath the practicalities of uneasy adjustment to a changing world there is a more deep-seated problem. In many Western cultures, where the word 'knowledge' has become shorthand for 'scientific knowledge', the value of non-scientific, experiential, knowledge is vastly underrated.

Some practical tips

Experience the challenge you are addressing
To gain further understanding in a complex problem, it is important to take into account the perspectives and practice of others. Often, this not only sheds new light on a problem, but also provides some firsthand experience of what a problem means in practice. In a neighbourhood where inhabitants were often complaining about the noise of a new factory, the responsible civil servant long stuck to the policy of sending someone with the necessary metering equipment and courteously informing the residents that the noise was within legal limits. Yet, when he finally visited the area himself, he was appalled by the noise and started doubting the way the legal norms were determined. He subsequently supported the efforts of others to replace the current norms with a more sophisticated way of measuring the 'nuisance factor' of noise. The more he learned about the psychology of sound-experiences, the more he was shocked that a combination of first class scientists and civil servants could have come up with this system which could be proven wrong by anyone taking the trouble to get out from behind their desks to listen and experience the burden of sound pollution.

Organise meetings at the organisations of the project participants
In one of the projects, an important turning point was the decision to organise their meetings at the organisations of the project participants. This assisted in gaining understanding in the point of view of the diverse project participant. Entrepreneurs reacted to this by saying, "so this is what a knowledge institution looks like", and scientists finally began to understand entrepreneurs' need for practical information. This may appear to be very superficial, but they are of utmost importance in creating acceptance for each other's situation and questions.

Ask broadening questions
Usually, specialists have the tendency to analyse and view a problem from a specific frame, which leaves little room for other stakeholders to put forward their ideas and notions. In such a situation it may be helpful to put some broadening

questions on the table, which are usually as fresh for the specialist as they are for the other stakeholders. For instance, in a project in which town planners were supposed to collaborate with the inhabitants of a certain area, the project manager was struck by the detailed and technical approach of the planners. He then asked some general questions, such as "what do you see when you enter the area?" "do you like what you see?" "where do you think the region will be in ten years?". The ensuing discussion proved helpful in gaining a more comprehensive outlook on the region, in which the experiences, hopes, dreams and visions of the inhabitants could be taken into account. Afterwards, the planners indicated: "Normally we are used to planning everything to the millimetre; the questions helped us see the bigger picture."

2   Too much process, too little impact

An ambitious farmer is involved in a project that strives to innovate agricultural practices in such a way that they strengthen the cultural-historic landscape, environmental quality, and regional economy. After months and months of meetings, discussions, networking, and research, he is done with this initiative as he still has no sight on concrete output. In the next meeting he will make clear that a concrete business proposition is absolutely needed, otherwise it is no longer interesting for him to carry on with this initiative.

It is common that a new project starts with meetings and discussions between stakeholders from different worlds. But it can become a pitfall as well, when this process takes too long, especially when it does not become explicit about how to create value. The farmer in this case is worried the process, which consists of ongoing conversations on policy issues, and no concrete plans. If the situation does not change, there is nothing in it for him and he will step out. As one project manager remarked "…entrepreneurs are not going to spend two years talking about something that might be possible."

For process managers, the crux is to link social and environmental challenges to entrepreneurial opportunities while the idea should be avoided that the whole process is just about making money. Doing research, co-creating knowledge and experimenting are part of the innovation space.

Some practical tips

Linking goals to the guiding idea

One of the leading ideas behind the Connected Value Development process is that in order to collaborate on a 3P value proposition, it is not a condition that all participants share the same objectives; in fact, they will usually have quite different goals. For example, in one project, local authorities tried to develop a region and to make it more attractive for businesses in order to create jobs. For the entrepreneurs taking part in the Connected Value Development process, these intentions and the forthcoming cooperation were a welcome support for their objective: realising a viable business proposition. The guiding idea is crucial for linking these intentions.

Large regional projects that stimulate innovations can create good preconditions for the development of 3P ideas. They often form the environment in which new ideas can emerge. An example from practice is a process manager who changed the focus of regional process from the applications of grants for conserving the agricultural landscape into business ideas focussed on new product-market combinations. These ideas developed into 3P value propositions using the Connected Value Development approach. This has finally led to new investments in preserving the regional landscape through profitable business activities.

Spark the entrepreneurial attitude in everyone

It is tempting to leave the formulation of a value proposition to the entrepreneurs. However, this is not the best strategy for turning the guiding idea into an actual value proposition. It is important instead that every participant thinks about the different kinds of investments that are needed and what the returns need to be on these investments to make the proposition attractive for all stakeholders involved. This not only reassures the entrepreneurs that the others do indeed understand their problems and questions, but also furthers the dialogue between entrepreneurs, (local) government and environmental or other societal organisations. Because they also need to make investments, for instance, by giving active support in the media or by giving legal permissions or even adapting the law to support the initiative. This requires an entrepreneurial mindset of each of the participants. One has to see the opportunities and actively search for ways to overcome obstacles in order to realise the potential. The Dynamic Learning Agenda (see Appendix, Tool III) will help participants to turn frustrations and assertions into knowledge questions and put them on the agenda of team meetings.

Make sure entrepreneurs are actively involved and check their willingness to continue

The active participation of entrepreneurs in the project is crucial. If entrepreneurs back out in the course of the process, it is essential to consider why this is the case. Are they not yet sufficiently involved, or are they on the verge of giving up, after initial enthusiasm? If so, this can be taken as an important signal that the business value of the process is not yet evident or not evident anymore. Such signals can also be picked up through reflexive monitoring.

3 Falling back to business as usual

When a new participant entered the project, an additional entrepreneur who was explicitly willing to invest, everything changed. Initially the whole team was happy because the realisation of their idea was much more probable with these investments. However after discussing the risks the new entrepreneur saw in the proposition and minimising those risks of the three P's everyone had committed to, just one, Profit, seemed to remain. Back to business as usual. The parties representing the other values felt not just disappointed, but downright cheated, and were left wondering how the project could have made such a drastic turn.

The innovative idea about the development of a new, sustainable, international supply chain for environmentally friendly agro-products was a complicated matter, since many different businesses and parties would have to be involved. The new participant joined the project in the implementation phase and immediately suspended the difficult parts of the process, for example the laborious relations with societal organisations, and concentrated on the profitability of the proposed supply chain, without much regard for the People or Planet values.

It could be argued that the very fact that it was at all possible to dispense with the people and planet aspects indicates that these values were not sufficiently embedded in the original guiding idea that gave rise to the project. Yet, that is not necessarily so: it could also be a lack of foresight or vision on the part of the newcomer entrepreneur. Or maybe his mindset was just on creating short term gains instead of long term sustainability. The other participants did not know, but because this entrepreneur was the one bringing in considerable investments, the project as a whole did indeed return to business as usual.

Some practical tips

Take time to co-develop the guiding idea into a value proposition
Take time to get a truly integrated 3P value proposition with all involved stakeholders. Ask yourself at the start whether the stakeholders who are developing the concept also are the stakeholders that will invest. Openly discuss the different values of the stakeholders and make clear what their

points of views are and their share will be. Make room for the network to develop, to learn, and to grow strong, both in terms of commitment to the guiding idea and in terms of strong personal connections.

It is almost inherent to the process of Connected Value Development that stakeholders will leave and join the process. It is crucial to invest in new stakeholders in the same way as was done with the stakeholders who were there at the beginning of the project. Their ideas and experience might change the proposition and lead to a stronger 3P value proposition. Once more, this illustrates the point that the process of Connected Value Development is a highly emergent process, with many feedback loops and learning cycles along the way.

4 Dealing with disciplinary silos

For one of the researchers in the project, this was the first time he was involved in a project with multiple stakeholders outside his own university. He literally had to move his workplace, as he realised that he could not do this job from behind his desk at the university. He had to adjust his all too academic language, as well. But even more problematic and unanticipated was the fact that the project demanded close collaboration with scientists from other disciplines, which proved very difficult in practice.

To participate in a Connected Value Development process, scientists need to have the willingness and competence to collaborate with participants from different backgrounds; when joining a multi-stakeholder group, they are prepared to do so. It is often assumed, however, that the collaboration with other scientists will be the easy part: they, at least, share the same background and values and speak the same language. Yet in practice, this may not be the case at all. As the scientific chair of the research concluded at the end of the project "It was difficult for scientists to cooperate in projects like this, because they have the tendency to stay within their own field." This is understandable, since scientists from different disciplines (and sometimes even within the same discipline) have different frames of reference and different views about methodologies and about what constitutes sound scientific research. These differences can lead to the same misunderstandings, frustrations and delays as are met with in collaborations between people from completely different backgrounds. In fact, the conflicts may even be more acidic. The frequent underestimation of these difficulties does not help, either.

When participants limit themselves to the approaches and assessments with which they are familiar in their own discipline, the integration required for Connected Value Development may be compromised. The new knowledge that Connected Value Development is looking for differentiates itself from traditional discipline-generated knowledge in the sense that when it is successful, it integrates various perspectives and fields of knowledge, and generates new ways of looking at a problem. One researcher concluded: "in my own research practice I have clearly stated that by broadening one's perspective, by listening carefully to what people in the community or in other disciplines have to say, one sometimes comes across unexpected things which we might not have discovered if we had sat in isolation in our offices".

If, as scientists, we want to benefit from the Connected Value Development approach, we must realise that our own perspectives and backgrounds are not universal, and we must be open to new insights and responses from other disciplines. However, even if the added value of an integrated perspective of Connected Value Development is recognised by the participants, it often proves difficult to maintain this shared perspective as the project moves forward. It is common in a project start-up that a process manager pays attention to the relationships between participants. Often, however, this attention fades as the initiative progresses.

Some practical tips

Build trust

The goal is to create a mutual engagement in which participants realise the added value of the other participants and open themselves to other perspectives. Paying attention to trust is an important element in this. To quote one process manager: "If you can bring the right people together, the next step is to get them to get used to each other. It is all about building trust: this is a step-by-step process." Spend enough time at the beginning of the process to grow familiar with each other's worlds, ideas, dreams, and expectations. Holding the group meetings at the various workplaces of the participants instead of at some neutral meeting place, and going to congresses and seminars together proves to be very valuable in creating an atmosphere of openness, togetherness, and trust.

Organise feedback on preliminary results

In an agricultural project where scientific collaboration proved difficult, the breakthrough came during the third meeting, when the scientists presented their preliminary ideas and results to each other. This produced a dramatic change to their working relationship, as it both fostered mutual understanding and allowed them to appreciate the value each of them was bringing to the project. They started to listen actively and to learn from each other. From that moment on, the scientists had a group meeting every six weeks, in which they gave feedback on each other's work[75].

6. Embedding and Alignment

Embedding is about implementing the 3P value proposition in such a way that it will sustain over time and is anchored in new business and supporting structures, communities and cultures. Commercially viable products or services are a very strong and robust way of anchoring 3P value propositions. To guarantee the optimal reciprocal connection between the economic, ecological, and social values created, developing a 3P value proposition into a business case that eventually leads to business development is a process of co-creation, which includes all the different stakeholders. It is a process that leads to tangible outcomes and economically, socially, and environmentally advantageous solutions. In this way, efforts to address wicked problems associated with sustainable development do not remain solely in the domain of policy or science (resulting in reports, policy documents, assessments, recommendations, etc.) but rather, are moved into new social spaces, where different actors co-create solutions, and in which entrepreneurs play a prominent role. Embedding these solutions takes the experimenting and prototyping described in the last chapter a step further into the market space and back to the institutional settings where all participants originated. This involves aligning processes occurring in the new practice with relevant parties and institutions in the environment of the new practice. Whereas the development of a guiding idea into a 3P value proposition can, at least to some extent, take place in an institutional vacuum, alignment is needed to root the initiative firmly in current practice. Strategies are proposed to help participants who experience discrepancies between the mode of working in the new practice on the one hand, and what they are judged on by their respective home-bases on the other hand. Without embedding and alignment, initiatives will remain isolated and slowly die out after the project funding is terminated, or when the initiators step back.

Embedding

3P value propositions are embedded not only in new businesses, but also in supporting structures, communities, and cultures. The relationship between tangible solutions and the structures in which they are embedded can be developed in many different ways. Let us give two examples.

One way is to start developing a common sense of direction, not only with the initial participants, but explicitly in a growing network of ambassadors and opinion leaders. According to one of the participants, in his project this resulted in "a common sense that we need to ensure that such a beautiful area remains a nice place to live in and we don't make such a mess of it." From this, a community of people developed (policymakers, entrepreneurs, scientists, local opinion leaders, etc.) who "don't just say, but also really feel, that they have to take care of this sustainable future." Along with this community, this feeling grows as long as one keeps talking about it. Eventually, a soil is created on which non-sustainable initiatives do not grow, because the community does not allow it. On this soil, 3P value propositions and business development based on them can flourish. This process snowballs, feeding upon its own momentum. Businesses start to see new product-market combinations inspired by the guiding idea. As other stakeholders recognise the contributions that these new business ideas can make to bringing the guiding idea into practice, they are willing to participate in developing and implementing them. The exact business opportunities that arise are not determined in advance, and initiatives take place across the entire network.

For example, in the case of Green Care Amsterdam, an initially broad challenge (to connect city needs to what the surrounding farmers had to offer) that was faced by farmers, politicians, retail and health institutions alike, gave rise to a variety of (unplanned) businesses, ranging from creating a consuming market for the products of regional farmers (MyFarmer) to professionally organising care farming around Amsterdam (Landzijde).

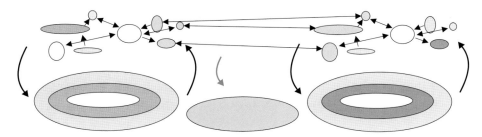

FIGURE 6.1A *Connecting people leads to new patterns*

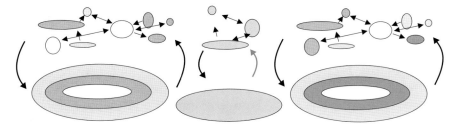

FIGURE 6.1B *New patterns lead to new business development*

In the examples above, connecting people from different settings led to new structures and patterns: a new discourse, a guiding idea, a shared sense of responsibility for a sustainable future (see figure 6.1a). This, in turn, affected the potential for new 3P business development (see figure 6.1b).

Let us turn to the second way in which concrete businesses can be embedded in broader structures. The idea for a New Mixed Farm also arose from a broad context: the discussions on intensive livestock farming led to the innovative idea of a New Mixed Farm. Whereas in the examples above a great deal of effort was put into the creation and stimulation of a new discourse in a certain region, which in turn enhanced the potential for 3P value propositions, in the case of the New Mixed Farm, the Connected Value Development process focussed primarily on developing the guiding idea (see figure 6.2a) into a 3P value proposition. This implied involving entrepreneurs who were willing to invest in the new company, building trust amongst them, and working out the actual design and business model of the New Mixed Farm, together with scientists and business developers. In this process, different alignment strategies are employed to ensure the anchoring and embedding of the initiative in current political and public discourse (see figure 6.2b).[74]

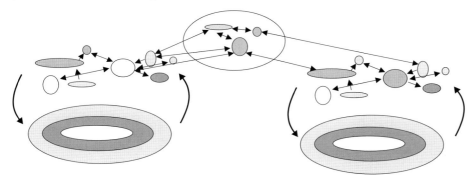

FIGURE 6.2A *A new value proposition is developed by connecting people*

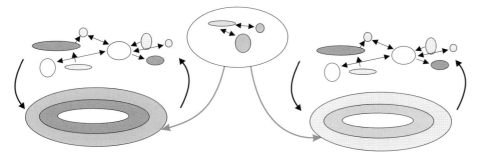

FIGURE 6.2B *The value proposition is aligned to existing patterns*

The same is true for the Rondeel: a guiding idea turned into a concrete 3P value proposition for sustainably-produced egg in an alternative henhouse. It built on the existing broad sense of urgency for the change of husbandry systems for hens. A new husbandry design faced three challenges. The first one was to design a socially desirable stable while providing enough profit for the farmer, the second was to shape concepts such as 'naturalness' and 'robustness' in an actual design, and the third involved a debate over indoor versus outdoor settings. To produce eggs that are able to compete on the regular market, the added value in terms of people and planet should be made visible, in order to make the needed profit to ensure the continuity of the business. For decades, the poultry industry chain had had the same structure. Rondeel presented a new opportunity for a business model based on shared ownership, and in April 2010 the first Rondeel opened. Rondeel's production model shrinks the distance from farmer to retailer and from retailer to consumer by doing things like on-site packaging. Also, because the poultry farmer receives a portion of the profit, it helps encourage a commitment to marketing Rondeel eggs. Other features of the project make it similarly attractive. The innovative design created a conference room above the stables, so that businesses may offer an original location for their conferences, and with its glass 'visitors tunnel,' citizens are invited to see for themselves the animals' well-being. Rondeel represents a new, more humane *and* commercially viable model for the poultry industry. It has truly intertwined the people, planet and profit aspects of the Triple P Value Proposition.

Letting go

For a new solution to lead to an actual innovation, it must not only be a good idea (inclusive, Triple P, etc.), it must also enable the actual creation of (monetary) value. Solutions that are realised in the form of business development, are a very strong and robust way of anchoring innovative ideas, as long as they incorporate people, planet, and profit values. Entrepreneurs play a crucial role here (they are the ones that invest their own money, and lie awake at night for the risks they take). If the original initiators of the guiding idea were not entrepreneurs (or are not the entrepreneurs who will invest in the implementation), they must realise that they are no longer in the lead. We have seen that this transition, from exploration (or idea generation, inspiration) to implementation (or development, realisation) requires that these kind of initiators to let go, which is not always easy for them to do. An initiator told us: "being an innovator, with enthousiasm and a vision, can be a pitfall too. [Believing that if] you keep up that enthousiasm, you should also be able to take the next step." And another: "I really like to start new things without knowing where we are going, to mobilise and connect people around a dream or ambition. It is great to see that people really start to pick up issues, and start to move the process into an implementation phase. That is what you want. But I also find it difficult. I think that different people are needed for this phase, people who like certainty, concreteness."

Guiding principle
Moving into phase of realisation requires the initiators to let go

The go/no-go moment

The realisation of a 3P value proposition often requires not only investments by commercial parties, but also investments by other stakeholders (e.g., a public campaign by an NGO, adaptation of regulations by governments). Entrepreneurs, who may have been brought into the exploration phase for their knowledge, views, and ideas, now must really start acting. A project leader: "I keep telling the entrepreneurs, you are now going into a new phase. You are going to build. I am not a builder, I am the person who kept the group together, who put in knowledge from unthought-of sources and acted as the spokesperson to the media. But I am really not a builder, so when the business really takes off, other people, project developers, will get involved." In this phase, real commitment is needed as a go/no-go moment appears. This moment is described by one of the entrepreneurs as: "After a year of planning, dreaming, and mutually reaffirming the intent to jointly go ahead, comes a moment of decision, where we ask ourselves: 'do we *really* want to do this? Do we *dare* to do this?'."

Guiding principle
Include a go/no-go moment; it will demonstrate true intentions

In the Rondeel case we also saw that moving to the phase of actual realisation of the new henhouse requires a different level of commitment from investors and farmers, but also from the involved NGO. A go/no-go moment emerges: are we really going to do this, and if so what are the consequences? What are the risks? One entrepreneur who was involved from the start backed out, because of the high uncertainties entailed in such an innovative husbandry system. Not only investors and farmers had to commit themselves fully to building the new system, the Animal Protection Foundation also had to commit to having its name linked to the project. And it had to do this upfront, which is usually not done by an NGO. They also had to decide how strict some of the criteria were, such as having an outdoor area, in the ranking of their label. A decision was taken to award the 'Better Living' animal welfare label for one year.

Value Creation from multiple perspectives

Obviously, for participants in a Connected Value Development process, being accountable in a bottom-line "what do I get for my money" manner on the one hand, while at the same time being urged to contribute freely to an emerging innovation whose deliverables have not even been well-formulated, may cause considerable tension.

Important for the embedding of a 3P value proposition is its translation in a business plan. In this way, the value proposition is tested in relation to the necessary investments; after all, realisation of a business plan implies considerable financial investment with a high risk. The Value Creation Model (see Appendix, Tool X) can support in making a business plan, by putting all the co-created ideas and aspects into a single, conceptual model, and in understanding the relationships between the aspects in the model. The distinctiveness (from the markets point of view) of an innovation is translated into a Unique Selling Piont (USP). When properly marketed this will finally lead to envisioned (tangible, monetary) results. These make it possible to do specific investments, which in turn lead to refining the USP and (re)consideration of competences.

It is not only important for businesses to root the developed 3P value propositions. At the same time it is necessary to root the 3P value proposition in the domains of other KENGI parties. These changes determine the system innovation character of Connected Value Development. Knowledge institutions invest by ensuring scientific recognition of the jointly developed knowledge. This entails risks, because knowledge developed in a transdisciplinary way is not necessarily appreciated by the scientific community, which is more oriented towards monodisciplinary knowledge production. Governments provide the required licences for the initiative. Since the initiative is highly innovative, it is likely that tensions occur with current regulation. Usually regulation will need to be amended to allow the initiative to grow. This can be risky since changing the rules is politically a sensitive endeavour. Civil society organisations invest by publicly supporting the initiative and setting an example for others. This also entails risks for those organisations since there are always critics who will emphasise that good is not good enough. In this phase of embedding, the KENGI parties invest each in their own way and they each run certain risks. To be able and willing to take risks, it is important that the value proposition is transparent and aligned with the values that are relevant in each of the different domains. While initially it is crucial that the process of Connected Value Development is not constrained by accountability mechanisms so as to provide room for creativity and co-creation, during the phase of alignment and embedding the focus is on setting standards in each of the domains of the involved stakeholders. Thus, for an innovative idea to make it to implementation, it is important to give ample attention to the various scales used to measure success.

To clarify, consider the case of care farming again. The idea is this: people with an acknowledged need for care (e.g. people with mental or physical disabilities) enrol in a program of regular visits to a farm, where they are offered a daily routine with farm activities. For this, the farmer receives compensation from the state, from the health insurance company, or from any other entity that is financially responsible for the care. The motivations behind the idea differ for the various parties concerned. For those responsible for the care, the fact that the care farm seems a very supportive and suitable environment for certain clients in that it increasing their capabilities, their self esteem, and their mental and physical health, is a motivator, as is the lower cost of the location when compared to intramural care in the city. For the farmers, on the other hand, the extra income is welcome, as is the spreading of the financial risk the program involves, since the risk factor for agricultural activities has been increasing for decades.

A care farm crosses the traditional boundaries of the agricultural sector, on the one hand, and those of the healthcare and welfare sectors, on the other. This has consequences for the way in which success is measured by different stakeholders. Farmers, for instance, traditionally measure and compare their success in terms of turnover per square metre. As care farmers often have a lower crop, dairy, or livestock yield than efficient, large-scale, industrial-agricultural entrepreneurs, they are sometimes regarded as less successful farmers. Care farming, then, requires rethinking the concept of 'value creation' for farmers. One of the early care farmers in the Netherlands and an enthousiastic ambassador of the concept, described it as follows: "I always ask sceptical farmers: what is your turnover per square metre? Then I divide my turnover (from both my farming and care activities) by my square metres. When I tell them the result they always fall quiet. I am doing far better than they are." The care farming setup also changes the farmers' customers or clients. In addition to the wholesale and retail sector, the principal clients of care farms are health care institutions, social services, and local welfare departments. Finally, it requires a rethinking of the competitive landscape, which now also includes other companies and institutions offering services to the targeted groups of clients, such as businesses that offer rehabilitation programmes for the unemployed, or health institutions offering daily activities to the mentally ill.

The values created by the care farmer consist of two very different components: the agricultural output, which is readily convertible to market prices, and the care output. Measuring the care component presents some challenges, since this value involves both the cost and the effectiveness of the care. Assessing the care's effectiveness is not a matter of tallying numbers but of integrating cost-benefit inputs from individuals who are, of course, influenced by personal and institutional values. In order to build sustainable relationships with health institutions that care farms needed, the new sector had to develop ways to measure health effects of care farming in a manner that would be persuasive to the health sector, and farmers had to obtain the credentials they needed in order to function as care institutions.

A third perspective is that of the local authorities. In the densely populated Netherlands, the rural surroundings of cities are under constant threat from housing projects, office blocks, and industrial development. Local authorities, however, recognises the value that a green environment holds for all city populations. It offers the city not only places for people to reconnect with nature and animals and physical labour activities on care farms, but it also offers city inhabitants an opportunity to reconnect with the origins of the food-production chain. Care farming is seen as one of the ways in which policy ambitions can be realised. It adds value for policy.

Equally, community organisations see in care farms a chance to retain smaller farms and prevent the sprawling of city boundaries. Another factor that is of particular importance to them is that Care Farms tend to be small-scale farms, which rely less on large-scale industrial methods. According to their reasoning, such farms stand a better chance of conserving the traditional agricultural landscape, as well as traditional labour-intensive agricultural practices. Thus, from their perspective too, the Care Farm idea is worth supporting.

Guiding principle
Make transparant and accountable how value is added to the different domains

The example of Green Care illustrates that Connected Value Development will lead to the value creation from different perspectives. The better the project is able to align to these perspectives, the higher the chances of success are. This may involve switching between discourses, but it may also involve creating measures of success that comply with these differing perspectives. Let us have a closer look at various alignment strategies.

Alignment

As described in the previous chapter, Wenger and Lave introduced the concept of Communities of Practice to denote the shared practice through which its members create meaning, and through which they make sense of the world around them. Participants of Connected Value Development processes are part of a new practice, one that evolves as they interact and co-create. At the same time, participants are members of their own professional communities, with their (unspoken) rules, their own ways of doing things, and incentives. "The process of alignment bridges time and space to form broader enterprises, so that participants become connected through the coordination of their energies, actions, and practices."[75] Alignment is about complying with expectations set by others, but also about belonging to broad systems of styles and discourses, such as political and social movements, or scientific disciplines. Wenger describes the bridging of different communities as a creation of forms of continuity between different communities of practice.

Two worlds

Most entrepreneurs involved in TransForum projects are self-employed individuals. As agricultural entrepreneurs, they are often the owners of small and medium enterprises (SMEs). They are accountable to themselves for the way they fill in their working time. This is different for the participants who are employed by institutions, with their specific cultures and working routines. These participants often have one foot in the new project and the other in the daily context of their own organisation. This can result in many different kinds of tensions. A participating scientist may take part in the joint formulation of the problem in the process of Connected Value Development, for example, but if the problem is not obvious to fellow scientists, it will be hard for him to get his work published. Publications in scientific journals, however, are the product for which scientists are held accountable. Therefore, a project requires an integrated approach to the problem, even when the so-called home base asks for a mono-disciplinary approach.

Another potential tension arises from the principle of there being a clear sense of direction within Connected Value Development, while the actual, concrete actions emerge along the way. This is in contrast with the practice and custom in many organisations of defining specific and tangible deliverables in advance. Many organisations (including corporations, NGOs, and knowledge institutes) increasingly work as project organisations, with project budgets lined up for a year in advance, and hours-per-project allocated to each employee. In one of the projects, events unfolded in a different order than had been anticipated in the project plan, which was to be expected. This required one of the scientists to work on his research later in the year than originally envisioned, to allow a certain entrepreneur to collaborate with him. He then found himself in trouble because "my hours in November have already been allocated to another project." The rigid project system of his home base made it difficult for this participant to go with the flow of emerging events.

The home base asks for concrete and unambiguous results, while the employee within the network, together with others, invests in exploring the problem, mobilising people, holding many conversations, et cetera. A participating policymaker says: "The government and entrepreneurs must work together in innovative projects, since together one can achieve more. Such collaboration dictates a different role for civil servants: not continuously sitting behind the desk writing papers that nobody reads, but actively plunging into the network. Only within the network can things be achieved. A civil servant operates in two worlds: the world of the network and the world of the local government. It is sometimes quite difficult to operate in both worlds: they often have different objectives and routines."

Accountability

Not only do participants have to be accountable to their respective home-bases for their contribution to the Connected Value Development trajectory, the project also takes place in the context of its financing partners. At the start of a project, a project plan is generally formulated. In a project plan, agreements between the sponsor and project participants with regard to the deliverables, mode of operation, project organisation, project planning, et cetera, are written down. We have already seen that developments in a Connected Value Development process are hard to predict. Responding to unexpected events and opportunities that emerge is crucial. As one participant commented: "At a given moment, the time is ripe, windows of opportunity for change open up, and you can't use these windows of opportunity when you don't have a solid plan." At the end of the project, however, the financing partners will judge whether the budget was spent according to prior agreement. As one of the financers says: "at the end of the day, we want to know whether the project was successful. It is public money, so it must be accounted for. And that is right and proper." The project team will then have to account for the choices that were made and for the form of the deliverables.

This can cause problems under two conditions. First, it may cause problems if the financing partner is very strict and intent on making the project focus on producing reports in order to account for progress and budget, rather than on the goals of the project itself. And second, and this is what we have encountered more often, a problem may occur if the project team itself develops a counterproductive loyalty to the initial project plan, even when it becomes clear during the process that the initially formulated deliverables are not meeting a demand in practice, or not contributing to the stated goals and objectives.

Possible alignment strategies

Different alignment strategies are possible for balancing between the two worlds. They range from not aligning at all by temporarily ignoring the home base, via making different types of connections between the two worlds, to achieving alignment through the instigation of structural change in the respective home-bases.

First, we have seen in the chapter Creating Innovation Space that it is sometimes necessary to take risks and act in a manner that is out of step with the expectations of the home base. The innovation space accommodates this by creating a free space for generating ideas, away from people's institutional settings. It may be wise to ignore the home base temporarily, outside of structured and facilitated meetings. To quote a policymaker: "Breaking through old routines sometimes requires unorthodox working methods: that way, one doesn't need to care about internal routines and ideas. While I am expected to spend my days behind my desk, I decided to spend my time outside of the office." But at the same time, people must make sure not to become isolated from what is going on at their institution. In the end, one wants to instigate a change there too, or at least be able to account for the new work being done in the terms and values of the institution. The sustainability scan developed by Blonk and TransForum could be a useful tool (see Apendix, Tool XI) in this respect.

Second, inherent to the concept of a 3P Value Proposition is that it embodies alignment between different worlds, value systems, and currencies. For instance, a solution to an environmental problem is in alignment with the discourse and expectations of entrepreneurs if it is also commercially viable. The value proposition then acts as a boundary object: it is recognised as relevant and valuable by different actors and communities, each in their own way. Or, as Grin and Van de Graaf propose: "Actors attribute *congruent* meanings to an artefact if they perceive the artefact's properties in such a way that the artefact has a sensible meaning to all of them".[76] By obtaining the AWBZ approval (the Dutch General Act on Special Medical Expenses), care farming became accepted as an official form of health care.

Not only can the outcome of the Connected Value Development be aligned with the various surrounding communities, but during the process itself, boundary objects can also overcome potential tensions between the new practice and existing routines. In some cases participants themselves have gone to great lengths to comply with the expectations of the institutions by creating these boundary objects. For instance, some scientists fully immersed themselves in projects, and co-created transdisciplinary knowledge together with others, while they also made an effort to align the

Guiding principle
Temporarily ignore the home base, so as to stimulate openness and creativity

Guiding principle
Give meaning to the Connected Value Development process in the respective home bases to increase support

Connected Value Development process with the scientific community by publishing articles in peer-reviewed journals. The published work then acts as a boundary object: it is recognised as valuable and relevant by the scientific community, and at the same time does justice to the development of the project. Similarly, in Streamlining Greenport Venlo, the four day working session resulted in a joint commitment, a clear sense of direction, and a lot of energy and ideas to further develop the region. However, the participants' institutions did not quite recognise these results. They requested a document with the vision for the region, which was subsequently produced.

Another requirement may be a concrete presentation of the initiative's sustainability performance. An evaluation method that combines both quantitative and qualitative analysis of different dimensions of sustainability may be employed as a boundary object that is recognised as valuable in certain contexts, even on the assumption that sustainable development is a discursive and emergent system property. On a smaller scale, individuals find ways to deal with rigid systems, such as hours allocated to projects in specific periods of time. According to one participant, "at the beginning of the year, I just fill in all the hours in the system according to the institutional plans, and then I feel free to act as needed throughout the rest of the year."

Third, instead of having participants moving towards the institutional context, the institutional context can be brought into the process by involving politicians and institutional leaders in the Connected Value Development process. For instance, in the case of New Mixed Farm, Connected Value Development implied involving entrepreneurs who were willing to invest in the new company, building trust amongst them, working out the actual design of the NMF together with scientists, but also involving policymakers to align with local and national policy, talking to neighbours and other inhabitants, and taking similar steps. Hybrid platforms, such as a task force and a steering committee, were installed in order to make these potential ambassadors part of the process.[77] We have already mentioned the example of Streamlining Greenport Venlo, where the third evening of the four-day session was dedicated to bringing the institutional representatives and local and regional politicians into the process.

Getting financers actively involved and included in decisions to diverge from the original project plan is a similar strategy. Project leaders who do not involve the financing partner throughout the process worry about the products they need to deliver. "When I had to make the final report I got nervous. I thought, 'well, we have taken a decision to go into another direction, or we were forced by circumstances to do things differently. How am I going to turn this into deliverables? We were experimenting, which is not very tangible. How will I show what has been achieved?'" In recent years, different evaluation approaches have been developed that focus on capturing the learning process of a project, rather than on evaluating outputs against intended goals. Capturing learning experiences implies turning an intangible process in a tangible one. The intervention process is like a continuous flow of decisions, observations, adjustments, etc. Showing these developments and the contingent factors in context is the objective of techniques like the (Audiovisual) Learning History and the Dynamic Learning Agenda (see Appendix, tool IX and III), but also the Most Significant Change Technique[78] and the Process Evaluation.[79] Giving meaning collectively to the project development and specifically including people who were not involved can be done by means of the Eye-Opener workshop (see Appendix, Tool VIII). This is particularly suitable for people who have their own perspective on the project; e.g. managers of programmes which include the project in question.

A final way to align an innovative idea with existing structures is by instigating changes in these structures. In other words, if the mechanisms for measuring success in different types of organisations (e.g. businesses, government, science and societal organisations) shift towards more inclusive measures, Connected Value Development initiatives find a fertile soil to grow on. For instance, instigated by the development of Greenport Venlo or concurrent with it, the Venlo municipality started an organisation-wide change towards becoming a learning organisation, working from the outside inwards, instead of the other way around. This made acting in an

Guiding principle
Involve institutional actors in the Connected Value Development process

Guiding principle
Instigate structural changes in the respective home-bases to accommodate Connected Value Development (change frames of reference)

unorthodox way easier for the civil servants involved in Streamlining Greenport Venlo. It aligned—or resonated—with the new discourse that was evolving within the organisation.

In conclusion

While value creation is a crucially important factor in the possible alignment between the innovative idea and the existing and powerful structures of the current institutions, other alignment strategies are developed along the way. They ensure that the effects of the project will be sustained over time, and contribute to a transition across domains and sectors. Connected Value Development results in 3P Value Propositions: economically, socially, and environmentally advantageous pathways to innovation. The result is more than that, though, since modes of thinking have been changed along the way, and dominant paradigms have been challenged. Naturally, the latter gains can hardly be quantified, but they are not less real for that reason. At the end of this chapter we present an intermezzo again, this time of the stubborn reality of embedding and alignment and possible strategies to cope with them or avoid them.

INTERMEZZO 4
The Stubborn reality of Embedding & Alignment

1 Do rules rule?

The point of the meeting was soon made clear; the new biological filter, that was much better in reducing fine dust emissions of stables than the old chemical air washer. All entrepreneurs complained: "...if we could make the rules, we would make them much easier".

These entrepreneurs have to find a way to deal with the maze of what is often seen as just bureaucratic red tape. In modern societies, the web of laws, rules, and regulations has become highly complex and intricate and it is, despite all the lip service paid to innovation, not well-geared to accommodate innovate ideas. The above example can easily be complemented by many others.

A condition for successful innovation is that the legal framework allows some room for experimentation. And even then, internal contradictions and inconsistencies can still turn out to be major obstacles. In one of the projects we studied, the guiding idea got caught between two governmental departments: one department took the position that the proposal was not really innovative, thus denying it subsidies and the legal exemptions associated with the status of innovation. Yet, when the project decided to forge ahead even without subsidies, it met with another department claiming the proposed procedure was untried and untested and could therefore not get the required construction permits. How to deal with such Catch-22s? How to make sure the rules do not hinder innovation and prevent other stakeholders from making the necessary investments?

Some practical tips

Involve government representatives

The idea of KENGI is to involve government representatives in the development process, too. The example above illustrates how crucial this is. While governmental agents experience the added value of the 3P value proposition, they are more likely to be inclined to give the necessary permits. Sometimes the project might even be reason for adapting the regulations and laws. This is the kind of investment the governmental parties involved in a process of Connected Value Development must be willing and able to make.

Status aparte

The Dutch government can assign a project a special status, the 'status aparte', which gives the project some legal leeway: less red tape and (temporary) exemption from certain regulations. In the case mentioned above, a status aparte can be designed to stimulate business development by offering flexibility and different options in the process of getting all permits. Also, the status aparte should further a cooperative attitude of public administrators in cases where a company cannot formally comply with current regulations, but its approach nevertheless fits in with the values and intentions behind those regulations.

2   No one is willing to invest

"This is unbelievable! Not one of these entrepreneurs wants to invest in the concept we developed!", a scientific participant reflected with his colleague on the last meeting they had with the entrepreneurs. Four months ago they had asked some entrepreneurs to bring in their expert knowledge in the development of an innovative concept. The plan they came up with turned out to be beautiful in the eye of the designers, but now that investments have to be made, all entrepreneurs backed out.

Co-creating a 3P value proposition is not the same as designing a new concept. The entrepreneurs involved were invited for their specialist knowledge. This does not mean that they feel committed to the design in such a way that they want to invest, nor that they are in a business situation that makes investment favourable.

This situation shows that if people want to succeed with a Connected Value Development process, they have to commit themselves early in the process in order to realise their goals. Goals will not be realised by selling a concept to a third partner. Do you want to develop a vision for an alternative agricultural practice? Or do you actually want to implement a design? One must focus early on the role that each stakeholder wants to play, and on what contribution each stakeholder is willing (and able) to make. This makes it clear right from the start whether a particular stakeholder has the role of knowledge co-creator, or also the role of investor. By focusing solely on the needs for the conceptual design, one may neither have enough support nor the right alliance for turning an invention into an actual innovation.

Some practical tips

Expectation management: co-creating plans together = investing together

It is important to invite stakeholders from the very start who will be crucial in the actual implementation of the concept and are committed to turn a guiding idea first into a 3P value proposition and finally into a business plan. First creating a plan, then looking for people willing to invest in it, is not usually the path to success. One must focus early in the process on the role each of the stakeholders is willing to play, and on the contribution each stakeholder is not just willing but also able to make. This clarifies beforehand whether a certain stakeholder has the role of knowledge co-creator, or is committed to investment. Forging ahead with the creative side of the project without people who are, in principle willing to invest is risky, at best.

Proof of the pudding

A strong 3P value proposition will improve the chance of attracting investors. Many, if not most, entrepreneurs would like their business to be sustainable and would like their business to be beneficial to as many people as possible. Yet, when push comes to shove there should be a healthy profit in it: of the three terms, profit is the only condition *sine qua non*.[80] In fact, as the proof of the pudding is in the eating, the proof of the quality of the 3P value proposition is in the willingness to invest. If only the government is willing to invest, this needs evaluation; it could be a sign of weakness of the 3P value proposition.

In the planning phase, innovation is sometimes supported by government subsidies. This entails the risk that plans will be developed that remain critically dependent on subsidies in the investment phase and that they will fail for this reason to provide a sufficient return on capital. The investment phase is marked by the truism that he who pays the piper calls the tune. The most effective course of action for parties cooperating in the planning phase and wishing to remain involved in the investment phase is to help share the investment costs.

3 Lack of loyalty

The project manager could hardly believe what had happened. A member of the city council was indirectly involved in the project. At the conference they both attended, she suddenly overheard him openly criticising the decisions made and complaining about the lack of results. Also, he was very dubious about the arduous collaboration between the different stakeholders in the project. This project "could have been done so easily," he said. The project manager was disappointed, everybody was working hard, and they all knew the project was very complex. How could this local politician show such lack of loyalty?

The project manager felt frustrated and betrayed by the local politician. She and the other participants had put a lot of effort in the project, with growing faith that this would, in the long run, result in a positive outcome. They had learned to appreciate and celebrate small victories, and had experienced that things are easier said than done. The local politician, on the other hand, had merely been indirectly involved in the project; he had been more of a spectator. He had not personally experienced the difficulties that had been overcome, nor had he learned to appreciate and celebrate the small victories of the project. His comment that the project "could have been done so easily" was not based on experience; rather, he simply did not appreciate how complex the project really was. Nevertheless, he was publicly associated with the project, and would be held accountable for the results, or for the lack thereof. This is a prospect which can be somewhat frightening when one does not really know what is going on, and does not see any concrete results.

Loyalty to the process, however, is one of the key elements of Connected Value Development. Participants must be able to trust that, in the end, some answers and viable plans will be delivered, or, at the very least, that the process itself and what has been learned from it is worth the trouble, in and of itself. Fear that a lack of results will harm one's reputation can undermine the trust of all of the participants.

Some practical tips

Be transparent and open when you are unhappy with the process

In the example above, the project manager was especially disappointed that the criticism was not voiced to the group, and could therefore hardly be discussed openly. This can be prevented by the process manager by giving regular and explicit attention to possible doubts and feelings of unease. As one team member described the experience: "it is important to acknowledge being stuck, to admit that one does not know how to continue, and to give direct feedback to the person of whom you get the sense that he is not participating well." It is equally important to include one's own part in the acknowledgement of being stuck. The process manager might consider initiating a plenary meeting to discuss progress and ask questions such as "What are we doing?", "Is there sufficient progress and if not why not?". This often inspires people to come into action. Make sure that the focus is on content, rather than power and authority, and reconnect with the expectations and images that were explored together at the beginning of the project, in order to get people focussed on what brought them together in the first place.

Make passive spectators into active ambassadors

There are usually, within a project, people who participate in some meetings but do not have the time or inclination to be fully involved. These may well be the higher authorities, carrying responsibility. A danger of any intensive network is that the participants who are deeply involved on a regular basis tend to forget what a meeting looks like to the occasional visitor.

The first thing to try is to involve these spectators and make them, if only temporarily, feel like they are part of the process. It is crucial to present the progress of the projects not only by written reports. Such reports can never carry over the learning done along the way and the energy and enthusiasm of the participants, nor their doubts and the challenges they face. Organising participatory meetings with your project's 'ambassadors' will help you connecting with them and involving them on a different level. Not just in their formal role, but also as individuals. Sometimes, it is helpful just to invite them to the actual workplace. Actually seeing the planning boards and all the sketches and scribbles on the flip charts tacked to the wall can convey some of the energy and the innovative atmosphere. In some cases, the meeting may actually be geared toward a kind of demonstration, tackling a limited and readily understandable but complex issue, and involving the spectator in the discussion, thus letting him experience the challenge.

Involve the opposition and the sceptics

Regulations and existing policies are often initially regarded as just a part of the landscape. The project team tries to deal with them as best as possible and may apply for exemptions from certain regulations or subsidies, or even for a legal 'status aparte'. Yet, as a rule, these parties are not invited to participate in the process. This situation understandably gives rise to some fears on the part of policy makers, and even of individual politicians, of losing control. Their well-established role as guardians of law and order is not easily inclined to accommodate the exceptional status of an innovative project – a status which is often crucial for the project to get off the ground. However, as one project manager said: "It would be a good thing if the Ministry would actually take part in this project. Right now, we can sense they are afraid to do so; they seem to think that their law enforcement responsibility would be compromised if they themselves got involved in the project. But that is not at all true, since we have learned that one can continue playing an independent role while participating." In fact, the Connected Value Development approach does not ask any participant to give up any values or to change any role. Instead, it tries to connect these different values and roles via a collective process resulting in a 3P value proposition, that adds value for each of the participants. Stressing this aspect of the Connected Value Development approach, and quoting people who already took part in a Connected Value Development process, may convince civil servants or politicians that actively taking part does not in any way compromise the values they represent; quite the contrary, in fact.

Demonstrate the wickedness

It is not just the great problems like global warming that are highly complex and fall into the category of "wicked problems". In fact, many small and local issues, which look rather simple to the untrained eye, can turn out to be highly complex and have all the hallmarks of a wicked problem. A project which looks simple from the outside may well take years to wrestle out from under sheer endless chicken-and-egg loops. But for those not actively involved, this may not at all be obvious. The remedy is, as we have repeatedly said here, to give sufficient attention to the exploration of the challenge. It might help to collectively produce a report reflecting the current state of affairs: the problems that have been overcome and the problems envisaged, in a wording understandable to any interested party.

4   Different reputational systems

A researcher is obligated by her university to publish at least one international scientific article a year in a peer reviewed journal. For the project she is in, she has written several reports, which were considered very helpful to analyse the problem and to define a shared vision. When the project decided that producing a video clip would be the most productive way to get their message across in the region, the researcher realised this would demand a lot of time and not add anything to her curriculum nor to her status in her institute.

The researcher in this case tried to adjust the results she produced for her project by making them suitable for publication in scientific journals. This is, however, a challenging task because the transdisciplinary research she conducted was aimed at solving specific, contextually bound, regional problems. They were a far cry from the questions considered relevant in her discipline. To connect her findings in the Connected Value Development process with theory and literature would ask a lot of her spare time.

Usually, the problem is worst for scientists. For the other participants, the proposed outcome of the project, a viable 3P value proposition, will necessarily fall within the broad range of what the participants are supposed to deliver. Not so for scientists, who are supposed to create knowledge, not solve problems. Thus, apart from their contribution to the Connected Value Development process, they must, as a kind of extra task, find ways to draw from the process such knowledge as will be useful to others and will be recognised by the scientific community. Despite the lip service paid to the necessity of transdisciplinarity, the organisational structures in scientific institutions is rarely conducive to such research. Scientific journals are often mono-disciplinary, each with their own epistemic cultures. This makes the publishing of transdisciplinary research more time-consuming, because the disciplinary bridges between the various sciences must be crossed. No matter how enthousiastic and committed one may be initially, it is hard to stay committed when it does not benefit one's career or may even harm it.

Some practical tips

Identify different evaluation systems and make their demands explicit

It is crucial to get to know not only the people, but also the worlds from which they come and the reputation system they have to work with, because this system also determines how specific actions and initiatives are judged. Questions such as "what is your personal interest in this project?" but also: "what are the expectations that your boss or your organization expect you to meet, and to which extent might these be satisfied through this project?" ought to be explicitly addressed in the beginning of the project. The answers can be listed and checked regularly throughout the project, when defining output, but also when people lose their motivation.

In particular, the publish-or-perish plight of scientists demands attention from all participants: when the input of scientists is required and appreciated, there should be willingness to cooperate in laying down the experiences of the process in order to gain (publishable) knowledge. This may require filling out questionnaires, participating in interviews, and so forth. In the processes we reviewed, many participants were actually quite willing to devote time to such tasks, as they felt the need to preserve the knowledge gained during the process.

Actively involve others

Just as at certain phases of the project it is necessary that everyone take on responsibility for formulating a business proposal, is it desirable that not only the scientist(s), but the whole group gets involved in the business of knowledge creation. As one process manager commented: "You have to organise a knowledge-creation process by formulating research questions with regard to the process. For example: 'Which actors are relevant for a certain issue to involve in an interactive process?', 'Can the parties change their existing behaviour?', 'Is the composition of the group important enough to break through firmly established institutional barriers?' I see this as an important step." Evidently, reflecting on those questions is not what comes naturally to, say, an entrepreneur, but then again: the whole Connected Value Development process is about bridging different worlds, and the mutual benefit this brings along.

"In our project there was one person who did not speak up about what he wanted. He wanted to participate in the project but he did not believe in certain aspects. He sold his assets within the company and a new director came in. This new guy participated more in the project and was much more honest. He said: 'listen, these are our goals within the project, nothing more nothing less.' The strangest thing happened. At first everyone was a bit annoyed because he limited his ambition. But his honesty allowed us to continue the conversation. We talked about how far he was willing to go and under which conditions we could take it a step further. In the end we were able to go a lot further than he initially wanted to, because he saw new opportunities in the project."

7. Reflections

Trying to agree on a generally accepted standard of 'sustainability', or setting up a grand design for a worldwide change is not possible. As wicked problems, issues related to sustainable development have no single owner and there is no shared perception of the problem. There may be different opinions on the seriousness of a (potential) problem or doubt how much mankind can do to solve it. There may also be vested interests to keep things as they are. There may be reluctance to invest in sustainable development because the benefits cannot be properly assessed. Although there is no overall remedy against these inherent tensions, fact is that projects *do* get off the ground and some lessons may be learned from those that were successful.

Connected Value Development 'projects' aim to provide more than just results. It is also the anchoring of the results in existing structures over the longer term that is part of the present endeavours to deal with wicked problems. Our experiences with the projects have shown that interventions at several levels are necessary to achieve the desired change. What is needed is first the ongoing acquisition of sensitivities and competences by individuals; second the development of a shared practice around a guiding idea at project level; and third supportive conditions in the multiple institutional settings and the broader social context[81] (see figure 7.1). These elements are indispensable ingredients for the desired changes. Successful intervention strategies are focused on these levels simultaneously. Applying the right instruments within the new practice is in-effective if the required competences and personalities are not present in the team. And a 'successful' project which is separate from the context(s) in which it is implemented will become isolated, will not be understood, and will have little success and minimal duplication.

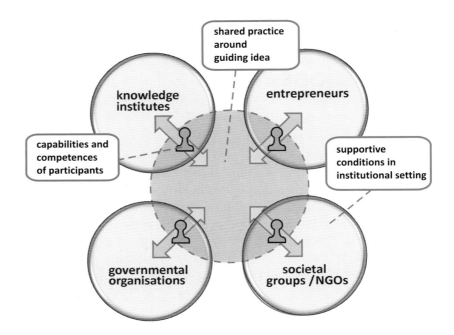

FIGURE 7.1 Intervention strategies at different levels in the Connected Value Development process

Paying attention to what is needed at these different levels simultaneously will enhance the chances that the collaborative efforts result in 'win-win-win-situations' (good for people, planet and profit). Success factors can be formulated for each of these levels of intervention. It is important to note that success factors are not to be interpreted as the necessary conditions for success that have to be present at the outset. These conditions will never (all) be present.[82] In the Connected Value Development approach, creating the necessary conditions at the different levels is part of the process.

The guiding principles formulated in the previous chapter show that developing *a shared practice around a guiding idea* involves creating an environment for knowledge co-creation, joint problem-solving and mutual learning. It is a process of communicating, co-operating, learning and building up a network between the different participants. It requires anticipating on problems which can arise as a result of differences in vision, language and power. An important aspect of this environment is promoting mutual trust between the participants. A certain degree of trust is crucial in order to gain access to sensitive information and implicit knowledge. Implicit knowledge is very personal and difficult to formalise. This makes it difficult to communicate such knowledge or to share it with others, while at the same time this knowledge is important in the case of wicked problems. Creating a safe environment is therefore essential.

Whether the Connected Value Development process is successful depends also on the *supportive conditions in the institutional settings* of the participants. Or on what 'task' people participating in a Connected Value Development process take with them from their home organisation. For a Connected Value Development project to succeed, attention has to be paid during the process to the boundary dynamics. The root of boundary dynamics lies in the relationship between the actions of an actor in the project and the framework on which his actions are based, that is, his professional and cultural background and the corresponding values, quality criteria and working method. The degree to which actors are able to participate openly, creatively and co-productively in a project is dependent on the degrees of freedom which are offered by the other networks of which the actor is a member, which in their turn are dependent on the way in which these networks are organised and the level of inclusion of this actor in the different networks.

Finally, the *capabilities and competences of participants* effect the success of the project. These too should not be seen as prerequisite conditions, but rather as elements to be developed over the course of the project. Our experiences have shown that sensitivity and experience are at least as important as methodological skills and competences. As each Connected Value Development process is different, project leaders and participants have to develop a sensitivity and awareness to the surroundings, the chances and the obstacles that are specific to their project. One way of doing this is by explicitly organising reflection, for example, by allowing a researcher to take part in the process and to reflect on it. By explicitly organising an action learning spiral, as indicated in figure 7.2, the reflection becomes part of the process.

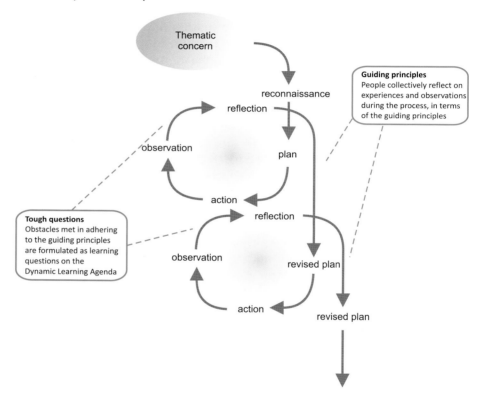

FIGURE 7.2 *Guiding principles and tough question in the action learning spiral*

Shared ownership of the Connected Value Development process is developed by formulating guiding principles that are specific to that project; these will be variations of the guiding principles that we have offered in this book. The guiding principles are in this way contextualised and embodied: they are brought in line with the words, language and activities of the project (and vice versa). These guiding principles will reflect the success factors on the different levels as discussed above. Regular reflection on this spectrum of issues that need attention in the process enhances the conducting of a multi level intervention strategy; it focusses our attention also on the blind spots. Especially when in the process default ways of working gradually and unconciously take over, reflection on the guiding principles is clarifying. Reflection then takes place on what obstacles are encountered and why things work out differently in practice than envisaged. This will lead to the formulation of issues on the Dynamic Learning Agenda on each of the levels, some of which will appear to be particularly tough.

In short, the approach Connected Value Development is focused on connecting values in a 3P value proposition by connecting people in a process. In this chapter we have emphasised that the participants of a Connected Value Development process bring into the collaborative endeavour their own skills, beliefs and attitudes, but also the expectations, stakes and current routines of their institutions. This implies that besides supporting the process of value cocreation, developing the capacities of both people and institutions are of great importance too in the Connected Value Development approach. The growing worldwide concern about environmental and social issues demands new ways of doing business, new ways of governing and of performing scientific research. These competences and capacities of our institutions are not developed overnight, but are part of long term proces. The question becomes whether these capacities are sufficiently present in our institutions to start realising value cocreation. To asses the situation at the moment we will look into current developments in these institutions in the next part of this book. This will show that strategies and practices are changing and will continue to change even more. Connected Value Development is an approach that provides a solid grounding for the embedding of the connection between values and actions of involved stakeholders in regular processes of business development, policy making and knowledge creation. It are these connections that provide the Licence to Grow.

Part II
The Bubbles

8. Changes in Sustainable Development Practices

Turning today's highly complex challenges in the field of sustainable development into 'win-win-win-situations' (good for people, planet, and profit) demands new ways of doing business, new ways of governing and of performing scientific research, which can only come about through collaborative efforts, involving multiple stakeholders willing to learn and build knowledge together in an interactive process. "Dealing with sustainability is […] a social learning process in which different individuals and (social) groups are involved. In this type of learning processes, there is no pre-conditioned route, but the interaction of different perceptions of different stakeholders to any given challenge results in a learning trajectory".[1] The realisation that complex issues can only be solved through the involvement of all stakeholders, as well as accepting the need for a continuous learning strategy, are the basis of the Connected Value Development approach.

The Connected Value Development approach obviously requires considerable effort: to overcome the boundaries between different perspectives, and connect and integrate the different perspectives, in order to develop a shared vocabulary and start searching for answers in a shared direction. The aim is for the separate KENGi–partners (Knowledge centres, Entrepreneurs, Non-Governmental Organisations and other societal groups and Governmental bodies, with the 'i' for their joint objective of innovation) to temporarily merge into one shared practice, resulting in an integrated perspective which can shed a radical new light on an issue. It is in this process of multi-actor cooperation that sustainable development is defined, shaped, and legitimated. The question, then, is whether the involvement of all stakeholders – traditionally separated or even antagonistic towards one another – is a realistic proposition. We have experienced that it is; in fact, we perceive a growing willingness (based on a recognition of a need) within various fields of society to rethink conventional strategies and overstep traditional boundaries.

In this part we will take a closer look at the four KENGi-partners and their respective home bases business, government, science, and societal organisations. We take a closer look at the appeals for new approaches to deal with sustainability challenges, as they have been made by leaders from these various fields. We describe sustainable practices that are taking place or are proposed, and demonstrate that, although the vocabulary may differ, there are many striking parallels between the developments in these different 'worlds', especially when it comes to dealing with the kind of complex problems which no single company or government can hope to solve on its own. This is the area where the Connected Value Development approach comes into its own. It can assist in creating '3P value propositions' (that is, solutions which provide a Profit, are beneficial to People, and respect the Planet), which can be developed with the cooperation of the four fields mentioned. First, however, we will take a closer look at the nature of these four worlds of business, government, science, and societal organisations, and their particularly complex demarcations.

These are the days of miracle and wonder

The Boy in the Bubble is a song by Paul Simon[2] about the difficult relationship between the suffering of people and 'the miracle and wonder' of modern technology. The boy in the song, having a severe immunodeficiency disease, is forced to live in a plastic bubble, a sterile environment without any direct contact with other people. The bubble becomes a metaphor for living and acting in isolation. The boy looks at the outside world from inside his bubble, and this determines the way he sees the world. We argue that, in a similar way, the four established worlds of business, government, science, societal organisations can be viewed as bubbles, which determine the perspectives on the 'outside world' of those operating within them.

A telling example illustrating this point is the tale of the squirrel and the oak tree. We often look at the interaction between the squirrel and the oak tree from the perspective of the squirrel. We say, for instance, "the squirrel collects the acorns (and other nuts) in late autumn and hides them in holes in the ground. During winter he will come out of his nest now and then to search for these hidden stores of food". In this sense, the squirrel uses the acorns to survive the wintertime of food scarcity. A very similar story can be told from the perspective of the oak tree. The squirrel is actually planting the acorns of the oak tree in the ground. The planted acorns are often not found by the squirrel and they sprout in spring to grow into new trees. From this perspective, the oak tree 'uses' the squirrel to plant its seeds. This perspective is often overlooked because we are used to attributing actions to humans and animals but not to trees or plants. Both perspectives are equally reasonable, and even from our vantage point as humans we could not say which description is the 'right' one. In the same way, the interactions of different actors can be told from different perspectives.

The societal landscape looks different when observed from the perspective of the entrepreneur or from the policymaker. A bird's eye view is impossible; any perspective implies a limited outlook. The different actors play in each other's 'outside world' and look at each other in a certain way, coloured by their own bubble. The segmentation and compartmentalisation of the past decades has created professional disciplines with their own approaches, ways of educating newcomers and handling problems. They function as bubbles through which individuals view society and define the way to go about things. From each perspective, the world and the other actors are perceived differently.

With the realisation that we live in a network society with complex interactions between societies and natural systems, attempts are made to address persistent problems in an integrated manner, crossing the boundaries of the bubbles. Society can then be viewed as a centreless network with multiple heterogeneous interactions, without a dominant power. Persistent or 'wicked' problems, such as most sustainability issues, are distributed over the whole network and are not confined to one policy domain, region, or scientific discipline. This implies that professionals cannot at the same time remain inside their own 'bubble' and instruct the actors in other 'bubbles' on how to act and make decisions. As Jeff Conklin puts it, "the antidote to fragmentation is shared understanding and shared commitment".[3] Luckily, individuals within different bubbles are increasingly aware that in order to effectively address these wicked problems, true collaboration is required between all relevant actors (be they companies, non-governmental organisations (NGOs), other societal organisations, academia, or governments). Accepting rather than regretting the multiple views of sustainable development can provide us with new ways for addressing the present challenges and transform them into opportunities. Next, we will elaborate on the appeals made for new approaches from within the business bubble, the policy bubble, the science bubble, and the bubble of societal organisations. In intermezzo's these appeals are illustrated by means of examples from practice.

9. The Business Bubble

The past century saw an acceleration of economic growth and a corresponding increase in the production of a large variety of goods, as well as the extensive use of energy sources and raw materials. The industrialised production processes, and the use of the products themselves, have in many cases led to a scarcity of 'goods' that used to be free and abundant. It has led to social damage as well. Today we are faced with the threat of climate change, a shortage of natural resources (such as clean water, unpolluted air, and unspoiled landscapes), and a loss of biodiversity. There is growing awareness that continuing with the one dimensional profit driven 'old' economy damages our planet and compromises the ability of future generations to meet their own needs. "Nature is the goose that lays all the golden eggs [...]; we squeeze it too hard at our own peril".[4]

Licence to sell

Because of the adverse effects of unlimited economic activities, the notion was conceived that companies require some kind of a 'licence', not just in the legal sense as has existed for centuries for certain products and services, but in a broader sense, as a 'licence from society'. To put it more precisely, in the past, before there was any concern about sustainable development, for companies to have such a licence was unquestioned and solely based on economic considerations. Whoever produced something (ranging from eggs to nuclear power plants) that customers bought because the product was useful to them, had in fact a 'licence'. This has been called by Casimir and Dutilh[5] the 'licence to sell': companies try to sell their products, and if the market finds them useful, and their price acceptable, these products are sold, yielding the profit which companies need to survive. The licence to sell is implicit and takes form in the continuous stream of daily transactions between consumer and companies.

Licence to produce

In the twentieth century, growing concern about safety and health (and later, sustainability) resulted in a 'licence to produce'. This demands from companies that their products should comply with existing rules and regulations regarding safety, contamination, labour conditions, etc. This licence to produce expresses itself in laws, regulations, permissions, and administrative demands. A licence to produce takes form in the interaction between government and companies. For example, the government requires (on behalf of the citizens it represents) that cars are sufficiently safe, and gives permission to sell certain types of car in the country. The discussion of what is 'sufficient' is negotiated between companies and the government, who seek a compromise between their different interests; in this example, 'profit margin' against 'reduction of casualties'. The licence to produce covers aspects of products that individual consumers are unaware of, ignore, cannot judge, or are simply not interested in. A licence to produce is often made explicit. Such a licence cannot be unilateral, as it is the outcome of reconciliation between different, often contradictory, interests. To obtain a licence to produce, the parties involved must be prepared to make concessions.

Licence to operate

Growing concern about sustainability has resulted in the notion of a third type of licence, the 'licence to operate'. In contrast to the licence to produce, this licence has no formal character, and it is not 'given' by any authority or organisation. A licence to operate reflects what public opinion (or rather the explicit opinion of certain groups in society) finds acceptable about the way a company runs its business, or about the impact of its products; for example, as an illustration, public opinion revolted against the 'Hummer', the car that became the symbol of excessive fuel consumption. A licence to operate can be considered as a mandate from the company's social milieu; though it is additional, since the company still needs a licence to sell and a licence to produce. Usually it only becomes clear when public opinion cancels the (implicit) licence to operate by boycotting the product, for example if a company becomes publicly implicated in sustainable development issues, such as causing pollution or environmental damage, or when it is exposed that a firm uses child labour. Societal organisations are the main mouthpieces for these opinions, but other social actors may play this role too, such as groups of neighbours who want to reduce the noise or emissions of an industrial plant. Increasingly, voluntary codes are drawn up in cooperation between non-governmental agencies and industry groups, such as the recommendations of the Forest Stewardship Council or the Marine Stewardship Council, co-founded in 1997 by the World Wide Fund for Nature and Unilever to oversee the sustainable and responsible use and management of these natural resources.

Another reason why a licence to operate might be questioned is through a more general shift in public opinion. Such a shift was recently noticed in the public attitude towards very high salaries, bonuses, and other remunerations in the banking sector (a pressure that is even extending to the government agencies and societal organisations).

Not having a licence to operate has no direct consequences other than the boycott itself. The company may still legally sell its products. But the absence of a licence to operate can be damaging in the long term. It may lead to actions being taken by societal organisations or local pressure groups, the boycott may spill over from one brand to other brands and even to subcontractors and licensees, or it may result in new legislation that enforces the behaviour that public opinion would like to see.

Toward a Licence to Grow: Value co-creation and next-practice platforms

The licence to produce and even more the licence to operate are manifestations of an underlying change of view: the insight that to improve a company's sustainable development performance, interactions between companies and other actors are increasingly relevant. Consumer activism is perpetuated by the increased accessibility of information worldwide and by networks of thematically organised consumer communities. The role of the consumer in the network society has changed, from being unaware to better informed, from passive to active. Greenpeace, for example, was able to mobilise a consumer boycott against Shell in 1995, when the oil company planned to let the Brent Spar oil storage and tanker loading buoy sink into the North Sea. Companies must now take increasing notice of the fact that societal expectations have changed, and they have learned that it makes sense to start discussions and consultations at an early stage instead of waiting for problems to arise. A sharply increasing number of companies routinely invite NGOs and other societal organisations to discuss sustainable development policy.[6] People are no longer satisfied with the 'trust us' stories offered by a company when it comes to strategies, plans, and activities related to sustainable development issues; they ask for 'show me' and 'prove it to me'. These demands require a more open attitude from the company; though it is not openness in the sense of the company telling the world about its points of view, but rather in demonstrating a willingness to discuss issues with other actors and follow up the discussions with changes in their mode of operation.

As a result, it has been advocated that companies must change their way of thinking about their interactions with customers and other actors, which in turn will lead to changes in products, processes, and business models. Business strategists have introduced the concept of 'value co-creation' as a new frame of reference for value creation.[7] Value co-creation is the process by which companies engage with customers as collaborators. There is a reward for being proactive: it pays for a company to undertake early voluntary steps to consult customers about their intentions regarding sustainable development issues, because in this process the needs and wishes of potential customers become more explicit and better understood, to the benefit of the company and its products. Together they can develop new business models, functionalities of products, and shape new technologies. The proposed model for value co-creation goes beyond consultations or consumer panels; "it implies shared learning and communication between two equal problem solvers".[8] Moreover, the uniqueness of the individual customer is emphasised, and each person's uniqueness affects the co-creation process as well as the co-creation experience.

Today, the concept of value co-creation has been extended further. Enterprises are building platforms that engage not only the firm and its customers, but also the entire network of suppliers, partners, and employees; creating a 'full theory of interactions'.[9] Others too advocate the development of so called 'next-practice platforms',[10] where value is co-created in a collaborative effort between companies, other businesses, consumers, non-governmental organisations, and governments. It has been argued that creating next-practice platforms creates promising innovation opportunities, particularly as the quest for sustainability is starting to transform the competitive landscape. Co-creative interactions trigger innovation, cut costs, increase employee engagement, and generate value.

These new practices, however, are not easy to realise, for they imply a change of paradigm. To develop sustainable innovations that lead to next-practices implies not only questioning the implicit assumptions behind current corporate practices, but also acting entrepreneurially to develop alternatives. While the goal should remain in constant focus, adjusting tactics along the way is crucial. Learning through experimenting as well as building collaborative capacity are key. Furthermore, taking a desired future as the starting point, rather than merely incrementally changing the present, will help companies' efforts to become sustainable.[11]

If asked what drives the choices to operate in a more sustainable way, many companies report various reasons,[12] including being less exposed to swings in prices, responding to public pressure, compliance to government policy, pressure from the capital market, and fear that competitors will catch up. However valid these reasons, they are primarily defensive in nature. Companies in a mature state of sustainable development performance think and act in terms of opportunities, added value, and cooperation. Expanding their scope to a new range of stakeholders that includes non-governmental organisations, media, academics, and the community at large gives businesses a 'licence to grow'.

Porous boundaries

Taken together, such interactions and dialogues make the boundaries between companies and their environment less distinct and more open. The activities and decisions of companies have an impact on the world outside their bubble. They trigger reactions (from governments, societal organisations, and consumers), which in turn affect the business arena. The boundary thus becomes more porous. "By better connecting companies' success with societal improvement, it opens up many ways to serve new needs."[13] In their considerations and decisions, companies allow the influence of other actors; and in turn, companies influence the activities and decisions of these actors. This process as a whole has an iterative character; in fact, it is about finding a new balance. To paraphrase Prahalad & Ramaswamy,[14] eventually, the roles of the company and the other actors converge toward a unique co-creation experience, or an 'experience of one'.

To put it in more general terms, through such dialogue a new cooperation model for sustainable development emerges, one based on interaction, collaboration, and co-creation. Importantly, the actors engage in dialogue, rather than attempting to convince each other. Companies can view other actors as potential allies and sources of solutions, not as adversaries or risk factors for their new plans, and their financial perspective on sustainable development will change, from one of 'expenses' to a view of 'investments for business opportunities'.

Companies that are open to interaction learn to understand the needs and interests of other actors, how to anticipate them, and how to draw mutual advantage from cooperation. In this situation it is no longer the company, or even a government, that can declare a product 'sustainable'. Rather, within the interaction between companies and society, 'sustainable development' is formed, defined, and legitimated.

The developments and trends described in the preceding paragraphs are summarised in table 9.1.

TABLE 9.1 Features of next-practice platforms as opposed to traditional operation within the business bubble[15]

	Traditional operation	Next-practice platforms
Goal of interaction	Ensure continuity by making a profit	Ensure continuity in a complex multi-dimensional environment
Role division	Company develops product in-house and obtains patents and copyrights Customer buys product Governments and societal organisations limit possibilities through license to produce	Company and stakeholders co-create product Companies form alliances with other business, non-governmental organisations, and governments Boundaries become porous: 'experience of one'
People	Customers are homogeneous target groups	Customers are unique individuals
Mode of operation	Routine	Cyclic development, adjusting goals and tactics along the way
Locus of interactions	Once, at the end of the value chain	Throughout the value chain, anywhere, and any time
Nature of interaction	One sided Firm initiated	Shared learning between equal problems solvers
Outcome (tangible and intangible)	Tangible: profitable business based on solid value proposition	Tangible: profitable business based on 3P value proposition Intangible: redefining business

INTERMEZZO 5

New practice: carpets for hire

The CEO of Interface Inc., the world's largest manufacturer of modular carpet for commercial and residential applications, realised he had been a 'predator' rather than a contributor to public welfare when in 1995 he read Paul Hawken's 'The Ecology of Commerce'.[16] Taking the idea of 'sustainable development' seriously, Ray Anderson set out to reduce the ecological footprint of his business by reducing the amount of energy and petroleum resources used in his products, thereby proving that paying heed to the environment, instead of being a 'cost factor', could actually reduce costs and thus be of direct commercial benefit.

Not content with this commercial success, he went on to develop a completely new business model for his products, which would ensure not only a commercial gain within the current framework of oil prices and legal limitations, but a business that is fundamentally sustainable; in his words, "taking nothing from the earth that is not rapidly and naturally renewable, and doing no harm to the biosphere".[17] Realizing, on the one hand, the needs of his customers (not really enthusiastic about paying for a whole new carpet just because a few patches looked well trodden), and on the other hand, that designing an optimally recyclable product is first and foremost in the interest of the one doing the recycling, he introduced a new business model whereby his carpets are hired out rather than sold. When used carpet tiles were brought in to be recycled (instead of being dumped, as they used to be), he made a direct profit. More importantly, this lent an incentive to researchers in the production department to make the product more recyclable. This 'short circuit' between production and recycling proved very profitable.

Anderson holds the opinion that in today's world, only business has the power to bring about the fundamental changes needed to encounter the 'wicked problems' we are faced with, and leave this planet to future generations in a state we will not be ashamed of.

10. The Science Bubble

Globally, scientists seek for solutions to reconcile social and economic improvements with the protection of natural resources. In recent years, a host of research efforts have been launched ranging from work on energy systems, ecosystem resilience, food security, and water and carbon management, to new initiatives in industrial ecology and earth system complexity. The focus of research has shifted from technologically oriented strategies for environmental protection ('end of pipe' technology) to prevention and increasingly to causal research and environmental systems research. Once the pure 'expression of human curiosity', science is now increasingly expected to deliver the basis for informed policy decisions. In recent years, appeals have been made on science to play a role beyond merely developing knowledge about the state of the environment; towards co-creating knowledge with others who are engaged in the practice of reconciling society's development goals with the planet's environmental limits.

Transdisciplinarity

In 2001 eight hundred people came together in Zürich, Switzerland, for a conference on 'Transdisciplinarity: Joint problem-solving among science, technology and society'. The discussions were about solving persistent, societal problems, such as the world's decreasing energy supplies, shortage of space, transportation, the environment, and climate change, all grouped under the common theme of sustainability. The definition for a new type of research paradigm, developed during the conference, was about transdisciplinarity as "a new form of learning and problem-solving involving co-operation between different parts of society and science in order to meet complex challenges of society".[18]

With regard to the assumed role of science, two things in particular stand out. First, there is no mention of research, but rather of learning and solving problems, suggesting that the linear innovation model of *basic research – applied research – development – production and diffusion* is shifting toward a more reflexive process in which the problem itself has to be continually redefined in the light of practical developments. Knowledge development and problem solving do not run sequentially. Second, the definition of transdisciplinarity refers to cooperation between science and society, implying that the primacy of science has to be abandoned. Scientists cannot solve these problems alone; rather, scientific knowledge has to be complemented by experiential knowledge.[19]

In the United States, a similar movement has been taking place, where initiatives to harness science and technology in the quest for a transition towards sustainability have been labelled 'sustainability science'.[20] Like the European transdisciplinarity movement, advocates of sustainability science say that "the research community needs to complement its historic role in identifying problems of sustainable development with a greater willingness to join with the development and other communities to work on practical solutions to those problems".[21] They also say that the goals of a sustainability transition should not be defined by scientists alone, but rather "through a dialogue between scientists and the people engaged in the practice of meeting human needs while conserving the earth's life support systems and reducing hunger and poverty".[22] Since the World Summit on Sustainable Development in Johannesburg in 2002, a rapidly expanding set of multi-stakeholder partnerships for sustainable development has been developing. It is exactly these local (place- or enterprise-based) practices that need to be supported. They result in usable, place-based knowledge for promoting sustainable development.

Co-creation of knowledge

These appeals for more interaction between knowledge producers and knowledge users, transdisciplinarity and sustainability science, can be seen against the background of new modes of thinking about the nature of knowledge production.

In the traditional view on science, knowledge development is considered an autonomous process in relation to other societal processes. Scientists are responsible for the production of objective, true knowledge, and are inspired by physical reality for the subjects of their research. How scientific knowledge is used in the societal domain is the responsibility of social actors. Scientific knowledge, according to this view, is neutral, and it is up to societal actors (policy makers, entrepreneurs, etc.) to use or abuse the knowledge according to their own moral or cultural values, ideals or questions. Thus, the responsibility for knowledge acquisition lies primarily with knowledge institutions (universities, research institutes, etc.), and the responsibility for how to approach societal problems lies mainly with government and industry. Yet scientific knowledge is seen as instrumental in resolving societal problems and stimulating the economy. In order to realise this, coordination activities have been developed to set the direction of scientific enquiry; for example, by giving financial incentives for pursuing particular research directions, but without influencing research design or execution. Both within scientific communities as in society at large, this traditional view on the functioning of the sciences has long been widespread.

Following the scientific sociological study of Kuhn,[23] however, the image of science as objective, independent, and as the producer of truths became open to discussion. Kuhn's idea that scientific knowledge is embedded in paradigms and value systems, and therefore has to be socially understood, shifted attention from the content of science to the structure and organisation of science. Kuhn introduced the notion that scientists make choices depending on what they are prepared to sacrifice, and on their value systems. The boundaries between what is and is not science were problematised, and because of that studying the boundaries became relevant.

The idea that scientific knowledge is embedded in paradigms, and therefore should be understood socially, paved the way for extensive research on the construction of scientific knowledge and science in action, as has been conducted over the past three decades within science studies. The assumption that scientific knowledge is not determined by the natural world, but that it is constructed, has provided the methodological basis.

On at least three levels, study of the boundaries between science and non-science contributes to the urge to rethink the role of science. First, on the micro level, ethnographic research has been conducted in and on laboratories.[24] French philosopher Bruno Latour describes the laboratory process in which facts and machines (the outcomes/products of science and technology) are "devoid of any trace of fabrication, construction or ownership".[25] Facts are 'black boxed' so to speak, when they appear without reference to the actors or context involved in their construction in manuals, textbooks, and newspapers. Before the black boxing happens, however, context (including 'lay' beliefs and knowledge) and contents do merge. Thus the rigid boundaries between scientific knowledge and 'lay' knowledge are constructed, in a process whereby context and content are separated until context dissolves into an invisible history.[26]

Second, on the middle level researchers have shown that the financial structures and reward systems of science play a crucial role in topic selection, choice of methodology, and the reporting of results. The chances to receive research funding seem to increase substantially if an individual, institute or (public-private) partnership is able to demonstrate its 'academic promise', and to fulfill this promise by producing output that can be measured via bibliometric quality indicators (e.g. high-impact articles and citations).[27] At the same time, scientists increasingly need to incorporate ideas of other disciplines and from outside the academic world in their research design, in order to obtain the resources necessary for their research. These types of activities are not yet addressed by evaluation mechanisms, i.e.

several authors demonstrated that bibliometric quality indicators overvalue disciplinary success and undervalue inter- and transdisciplinary research activities.[28, 29] Third, when looking at the macro level, a strong intertwinement between science and society is visible. Schwarz[30] introduced the notion of a 'technological culture', by which he argues that (the products of) science and technology are so deeply rooted in our society that they become our natural habitat – we have transitioned from a biotope to a technotope.

According to science scholars, positivistic notions of science on the one hand restrain the democratising development of science and technology; while the image of science and technology as contingent, as socially constructed, leaves room for other voices in scientific and technological decision making on the other. The co-evolution between science and society offers the basis for the construction of a new social contract between science and society, through which people have a stronger voice in the agora where science and society meet, and all 'experts' (certified and uncertified) should contribute to technological decision making.[31] "Co-creation of insights and solutions in the midst of academic and non-academic expertise is facilitated by various tools and aims at becoming a part of the competences learned in the process. This style of knowledge production is most appropriate if the decision-making process and its implementation depend on a number of different actors within academia, civil society, governmental agencies and the private sector, and if knowledge needed to address the issue is distributed among these actors".[32]

With an increased sensitivity for the actual processes involved in scientific practice, numerous examples have been given in which the traditional view on the relationship between society and science, and the conviction that science produces certain and independent facts of reality, have been questioned. For example, over the last century scientific studies paid for by industry have been on the increase. In the past decade especially, the independence of this research has been called into question, not least from within the science community itself, particularly after the appearance of reports of scientific evidence being deliberately suppressed by funding companies. But it is not just the exposure of deliberate wrongdoing which has urged a rethink of the role of science. Collins and Evans,[33] for instance, emphasise the fact that scientists do not have the sole right or claim to knowledge. A well known study that supports this position is that of Brian Wynne, who investigated the reaction of sheep farmers to the danger of contamination of their livestock as a result of the nuclear disaster in Chernobyl.[34] Wynne studied the relationship between scientists and sheep farmers, and saw that the local knowledge of the farmers about the effects of raised radioactivity on the fields and sheep was not recognised by the scientific specialists, who subsequently turned out to have been mistaken in their conclusions.

The borders between scientists and non-scientists are blurred by these insights. Increasingly, the need is felt to incorporate other types of knowledge aside from the strictly scientific, such as 'tacit knowledge' or 'personal knowledge',[35] 'implicit knowledge',[36] etc. This need is epitomised by the call for transdisciplinary research, which, by definition, engages other societal groups in the processes of problem solving and knowledge building.

According to this newly proposed role of science, the primary and main responsibility for resolving persistent societal problems does not lie with a single established institution. Rather, different societal actors, including scientists, must search in a joint deliberative process to find solutions. The knowledge which scientists contribute to this process complements the knowledge which other participants contribute on the basis of their experience, resulting in the co-creation of knowledge. The transdisciplinary approach enables researchers to perform very different roles and provide new contributions to the knowledge creation process. The different perspectives on the issue are combined in a learning process, whereby in the course of the interaction, implicit knowledge is made explicit and new knowledge is construed, shared, and tested. In this kind of process, 'socially robust knowledge' can be generated, which Nowotny et al.[37] indicate is not only scientifically reliable, but is also acceptable and applicable in the societal contexts pertaining to the issue at hand. In fact, the complexity of the problems, the complementary knowledge brought in by non-scientists, and the frequent feedback from 'outside', call for a highly reflexive process, in which not only the research agenda but the definition of the problem itself is continually adapted.

TABLE 10.1. Features of transdisciplinary platforms as opposed to traditional operation within the science bubble

	Traditional operation	Transdisciplinary platforms
Goal of interaction	Providing knowledge which may or may not be used for the benefit of social and economic progress	Contributing to the solving of complex societal issues (wicked problems)
Role division	Mono-disciplinary knowledge Develop knowledge and technology and have sole right to knowledge Societal actors (policy makers, entrepreneurs) decide how to use knowledge	Science and society co-create transdisciplinary knowledge
People	People are categorised as either 'scientists' or 'laymen'	Non-scientists are recognised as 'uncertified experts'
Mode of operation	Seeking solutions according to well-documented methodologies	Non-linear research path
Locus of interactions	Valorisation and diffusion of knowledge once and at the end of the research chain	Valorisation and diffusion of knowledge throughout the design and execution of the research
Nature of interaction	Transfer of knowledge from science to society	New forms of co-learning and problem solving
Outcome (tangible and intangible)	Tangible: peer reviewed knowledge in scientific publications	Socially robust knowledge in innovative solutions Intangible: rethinking science

INTERMEZZO 6

New Practice: Synergy[38]

Synergy has successfully implemented the transdisciplinary approach. It is one of the over thirty innovative practice projects of TransForum and aims to stimulate the adoption of the 'closed greenhouse'. In a closed greenhouse excess summer heat is stored underground and recycled to warm the greenhouse in winter. This makes the innovative closed greenhouse, unlike the traditional open greenhouses, independent of the limited capacity of natural resources and thereby contributes to the call of society for sustainable food, the reduction of CO_2 emissions and the sustainable production of energy.

To stimulate the implementation of the closed greenhouse, a learning community was created to facilitate transdisciplinary collaboration between civil servants, scientists and entrepreneurs (growers that implemented a closed greenhouse or had the ambition to implement a closed greenhouse). A key activity of this learning community was organising a platform to stimulate knowledge exchange both between growers, and between growers and scientists. During these platform meetings growers shared their experiences and common challenges, which were reformulated by the scientists into research questions.[39] Moreover, growers were consulted by the researchers when designing a research approach. These short feedback loops resulted in congruency between science and practice and joint problem solving.

An example of this cooperative problem solving concerns the folding of the tomato leaf. When the leaves of a plant are folded, they cannot absorb enough light to transform into food for production. This failure of the leaves to convert productive energy from the sun means that the plant doesn't grow enough tomatoes, and this, in turn, hurts the grower, since costs of electricity, labour and more remain the same. The growers were flabbergasted by the folding of the leaves since they had never seen such crop behaviour before. In pursuit of explanations, other growers, researchers and literature were consulted. Eventually they found out that the change in the vertical temperature gradient in a closed greenhouse caused the folding of the tomato crop leafs. The feature of vertical temperature had never been considered a relevant climate parameter. This specific case shows that experiential and scientific knowledge are intertwined and knowledge cocreation and collectively developing knowledge is essential in implementing sustainable innovations.

11. The Policy Bubble

Despite increasing knowledge, despite environmental regulations, despite international agreements, despite all these efforts, the problems that we are faced with today seem more urgent than ever, and the unlimited growth of production and consumption worldwide is not helping. The realisation is growing that in our complex society the existing order and traditional bodies of policy making are not well suited to address the issues of our times. In Western post-war society, the systems of policy formulation and political decision making became consolidated within established authorities and institutions. Considerable progress was achieved in the previous century with the segmentation of policy themes into departments and the specialisation of expertise. These formal structures, however, are facing difficulties in managing the indeterminate boundaries and borders of international global problems. Specialised knowledge is not sufficient; rather, knowledge has to be co-created, different policy areas have to collaborate, and innovative solutions have to be sought.

To complicate matters, under the influence of globalisation and individualisation, governmental bodies are losing their authority. Important decisions are no longer primarily taken in the political centre, but by scientists in laboratories, by managers in business, by the media that select news items, by consumers, by marketers, and by societal organisations. Equally, knowledge is distributed throughout the system, thus there is a much greater variety of sites where knowledge is produced (think tanks, consultancies, businesses, societal organisations), and a much greater variety of skills and expertise brought in by the multiple actors in a network, compared to traditional scientific systems. It is a feature of networks that power, control, and authority are distributed throughout the system. Naturally, these changes are not confined to national or local government. In fact, nowhere is the need for change more clearly perceived than in the field of international policy. From regional border problems to global environment and health issues, the need is perceived for international cooperation, not just between governments but between peoples, in a way and on a scale never seen before.

With the increasing realisation of the complexity of certain issues, such as those relating to sustainable development, pleas are being made within the policy bubble for a new kind of governance. The classic central role played by the government, whereby it defined a problem and subsequently developed, implemented, and evaluated the policy, is making way for a more interactionist and interdependent view on how a government should function.

From government to deliberative governance

The complexity of wicked problems, such as those surrounding sustainable development, imply another type of governance. Consider, for instance, issues such as climate change or the investment in biofuels. Due to the complexity of these issues, a policymaker is confronted with incomplete knowledge, scientific uncertainty, limited resources, and uncertain public consensus. Moreover the developed policy usually does not affect one single actor, but a policy arena filled with actors, who all hold a different perspective on the policy issue at hand. On top of this, the global character of the problems and the ongoing efforts to address them internationally limit individual countries' divergence from international regulations. Learning and reflection appear indispensable when dealing with the highly complex issues discussed here.[40]

Governmental bodies are increasingly sensitive to the societal dynamics surrounding such complex issues and the need to develop strategies with other societal partners. Next to the traditional lobbies, the advisory councils, and the well known actors in the socio-political arena, the citizen is becoming increasingly engaged in policy making. After interactive expert workshops, focus groups, or public forums, we now see the emergence of "citizen participation and deliberation in public policy premised on the fundamental democratic principle that government decisions should reflect the consent of the governed, including rights to meaningful participation in decision making and to proper access to information about policy rationales".[41] In addition to citizen participation, new concepts must be forged to describe complex issues and proposed solutions, and new alliances with relevant market parties, societal organisations, citizens' initiatives, and (last but not least) the media, must emerge and will have to be extended.

Governments today, for instance, create spaces for social or technical experiments. This implies the necessity for a culture of 'learning together', in which there is respect for the values of all players and whereby individual self interest can be (temporarily) suspended. It also implies a capability for handling inherent uncertainties. Because of the experimental character of the innovations, mistakes are inevitable, but they are acceptable as long as one learns from them for future reference. This means that innovative experiments should not be judged solely on project outcomes but also on their exploration of the technical and institutional possibilities for dealing with a certain issue. In the heterogeneous networks that are formed in these experimental spaces, governments and governmental institutions are becoming 'participants' while at the same time redefining the role of government itself.

The relevant competencies of civil servants shift from expertise on a certain policy or issue to being able to bridge gaps between various societal actors, sectors, and disciplines.

What emerges is a shift from 'government' in the traditional sense – of centralised and hierarchical decision making – towards a more inclusive model known as 'deliberative governance'. According to scholars of politics, "deliberative democracy now dominates the theory, reform, and study of democracy".[42] This approach promises political benefits on the one hand and practical operational benefits on the other. Moreover, according to its proponents, decisions reached through inclusive deliberations assert democratic legitimacy[43] and foster civil society,[44] thus furthering forms of social capital such as trust, cooperation, norms, moral obligations, and community resilience.

TABLE 11.1 Features of new forms of governance as opposed to traditional operation within the policy bubble

	Traditional operation	Deliberative governance
Goal of interaction	Develop policy and regulations to achieve set policy goals	Managing intractable policy controversies
Role division	Policymakers define the problem, define a solution, and implement it	Government co-creates policy with citizens and other stakeholders
People	Citizens are subjects to be governed	Citizens are active agents
Mode of operation	Seeking solutions for graspable problems according to well documented methodologies	Iterative, interactive policy making
Locus of interactions	At the beginning, with the gathering of information In the policy preparation phase At the end, in the evaluation phase	Continuously and 'on the spot' during the policy making process
Nature of interaction	One sided consultations of views and evaluation	Two sided, multi-layered Shared vision building
Outcome (tangible and intangible)	Tangible: policies based on political agendas	Tangible: credible solutions based on societal agendas Intangible: rethinking democracy

New Practice: Dutch Environmental Policy[45]

The change from 'government' to 'governance' is highly visible in the different generations of environmental policies in the Netherlands over the past four decades. The first generation of environmental policy was developed in the Netherlands around 1970 as a reaction to distressing reports about air, soil, and water pollution. Although there was a consensus at that time on the systemic character of environmental problems, the risks for public health provoked by emissions was the dominant theme and reducing emissions to an acceptable level the overall goal. This policy, enforced by regulations, was moderately successful in that it led to marked (short term) improvements in the quality of the air, soil, and water. However, it left the root of the problems unaddressed. The height of chimneys, for instance, was raised in order to avoid pollution of the direct environment, but led to increased air pollution in neighbouring countries. More significantly, a number of 'wicked problems' like climate change, loss of biodiversity, and shortage of natural resources, seemed to escape the grasp of the measures taken.

The most recent generation of environmental policy tries to account for these shortcomings by changing the policy goals, from the reduction of emissions to a predetermined level, to structural societal change in the long term. The need for system change has been recognised within the policy agenda in various areas. In the economic arena, change is being pursued not just in production methods, but also in consumption patterns. At the institutional level, the policy strives to broaden the scope and competencies of international environmental bodies. Vis a vis science, diverse incentives – funding but also enhanced cooperation – are used to steer toward practical solutions. Finally, and most importantly, change in the perceptions and attitudes of the general public is furthered by informing citizens and by actively engaging them in working toward the kind of solutions which can never be forced by regulations, but can only work when new attitudes become an ingrained part of our culture.

Comparable changes have taken place in several other countries, notably Germany and Britain, and have been summarised under the heading 'ecological modernisation'.[46] This new encompassing approach was picked up and advocated within the EU and elsewhere.[47]

12. The Bubble of Societal Organisations

We use the term societal organisations instead of the more common term NGO to denote a broad range of organisational types, from small local pressure groups or citizens' initiatives to large, well funded, and influential multinational organisations. Many focus on sustainable development issues such as protecting the environment, health, wildlife, biodiversity, the development of poor countries, fair trade, human rights, and animal welfare. They are often actively on the lookout for abusive situations, 'greenwashing', and behaviour that goes against organisations' stated good intentions. Such societal organisations have given – and still do give – an important impulse to improve sustainable development. Major activities are lobbying with (inter)governmental bodies to promote more sustainable laws, regulations, and subsidisation, informing consumers and citizens about sustainability issues, and mobilizing citizens to show their concerns through letter writing campaigns, boycotts, etc.

Thus, societal organisations can be active in giving (or cancelling) the various licences discussed in the section on the Business Bubble. Casimir and Dutilh[48] provide some examples of the roles NGOs play in this process. First, they can use their influence to change the terms of the 'licence to sell', for example, by organizing consumer boycotts of environmentally damaging products. Second, they can influence the 'licence to produce', for example through citizen suits or political pressure on governments for regulatory initiatives or more ambitious targets. Third, NGOs can directly influence the 'licence to operate' through taking an active role in public discussions and (negative) publicity.

Professional and well equipped organisations have the expert knowledge, which, in the past decades, has led to a new additional role: that of expert consultant. Going one step further, many societal organisations are involving themselves in partnerships with companies and governments. The goals of such partnerships may vary, from developing sustainable business concepts, promoting the use of sustainable products and services (for example, the use of clean energy), or developing eco labels (such as the Forest Stewardship Council and Marine Stewardship Council).

Cooperation or opposition?

There is a dichotomy with respect to the fundamental issue of whether (and which) societal organisations are willing to cooperate and negotiate with other actors. Most organisations have changed (or are changing) their strategy from one of opposition to a more cooperative attitude, open to interaction, dialogue, and joint projects with companies and governments. They opt for collaboration because they believe that they can reach their goals better following a win-win strategy, even if this implies compromise. However, a smaller segment of societal organisations is moving in the opposite direction. For these activist organisations, opposition is a matter of principle. They refuse to cooperate with other actors and instead follow a strategy of confrontation, seeking media attention around sustainable development issues, and organizing demonstrations and 'naming and shaming' campaigns. They make use of the fact that companies are increasingly sensitive to reputation damage.

The challenge for the collaborative organisations is to explain their compromises and choices to their rank and file. They must be capable of clearly explaining why the outcome of cooperation is better (in terms of what their members find important) than the outcome that can be reached by opposition. The challenge for oppositional organisations is not much different: even the majority of their hard line supporters ultimately expect changes for the better, and realise that more often than not these cannot but come from the side of government and business, supported by science.

Changing attitudes

Within the category of collaborative societal organisations, different attitudes with respect to cooperation are discernable. Somewhat simplifying, one can identify the 'defensive attitude' and the 'open attitude'. The former is one of defensive cooperation; both sides aim to convince the other, whom they see as potential adversaries rather than sources of options, solutions, and useful knowledge. The latter is that of having an open mind, whereby the point of view and interests of actors are acknowledged by both sides, and responsibility is collectively assumed for a negotiation process to find the best solution.

To illustrate how the outcome of cooperation is influenced by attitude, van Huijstee[49] describes two different scenarios for dialogue between NGOs and companies. The starting point is a company which wants to build a factory on a specific location with strategic benefits. However, the location is situated in an area with a large biodiversity, upon which a nearby community depends. The building of the factory would have a large impact on the biodiversity in the area, and consequently on the community. The company is aware of the sensitivities surrounding the building plan.

In the 'defensive attitude' scenario, NGOs are invited by the company to voice their concerns. There may, for instance, be concerns that certain limits set by law will be exceeded. The NGOs meet with well prepared answers but, relying on their weight in forming public opinion, are nevertheless able to negotiate a number of amendments. Finally, the factory is built with just enough concessions to forgo further actions by the NGOs.

In the 'open attitude' scenario, the company invites NGOs that have knowledge about ecosystem dynamics, the specific area, community development, and ecosystem friendly technologies. Through dialogue, the company and the NGOs share their interests: business continuity, poverty alleviation, biodiversity protection, etc. The next step is that they search for solutions in which all interests are taken into account. This may involve looking for alternative locations, new factory designs, or maybe even a new business approach that would make the factory redundant. Because this type of dialogue starts with the problem instead of the possible solutions, actors with diverse and seemingly contradictory interests become true 'owners' of the problem, which promotes creativity and innovation.

Overcoming prejudice

Within the bubble of societal organisations, there has been a noticeable shift towards engagement in constructive dialogue with business and government. This requires an 'open attitude' which asks for an essentially different mindset. As environmental consultant Mark Rudolph has remarked, such cooperation requires all actors to "check their biases at the door".[50] Societal organisations following the open attitude approach will become part of an uncertain, emergent process (though obviously this will only work if the other actors participate with an equal degree of openness and willingness to reach a shared vision and shared solutions). They should not aim to convince other actors of their point of view, but instead must be willing to understand others' interests, and feel co-responsible for the process and its outcome. The organisations must engage with other actors to develop a shared vision of the problems and shared options on how to reach a solution.

To participate effectively in such a process demands flexibility and trust amongst all actors,[51] who are all engaging in a process with an uncertain outcome, the parameters of which may well change in the course of the deliberations. Trust is important to overcome prejudices. Such prejudice on the side of the societal organisations, for example, may be that they think that companies abuse them and their standing to obtain societal legitimacy for their plans, and are not sincerely interested in sustainable development. On the other hand, companies often think that societal organisations will not participate fully in the process but stick to their vested interests. Pleas within the bubble of societal organisations for leaving this traditional enmity behind, and collaborating in joint efforts for change in a shared direction, are becoming louder.

TABLE 12.1 Features of new social practice as opposed to traditional operation within the societal organisations bubble

	Traditional operation	New practice
Goal of interaction	Representation of public values	Search for win-win solutions for complex societal issues
Role division	'Watchdog' of businesses and governments Traditionally adversarial	Collaborative search for win-win alternatives
People	Homogeneous group of supporters	Citizens are articulate, well educated individuals
Mode of operation	Seeking media attention 'Naming and shaming' mail and media campaigns Direct action Forming temporary alliances	Constructive dialogue Collaborative search for win-win alternatives
Locus of interactions	At the end of a process (the criticised pattern is already established)	From conception of a process and throughout
Nature of interaction	Passive Representing the public Criticizing patterns	Creating values together Prioritizing together
Outcome	Increased public awareness Polarisation of society	Increased public awareness Viable solutions with broad support

New Practice: Tony Chocolonely

"There is a good chance you are an accessory to slavery", starts the story on the website of Tony Chocolonely's chocolate. It is representative of the approach of TV maker turned businessman Teun van der Keuken, who from 1992 has tried to gain public attention for the way in which chocolate is produced. The word 'slavery' is not to be taken as hyperbole. "Contemporary forms of slavery remain a "grave" and unresolved problem across all continents", confirmed UN Secretary General Ban Ki-Moon in his 2009 address on the occasion of the International Day for the Abolition of Slavery.

Several other NGOs, like the Fair Trade and Max Havelaar foundations, and a number of others, had already made considerable efforts to draw attention to the miserable circumstances of the producers of cocoa beans, and the generally predatory means of production. These NGOs have sought to influence public opinion, as traditionally all NGOs do, but went a considerable step further by setting up a collaborative network with producers on the one hand and travelling experts on the other, granting a well protected label for chocolate which has been produced under acceptable circumstances. This was done, of course, in the hope that the consumer would be willing to pay a bit more for chocolate carrying their label.

Although these labels have had a moderate degree of success, mainly through the pressure they exert on other brands, this apparently was not enough for Tony Chocolonely who, after gaining much TV coverage in his (failed) effort to get himself prosecuted as a "chocolate criminal, guilty of furthering slavery", started his own brand of "100% slave free chocolate". The project 'Tony in Africa', launched in February 2009, is dedicated to setting up a model supply chain for West African cocoa, and is aimed at improving farmer incomes and reducing the occurrence of extremely poor labour situations, in particular child labour. This is but one example of an idealistic NGO, evolving from signalling and protests to cooperation, and from there to a viable new business model, relying on a responsible and responsive citizenship.

13. Implications for Connected Value Development

When comparing the trends in the four 'bubbles' discussed above, perhaps the first thing that stands out is the similarity between emerging next-practice platforms in business, the calls for transdisciplinary practices in science, the pleas for deliberative governance in policy making, and the movement towards collaborative practice by societal organisations. Clearly – though clearest in the field of business – there is growing support for the idea that a complete shift in the usual way of doing business is necessary. In all fields, a multi-stakeholder approach involving customers, citizens, pressure groups, and scientists is considered key to bringing about such a shift. In this new paradigm, neither the definition of a problem nor the direction of the solution is unequivocally known a priori; rather, it is about common searching and learning processes, whereby all stake-holders jointly try to find a shared problem perception and redefine the questions along the way.

Although 'sustainable development' is a keyword in all arenas, motivations are not necessarily the same. Businesses are confronted by rising energy prices and scarcer resources, pulled by the demands of an increasingly environmentally aware clientele, pushed by the growing power of internet enabled societal organisations, and fenced in by government regulations. Apart from all that, there is growing awareness within the business community that 'we just can't go on this way forever'. Scientists, on the other hand, are sometimes urged into sustainable development practices by developments within their own discipline – for example, in order to tackle (global) health issues – though pressure more often comes from the demands of businesses (small innovative businesses as well as large corporations with a eye on the future) and by governments seeking ways to solve those highly complex, intractable, wicked problems which seemingly cannot be solved within the existing frameworks.

Confronted with these problems, and with the diffusion of power towards business, pressure groups, and even science, governments too are increasingly dependent on collaborative networks and the direct involvement of citizens. There are no longer clear, generally accepted rules and norms regarding which form of politics is to be conducted or which policy measures are to be agreed upon – a state of affairs dubbed the 'institutional void,[52] as introduced in the introduction. Though seemingly negative, this 'void' can be regarded in a positive sense as a new social space, offering new opportunities for societal innovation. Whatever the motivations of the various players may be, in all bubbles there is a movement toward collaboration, the participation of societal groups, co-learning, co-development, and a willingness to review goals along the way. In this way the knowledge produced becomes embedded in and is intertwined with the demands and goals from business, policymakers, scientists, and societal organisations.

Finally, through raising public awareness, all societal organisations concerned with environmental issues contribute to the participation of citizens and thus push businesses, governments, and scientists to 'do something about it'. The willingness to collaborate and co-create knowledge and solutions clearly extends to most societal organisations who recognise the complexity of the problems and see contributing to a possible solution as their best course of action. Even the actions of those organisations which continue to choose for opposition might have the indirect effect of stimulating others to collaborate towards a solution. Connected Value Development purports to encompass all the emerging trends discussed in this Part in a coherent model for structural change. In particular, it is based on the striking convergences between the various 'bubbles' as they appear in table 13.1.

TABLE 13.1 New proposals developed in the four different bubbles

	Business bubble Next-practice platforms	Science bubble Trans-disciplinary platforms	Policy bubble New forms of governance	Societal organisations bubble New social practice
Goal of interaction (managing complex problems)	Ensure continuity in a complex society	Contributing to the management of complex societal issues	Managing intractable policy controversies	Search for win-win propositions for complex societal issues
Role division (multi-stakeholder)	Companies form alliances with other business, societal organisations and governments Boundaries become porous: 'experience of one'	Science and society co-create knowledge	Government co-creates policy with citizens and other stakeholders	Collaborative search for win-win alternatives
People (unique individual)	Customers are unique individuals	Non-scientists are recognised as 'uncertified experts'	Citizens are active agents	Citizens are articulate, well educated individuals
Mode of operation (action learning)	Cyclic development, adjusting goals and tactics along the way	Non-linear research path	Iterative, interactive policy making	Constructive dialogue
Locus of interactions (anywhere, anytime)	Throughout the value chain	Throughout the design and execution of research	Continuously and 'on the spot' during the policy making process	From the conception of a project and throughout
Nature of interaction (co-creation)	Shared learning between equal problems solvers	New forms of co-learning and problem solving	Two sided, multi-layered Shared vision building	Creating values together Prioritizing together
Outcome (intangible & tangible)	Profitable business based on 3P value proposition Sustainable businesses	Socially robust knowledge Structural changes	Technical and institutional possibilities New discourse	Increased public awareness Viable solutions with broad support

As table 13.1 summarises, there is considerable convergence in some areas, notably in the goal of establishing sustainable practices and in the way to go about doing so. On the other hand, businesses will continue to make a profit, politicians will continue to feel responsible toward their electorate, scientists will continue to aim to publish papers in peer reviewed journals, and societal organisations will continue to sting like bees. Yet, co-creation of new values can lead to finding new 3P (people, planet, profit) solutions, which combine sustainable development – in the environmental, economic, and social sense – with broader, and therefore more robust, knowledge and understanding. It is against this backdrop that the concept of Connected Value Development proves its worth.

Epilogue: Looking Ahead

Today's complex societal problems, and more in particular the so-called wicked problems we mentioned in the introduction, require new innovative approaches to tackle them. In the past decades, a great number of efforts have been made to develop new methods to respond to this challenge. From these efforts, many valuable lessons can be drawn, hopefully leading us from incidentally applicable methods to unifying concepts and eventually to a more generally useful methodological framework.

In this book, we took the TransForum programme, explicitly aimed at tackling the complex problems met with by innovators in the agricultural sector, as our object of study. These projects are particularly suited as they were executed in the context of explicitly described assumptions, addressing the systemic nature of efforts to addres sustainable development, the need for transdisciplinary knowledge creation and multistakeholder collaboration and the importance of reflexive learning. TransForm did not merely support projects that were to meet a set of predetermined criteria. Rather, TransForum acted as a change agent itself by actively participating in projects and stimulating a learning-by-doing approach. The Connected Value Development approach described in this book is an attempt to formulate generic features of and lessons about successful approaches to sustainable development. They are drawn from the great diversity of strategies, experiences, and tools developed and used in the projects that together comprised the TransForum programme.

In the last chapters, we considered the all important question of whether or not there is indeed sufficient support for this kind of new approach and, if so, whether there is sufficient know-how available to practically implement it on a wider scale. In "The Bubbles" we signal that the trends in all sectors of society seem to converge in this respect. In business it is recognised that consumers base their choice on considerably more then just the product itself and consequently the key concept of 'innovation' has been broadened to comprise not just new technical inventions, but 'new ways of doing business' and new trends in management, based on value co-creation. In government, the notion of 'participative governance' is ubiquitous. In science, the need for more 'transdisciplinary research' is becoming increasingly apparent.

The observation of such convergence gives rise to optimism in the face of the challenges our modern society poses. But is that justified? Can we, for example, be confident that in the future our society moves toward a more sustainable state? It seems probable that an increasing number of businesses will learn to grab not just the profits that can be reaped from new technologies, but also from the changes in the public stance and the increase in public awareness of global problems. Sensitivity for such trends simply mean 'good business' and will no doubt require, and lead to, changes in the way the business is managed and new employees are recruited and trained.

While analysing the Connected Value Development approach applied in practice, and observing the progressing changes within businesses, governmental bodies and other institutions, we of course asked the question whether these developments should be seen as 'niches', determined by locational and timely circumstances, or whether they could be seen as heralds of deeper changes taking place within the contributing institutions and societal sectors. This last interpretation would fit well within the theory of transitions, according to which *system innovations* emerge from a wide variety of innovative practices. In this view, changes within institutions, and institutional roles, will follow changed practices until, after the success of the new practice and its general adoption as a consequence thereof, finally a new equilibrium is reached. However, transition theory describes other, less successful, pathways as well: developments may strand in a 'lock in' or even completely fail even after initial success. Thus we need continue our efforts to experiment with and study Connected Value Development and further develop the effectiveness of the strategies used to deal with obstacles which 'stubborn reality' tends to put in the path of brilliant ideas.

For now, we conclude with the observation that all efforts to bring about changes which are desired by citizens on the one hand, and create a viable business value on the other, seem to center around *collaboration and co-creation* across the boundaries between professional and societal sectors, between business, government, academia and societal groups and lobbies. Dialogue is the *conditio sine qua non* for collaboration and co-creation and the difficulties of bringing it about are often underestimated. As professor Rudy Rabbinge of Wageningen University puts it, speaking of the academic world: "researchers tend to specialise further and further – that is something occurring naturally, you don't have to do anything about it. Yet, what you *do* have to organise is some way to bring them all together again."

We hope this book contributes to showing the need for such collaboration, offers some practical advice in furthering it and contributes to the growing practice base about ways to approach the great challenges of modern society: sustainability, equity and freedom. The only way forward is: step up and do it!

Prof.dr. Joske Bunders – Director Athena Institute
Dr. Henk C. van Latesteijn – CEO TransForum

Appendix
Tools

Introduction

Connected Value Development processes are like expeditions; we learn our way towards innovative solutions. Along the way, different stakeholders explore and experiment, and together they develop 3P value propositions for (new) business development. Bringing a diverse group of people together is not just a matter of employing straightforward techniques or conducting an analytical exercise. It is an approach of experiencing, acting, reflecting, learning, of transformational leadership, and of connecting people to each other, to their underlying values, and to the challenges that lie ahead.

This systemic, participatory, and emergent character of the Connected Value Development approach requires different tools from those used in regular project management and business development, although more straightforward tools such as SWOT analysis, confrontation matrix, brainstorming techniques, visioning techniques, and marketing and communication tools are also very helpful to co-create knowledge and transform this into concrete information for further development, action or decision making. We have not included these tools in this book, since they are not specific to the challenges we are dealing with in Connected Value Development, and because they are well-documented elsewhere. We have made a selection of tools that are particularly suitable to support Connected Value Development and other system innovation processes.

In this appendix we present the tools that have benefited us in our experiences with innovative projects where the Connected Value Development approach was used. Some tools have been specifically developed for this purpose (Dynamic Learning Agenda, Eye Opener Workshop, Audiovisual Learning History, Sustainability Scan), while other tools are modified versions of existing tools, adapted to make them applicable in our context

(Causal Analysis, Actor Analysis, Timeline Workshop, Value Creation Model). To emphasise the importance of dialogue and conversations in Connected Value Development, we have also included two well-documented tools that have been used successfully in the context of TransForum; the Open Space Workshop and the World Café. Both tools enable a group of people to engage in a dialogue about a central issue. The techniques are inspired by how people normally, in informal settings, interact in a meaningful way. We present them here to honour the valuable work others have done in this field. And yet, this toolkit is far from complete. Naturally, many other tools and methods can be applied in the process of Connected Value Development, depending on the challenges that you may encounter in your project. Probably you already know many of them and possibly you even use them in practice.

The following tools are described:

Phases/Tools	Tools for Exploration & Alliance Building	Tools for Co-Creation & Experimentation	Tools for Embedding & Alignment
I. World Café	x	x	
II. Open Space Workshop	x	x	
III. Dynamic Learning Agenda	x	x	x
IV. Focus Group	x	x	
V. Actor Analysis	x	x	
VI. Causal Analysis	x	x	
VII. Timeline Workshop		x	x
VIII. Eye Opener Workshop		x	x
IX. Audiovisual Learning Histories		x	x
X. Value Creation Model		x	x
XI. Sustainability Scan		x	x

The tools presented in this toolkit can be used by the process manager in the project, but some of the tools are particularly suited for use by a dedicated reflection monitor. For 'project leader' or 'process facilitator' you may also read 'evaluator' or 'reflection monitor'. We hope this selection of tools helps you on your journey of Exploration & Alliance building, Co-creation & Experimentation and Embedding & Alignment, to create a toolkit that works for you.

I. The World Café

Purpose of the tool

The World Café is a tool for designing meetings that is much more effective in creating common ground for change. The World Café is a relaxed and inviting space in which a large group of people think together about meaningful questions, and thereby collectively create new insights. The underlying assumption of the World Café methodology is that the knowledge and wisdom that we need to solve issues already exist. It is in our collective brain, we just don't know it yet.

In Connected Value Development we have used this tool for instance to explore the guiding idea with a much larger group than the core project team. It intentionally creates a living network of conversations around important questions and enables as few as 12 or as many as 1200 people to discuss and share ideas. The World Café can help to bring out our collective wisdom and use it to create positive change.

Although this way of meeting and discussing important issues has been done informally for ages, the World Café was formalised as a methodology in 1995 by Juanita Brown and David Isaacs. The methodology is especially valuable in situations that aim to engage people and to generate input, sharing knowledge and innovative thinking around important questions or issues. The method can be used for large groups to create meaningful interaction, and to create common ownership of the outcomes in a group. People who have participated in a World Café speak of a highly energetic and almost 'magic' atmosphere that arises during the conversations.

We have found that the World Café is an excellent tool to connect ideas and connect people.

How It Works

STEP 1. Organise a Café setting in the meeting room
Being a Café, the room in which the World Café takes place is actually set up like a café: people sit around different tables in small groups. Preferably with four people per table, to enable participatory and high-quality conversations.

STEP 2. Share the Café etiquette with all the participants
To optimally engage all participants in the World Café, the 'World Café Etiquette' is shared with participants by the facilitator before the start (see box 1.1):

BOX I.I   World Café etiquette[1]
- Focus on what matters
- Contribute your thinking and experience
- Speak from the heart
- Listen to understand
- Link and connect ideas
- Listen together for deeper themes, insights, and questions
- Play, doodle, draw—writing on the tablecloths is encouraged.

A generative dialogue is the most effective mode of having conversations in the World Café. You might want to note when the conversation falls back to downloading and/or debating, and stimulate reflective dialogue by empathic inquiry of the other participants.

STEP 3. Formulate a central question or challenge

The meeting consists of series of conversational rounds around meaningful questions or challenges. Because of the number of people and diversity of the group, you can use one central question or challenge. The facilitator can pose this central question which is then elaborated upon at each of the tables. You will notice that the dialogues at the various tables will also lead to a rich diversity of ideas and possible solutions. Encourage people to write down their ideas, thoughts, notions, either in words or as pictures. Use a large sheet of paper for this, or even the table cloth. Invite people to put reflections next to drawings or words of other participants.

STEP 4. Move to another table

After every round, one host stays at the table while the other participants move to another table to connect to the conversations of the other tables. The table host shares the essence of his/her table's conversation with the new participants at his/her table. The new participants build on the input that was provided by the first group. In this way, the conversations are cross-pollinated and the collective intelligence evolves within the group.

STEP 5. Share the results

The best way to share the results of the various groups is to have the host give a small presentation at his table for the whole group. Walk with the group along each of the tables, or put the sheets of papers on the wall as a display.

Further reading

Brown, Juanita and David Isaacs (2005). *The World Café: Shaping Our Futures Through Conversations that Matter.* San Francisco (CA): Berrett-Koehler Publishers.

http://www.theworldcafe.com

Bojer, M., Roehl, H., Knuth, M. and Magner, C. (2008), *Mapping Dialogue: Essential Tools for Social Change*, The Taos Institute.

II. Open Space Workshop

Purpose of the tool

Open Space is a tool to enhance creative solutions to central themes of strategic importance. In Connected Value Development we have used this tool to combine knowledge, experiences, and visions of the diversity of stakeholders in an effective way. Open Space methodology originates from the idea that at conferences, the best conversations and deals are being made during the coffee break. During coffee breaks participants speak with each other freely about subjects of their interest. They introduce new topics or move away to another group if the topic discussed is no longer of interest to them. Those breaks are often characterised by a combination of synergy and excitement. Moved by the question of whether it was possible to create a methodology that combines the atmosphere of a coffee break with the result-oriented characteristic of a meeting, Harrison Owen initiated the Open Space Technology in the 1980s.

Open Space workshops allow small and large groups to deal effectively with complex issues in a short time. They create their own agenda of parallel working sessions around a central team. Open Space relies on a high level of self-organisation of the participants. Key in such Open Space workshops is that the central theme must be of importance to the participants. In that way, participants will be engaged and passionate to contribute their knowledge to the central questions. This further strengthens the individual commitment to the shared practice that is created via the Connected Value Development approach.

BOX 11.1   **Four principles and one law[2]**

Principle 1: Whoever comes are the right people.

Participants are encouraged to let go of any need to get specific people, e.g. people with specific expertise or people in a certain position, to join their group. Instead, this principle encourages freely inviting and welcoming people who care enough, or who are passionate about the topic. The people who choose to join a conversation freely are the best ones to be involved in the conversation.

Principle 2: Whenever it starts is the right time.

Creativity and inspiration do not always come at the desired time of a meeting. This principle recognises that conversations really start when the time is right.

Principle 3: Whatever happens is the only thing that could have happened.

This principle encourages people to be free of expectations as to how things should go. Rather than thinking about expectations, participants are encouraged to pay attention to what is actually happening and to what is actually being achieved in the group.

Principle 4: When it's over, it's over.

In line with principle 2, which says that whenever it starts is the right time, the conversation is over when it is over. We do not know in advance how long a conversation will be. The timeslot is less important than the topic. If the conversation is finished before the time is up, participants can finish this conversation and move on to another topic. It also works the other way around: If the allotted time is over, but the conversation is not yet finished, participants may continue their conversation at another time or self-organise to work on the topic beyond the workshop.

The law of two feet

This law is essential in Open Space workshops. The law of two feet acknowledges participants' responsibility for their own contribution and learning. The law of two feet encourages people to use their feet during the workshop by joining in conversations in which they can contribute or learn. Participants are free to move to other groups if they feel they can contribute more, or even if they just feel more engaged with the other topic.

As a result of this law, Open Space workshops can identify different participants. Some participants will stick to one certain conversation or topic while others will become 'honeybees', fly from one conversation to the next, touch on all topics, and cross-pollinate the sessions. Other participants will behave more like 'butterflies'. They choose to skip sessions and go outside instead or meet up with other butterflies. In these conversations, new topics and sessions may arise.

Open Space workshops have four principles and one law that help these workshops being effective. These principles and law encourage participants to take responsibility for their own learning and contribution. It enables participants to work hard and to remain focused, while being flexible and open at the same time (see box II.1).

How it works

An Open Space workshop is built around one central theme of strategic importance to the participants. The topics that are actually discussed and the agenda of the workshop are decided by the participants themselves. There are different ways of organising an Open Space, but the self-organisational aspect of the workshop is key. An Open Space workshop might have the following set-up:

STEP 1. Inspirational introduction of the central theme

Ask someone who is personally confronted by a problem or a challenge to tell his/her story, so as to illustrate the central theme. At best, this will lead to a burning question to work on during the workshop.

STEP 2. Establishing the agenda

All participants are invited to propose sessions on topics they feel the need, urgency, and commitment to work on, in order to better deal with the burning question. list these suggestions on a large, blank screen. The proposed topics are the agenda around which the discussion sessions take place. Ideally, the number of topics is approximately the square root of the number of participants.

STEP 3. Dialogue sessions

The persons who proposed a discussion topic will serve as hosts during the session on that topic. They do not act as facilitators, but they help the group have a conversation about the topic. Dialoguing is the perfect mode of conversation in this setting. Participants are free to join in any conversation that they feel passionate about, and switch between different conversations (see 'one law'). The host of each group compiles a small report, describing the results of the conversation.

STEP 4. Reporting

After the discussion session, the host of every session shortly reports the discussion and outcome to the whole group.

STEP 5. Optional second round of discussion

Start again at step 2.

STEP 6. Closing

The owner of the burning question that was posed in step 1 reflects briefly on the outcome of the discussion sessions and on its contribution to the central theme.

Further reading

Owen, H. (1997). *Expanding Our Now: The Story of Open Space Technology.* San Francisco (CA): Berrett-Koehler Publishers.

Owen, H. (1997). *Open Space Technology, A User's Guide.* San Francisco (CA): Berrett-Koehler Publishers.

http://www.openspaceworld.com

Bojer, M., Roehl, H., Knuth, M. and Magner, C. (2008), *Mapping Dialogue: Essential Tools for Social Change*, The Taos Institute.

III. Dynamic Learning Agenda

Purpose of the tool

The dynamic learning agenda is a tool that helps the Connected Value Development process link long-term aims to concrete action perspectives by formulating the challenges that arise, recording them, and keeping track of them. The dynamic learning agenda defines the learning pathway during the project itself, so that reflection and learning can become an integral part of the project. The agenda can also be used for a joint review of the entire project history as well as for reporting purposes.

The dynamic learning agenda encourages participants to continue working on change. The learning agenda is a brief document containing the challenges, summarised in learning questions, that the project is facing at that moment. It is also a tool for commencing and supporting the dialogue about the challenges faced by the project. The agenda is dynamic because it is modified over the course of the project. As soon as a challenge is dealt with or is no longer relevant, the associated learning question disappears from the agenda. It often turns out that questions have to be formulated differently over the course of the process. In addition, new challenges are added to the agenda. Questions that remain on the agenda for

An extended version of this tool was first published in Van Mierlo, Regeer et al. (2010) *Reflexive Monitoring in Action. A Guide for Monitoring System Innovation Projects.* Wageningen/Amsterdam: Communicatie en Innovatiestudies, WUR; Athena Instituut, VU.

a longer period (months) will probably represent persistent problems which require further analysis, attention, and intervention.

The Connected Value Development process facilitator helps put into words the problems that the project participants are experiencing. The problems and challenges have to be expressed as system properties, without losing track of the words and vocabulary of the project participants. Not all problems experienced by the project participants are learning questions that should be on the learning agenda. The learning questions on the learning agenda are so-called tough questions, issues that are often swept under the rug because they are hard or even painful to deal with. Moreover, tough questions are often second-order learning questions. Second-order learning involves changing underlying beliefs, norms and assumptions, whereas first-order learning involves doing things better through incremental improvements of existing routines. It is important that one frames the system changes as learning questions of the group itself, so that working on these changes becomes an integral part of the project. This way, environmental factors that are hampering the project will no longer be seen as properties of an external system, but rather as points of leverage for the strategies that the project needs to develop.

A practical example: A representative of an NGO is working on a system innovation project in sustainable agriculture. At one of the project meetings, he cries out, "But the farmers aren't cooperating! All they want is increases in scale!" This situation ends up as a question on the dynamic learning agenda: "How can I ensure that the farmers cooperate?" Those present at the meeting note that this formulation gives too little insight into possible solutions. Following on from that, the facilitator guides a dialogue in which the situation is clarified using questions such as "Why do farmers want increases in scale?" and "What benefits will a farmer get from this project?" Finally a number of specific questions are placed on the learning agenda, such as "How can we link the goals of this project to farmers' concerns?" This has changed the farmers' reluctance, as experienced by the NGO representative, from an external system characteristic into a point of leverage for the project to help shape the interaction between the project and the farmers. The frustrated outburst evolves into a second-order learning question: a question that reflects on your own framework and actions.

It is part of your role as a facilitator to help formulate the challenges experienced by the participants and use them to formulate the desired system changes using the language and world view of the participants themselves. The project participants will then interact with other actors in the same way. This initiates learning processes in the wider network. It is also possible to maintain a dynamic learning agenda for this broader network. This renders the broader anchoring of learning within the network visible.

A step by step description

The questions that are on the dynamic learning agenda are based on the challenges mentioned by the project members. As a facilitator, you can help reconstruct these challenges on the basis of participatory observation at project team meetings or interviews. Another option is to have the challenges put into words during a network meeting. Causal Analysis (Tool VI) is also a suitable method for getting a picture of the challenges.

A description is given below as to how you as process manager, can use a dynamic learning agenda.

STEP 1. Identify the initial 'tough questions' with your team
From the very first interaction with the project participants onwards, listen to what they experience as hindrances, struggles, and challenges. Identify the aspects of their comments that can be meaningful from the system innovation point of view. These are often aspects that are difficult to deal with, since they are at the heart of the change that is hoped for. An example of such a tough question within the context of the New Mixed Farm TransForum project is shown in the figure below. The New Mixed Farm aims to set up an innovative way of combining different agricultural disciplines. Since Dutch legislation is very strict regarding emissions and other

agriculture-related aspects, there is little room for new innovative approaches like the New Mixed Farm. Therefore, for the innovation to succeed, either the legislation must change, or the New Mixed Farm must operate completely in line with Dutch legislation. This challenge of how to make sure that system innovation does not reach an impasse as a result of incompatibility with prevailing legislation is an important part of the Connected Value Development process. Express the challenges that are relevant from the system innovation point of view as second-order learning questions. This is important because system change also requires changes in your own framework and actions. Often, second-order learning questions can be phrased as dilemmas or as tensions between two positions, between conditions and objectives, or between the actual and the desired situation. You can do this by analysing notes or reports. You can also formulate the questions together with the project participants by probing further in order to uncover the nature of the situation. Combine your own knowledge of Connected Value Development here with sensitivity to the project participants' point of view. The result of this first step is an initial version of the dynamic learning agenda.

STEP 2. Put the tough learning issues on the project meeting agenda

Make use of the list of tough questions as an agenda-setting instrument for project meetings. A whole pile of statements, actions, plans, ideas, and annoyances will be mentioned in such meetings. The dynamic learning agenda can help structure and order this 'clutter' using second-order learning questions. You can carry out this analytical activity afterwards, but the dynamic learning agenda will additionally help you to intervene during meetings in order to keep making the connections between the clutter and the second-order learning questions. The two activities will give rise to a new version of the learning agenda. Some questions are persistent and will remain on the agenda. Provisional answers will be formulated for others, often phrased in terms of activities. Yet other questions will disappear from the agenda because merely stating the question provides enough insight for effective action to be taken.

STEP 3. Collectively plan and record interventions in order to deal with tough issues

If a question remains on the agenda for a long period, it is worthwhile making an effort with the project team to consider this tough question thoroughly. The greater depth of understanding that is achieved thereby may lead to various large or small interventions for dealing with this particular issue. It can also result in a meeting of the people and organisations concerned, at which the question is tackled. In your role as facilitator, you are also able to bring in new expertise by doing your own research and by giving a presentation about it, or by calling in an external expert.

STEP 4. Formulate lessons learned together and evaluate interventions

The project team discusses the dynamic learning agenda and the executed intervention strategies in all its subsequent meetings, and adjusts the agenda as necessary. To what extent were the interventions successful? Does this mean that the question on the Dynamic Learning Agenda is tackled? Or are additional interventions needed? If questions are tackled, final lessons learned are formulated. These resolved questions will disappear from the updated versions of the Dynamic Learning Agenda (to keep it readable). The lessons learned will be recorded and archived in the older versions of the Learning Agenda. The old versions should be kept, because they describe the results and the lessons learned. They are also useful for accountability purposes and for other Connected Value Development processes. You should always include a new date on the agenda.

STEP 5: Permanently update the learning agenda

Get the project participants to update the agenda themselves after each meeting. The Learning Agenda is dynamic. The project team must examine whether new questions must be added to the agenda. As such, steps 1 through 4 are cyclically repeated, and updated versions of the Learning Agenda are created. The *new* questions do not constantly exemplify new problems, but may also be a specification or re-formulation of an earlier, recognised problem.

Further reading

Hoes, A.C., B.J. Regeer, J.F.G. Bunders 2010. *Facilitating Learning in Innovative Projects: Reflections on Our Experiences with ILA-monitoring.* Paper presented at the International Conference on Organizational Learning, Knowledge and Capabilities (OLKC). June 3-6, 2010. Boston, Massachusetts.

Mierlo, B. van, B.J. Regeer et al. (2010) *Reflexive Monitoring in Action. A Guide for Monitoring System Innovation Projects.* Wageningen/Amsterdam: Communicatie en Innovatiestudies, WUR; Athena Instituut, VU.

Regeer, B.J., A.C. Hoes, et al. (2009). Six guiding principles for evaluating mode-2 strategies for sustainable development. *American Journal of Evaluation* 30 (4): 515-537.

IV. Focus Group

Purpose of the tool

In general, focus groups are used to focus on a topic in three different ways: focusing, progressing from a vague image to a clear image; converging from a general notion to a particular relevant notion; and detection, coming from a variety of notions to the essential one. Therefore it is a tool recommended for the examination of the deeper structure of concepts that play a role both in the arena of experts and in the common-sense language of non-expert citizens.

Focus group designs can be applied to all types of groups, as long as one avoids participants who have a vested interest in the issue at stake or who are authorities (by behaviour and/or institutionally). For these persons, the process of focusing is already far behind. They have already made their choices as technical experts. Our experience is that they will be disappointed by what they consider the low level of knowledge among the participants. They tend to take the role of teacher and therefore block the open exchange of non-expert positions towards the topic (hesitations, ideals). An interview with an expert is a far more efficient way to collect this information. This does not mean that one could not invite intellectual and academic participants to a focus group, as long as one avoids experts on the issue at stake, who might also blur the information by having an

An extended version of this tool was first published in De Cock Buning, Regeer and Bunders (2008). *Biotechnology and Food. Towards a Societal Agenda in 10 Steps.* Den Haag: COS, RMNO.

hidden agenda (or institutional constraints), such as an emphasis on economic or legal aspects.

The actual implementation of the focus group method is driven by three principles: (a) inviting people to engage in a joint exploration into 'the new', (b) creating a safe environment to exchange ideas freely (c) supporting co-creation of knowledge.

Assumptions
- the setting (location, invitation) is neutral, avoiding restraining (political) bias;
- the participants do not have topic-related interests (the urge to convince is absent);
- new knowledge is expected to emerge through mutual interaction;
- participants are welcome to share their opinions and knowledge (atmosphere of equality);
- the facilitator acts as catalyst of group work and refrains from becoming personally involved in the discussion.

How it works

STEP 1. Selection/invitation of participants;
Participants can be recruited by either randomised selection or by non-randomised selection (e.g., through existing social networks). Using non-randomised selection, the project team starts to explore the pros and cons of various options for recruiting possible participants. The rough list of individuals and clubs thus composed is the first step in the 'snowball method' to trace potential participants that meet the set constraints via informal networks of staff members (or from relatives and friends from staff and trainees): intellectually interested in the topic in general, absence of vested interest in the outcome of topic to be discussed, having some related background knowledge regarding the topic but not being an authority.

The invitation process consists of three stages. Stage 1: invitation by telephone, Stage 2: confirmation by letter of invitation, Stage 3: reminder the day before. It is important that step 1 is carried out personally by the process manager, because the initial response of prospective participants gives a first impression of their intuitive position regarding the topic. Not only are the positive responses interesting, but also arguments why people prefer not to participate are important to record. Step 2 is crucial in order to assure that all participants have received the same information regarding the meeting before they arrive. Step 3 is important because invitees who do not have a vested interest in the topic at hand may be more likely to prioritise other upcoming events. It appears to work out best when the invitation is extended not too long before the meeting: two to three weeks in advance is enough.

As the focus groups aim to explore a number of themes in depth, typical demographic representation criteria for quantitative research – such as balanced share of gender, age, ethnicity and income – are less relevant. Furthermore, the size of the group should support the goal of the exercise. A group of 5-8 participants is adequate to ensure a rich, efficient and dynamic meeting, and still capture the attention of all participants throughout the session (around 3 hours).

STEP 2. Design of the session

The general plan should support a maximum exchange of information and a safe environment to speak out. This implies that the location does not induce particular associations (institutions with a political or lifestyle flavour) that may restrain the dynamics of the focus group. An informal welcome (tea/coffee or a snack) will put participants at ease. Attending to the room (not too small) and to a functional chair/table plan (one round table or a cafeteria setting with three small tables) is also important. Individual expectations and attitudes become more aligned when the main programme starts with an introduction (aim, rules for an open deliberation, time scheduled for breaks, closing time).

The programme itself consists of a series of exercises (e.g., associations, list of pros and cons, clustering, prioritizing) that are scheduled one after another in such order that the issue can be explored both widely and deeply. Within each exercise the sequence collection-articulation-systemisation-focusing is a very fruitful recipe. The final closing may serve to evaluate the meeting and solicit reflections and also to raise issues not yet discussed during the structured exercises. It is much appreciated if a small gift is presented and arrangements are made for an informal, post-session gathering, with refreshments provided.

When multiple groups are meant to follow the same design, it is especially important for the sake of methodological consistency and data interpretation that the groups follow the same design and meet the same time constraints. It is therefore recommended that the designs are written down in detail in a "script" containing the exact wording of the opening questions of the exercises, the purpose of the exercise, the way the answers have to be visualised during the session (e.g., Post-it notes with keywords in two columns, with pros & cons) and the anticipated pitfalls that may obstruct the open deliberation in a specific exercise (e.g. "Do not allow a detailed discussion between the participants yet, this is scheduled for the next exercise.") A timeline is helpful to ensure that the scheduled steps are performed on time. The monitor and/or secretary can be an extra help to keeping on schedule.

STEP 3. Execution of the session

The goal is to create a safe context and facilitate a joint exploration into 'the new' by respectful sharing of perspectives (experiential knowledge, values, deliberations), leading to the co-creation of new insights and knowledge. The facilitator has to safeguard these conditions and should be alert to participants who want to challenge the orchestration or who are inclined to play a power game, or 'blackmail' vulnerable statements made by others by means of ad hominem comments (Greenbaum, 2000). This safe context can be achieved by applying general principles such as: postpone judgment to avoid hasty conclusions that block an open exploration of the issue ("My name is Martha and I am fundamentally against biotechnology"); maintaining a consistent level of inputs to avoid contingent dominance of perspectives, for instance by applying 'go-rounds' (each participant answers the same question in turn); feedback-reflection-feed forward by constantly inviting the group to reflect upon individual and groups positions (i.e. "Is this shared by all?", "Would anyone like to comment on this?", "Is this clear to everybody?").

Circling-in is a design typically applied in the context of focus groups to find a 'focus'. One starts the first exercise with a go-round in which participants are each asked to write down on three different Post-it notes three associations (or options, challenges, problems and so on) related to a general theme (food, North-South inequalities, regulations). One by one these Post-it notes are explained in the group and placed on a flipchart. Some are identical and can be placed on top of each other. This results in a rough and broad problem definition of the issue at stake. The first round also serves three additional goals: breaking the ice, encouraging participants to become active by speaking up, and obtaining a sense of the positions and characters gathered around the table.

In the next exercise the facilitator takes the flipchart from the wall to a separate table, invites the participants to stand around the table and discuss with each other whether these statements could be clustered with regard to the topic. Then he or she steps back and lets the participants discuss their arguments for arranging the Post-it notes (the secretary and monitor take notes and the tape/video recorder captures the actual discussion). After some time the group is satisfied with the clustering and the facilitator asks the participants to explain their rationale behind the clustering. The problem definition is now structured, and narrowed down to issues relevant to the topic. Some Post-it notes are set aside as being irrelevant for the topic.

In the third exercise the participants might be asked to prioritise for themselves what cluster (or sub-clusters) are most important, and why. Each participant writes down three of the most important aspects, or alternatively, participants are given three stickers to distribute over the clusters.

The result of this exercise is discussed (What is remarkable, and why is it? Is the order shared by everyone and, if not, why not?). Although all the input from the participants is visualised by means of keywords on Post-it notes and flipchart sketches, the story behind those keywords and drawings must be recorded for proper post-hoc interpretation and in order to make reliable comparisons with keywords and discussions in parallel groups. For this reason, a secretary takes notes and a monitor observes group-dynamic (nonverbal) responses during the deliberations, in order to register the level of consent.

At the beginning and end of the session, participants are asked for their consent to use the recording of the meeting for research purposes. It is important to hold an evaluation go-round, for the sake of one's own methodological reflection and to collect additional information regarding the issues not discussed due to a possible design bias or to time limitations of the meeting. Usually, 10-15 minutes will be sufficient to schedule for 10 participants.

STEP 4. Session report
The goal is to produce a reference dataset by means of a session report, including the constructed schemes and visualisations. It is efficient to make this session report as rich as possible, as this will be the hard-copy reference for further analysis. Integrate notes and citations from tapes to reconstruct the contextual stories in which the schemes and visualisations are grounded. Three types of information are included: the results of the exercises (schematic drawings, matrixes), the positions which typically emerged as co-created insights/knowledge in the session, and some preliminary observations that struck the team, in our case, for instance, the perceived deviations from the positions of the institutional level as emerged from the previous steps

STEP 5. Summary to the participants
In order to verify the session results, the main findings are selected for comments. This mailing can be also used to double-check a specific finding

or to add questions relating to feedback on new findings which emerged in a parallel group.

Further reading

De Cock Buning, T., B.J. Regeer et al. (2008). *Biotechnology and Food. Towards a Societal Agenda in 10 Steps*. Den Haag: COS, RMNO.
Roelofsen, A, et al. (2010) *Engaging with Future Technologies: How Potential Future Users Frame Ecogenomics*. Science and Public Policy, 37. 167-179 (13)

V. Actor Analysis

Purpose of the tool

As a process manager, you may get the feeling (usually at the beginning of a process) that some of the members of the project team have a restricted view of their contribution and role. One member may see himself only as an adviser on various substantive aspects; another only takes action when something needs organising. As a result, there is no clear guiding idea on the role that this project has in contributing to a longer-term ambition: system innovation. One of the reasons for this superficiality is having a limited picture of how the project is embedded in a wider system (i.e. the various societal parties and institutions). This insight is needed in order to obtain a better understanding of the role of the fields of expertise within the project team. This may also identify particular fields of expertise that are missing. Expansion of the project team or the network of participants may then be necessary.

An actor analysis gives a picture of which actors are playing a role within the system, who needs to be involved in the project, and in what way.

An extended version of this tool was first published in Van Mierlo, Regeer et al. (2010) *Reflexive Monitoring in Action. A Guide for Monitoring System Innovation Projects.* Wageningen/Amsterdam: Communicatie en Innovatiestudies, WUR; Athena Instituut, VU.

How it works

An actor analysis can be a useful tool when it comes to learning together and sharing insights on the Connected Value Development process. The actor analysis is most useful when it is done within the team. However, the project manager can carry out the same analysis steps by way of homework. He or she may then introduce the results as a discussion item in various project phases. In this description, the group context is the main focus.

STEP 1. List all relevant actors involved

When the actor analysis is carried out within a group session, a matrix of four rows by four columns (see table V.1) is drawn on a large sheet of paper. Discussing it as they go, the participants can put the names of actors in the matrix by using Post-it notes. This may take about 20 minutes (for 4 to 5 participants) to three quarters of an hour (10 participants). Allow plenty of time immediately after this first brainstorming session for reflection, and for operational conclusions and agreements. Within the matrix three organisational levels are shown:

- individuals and small niche initiatives (e.g. 'farmer X')
- the institutional level, such as municipalities, Chambers of Commerce, banks, water boards, charitable foundations, associations, NGOs;
- the governmental level: regional and national authorities, regulatory authorities, etc.

The headers of the three columns are based on the interests of these actors in sustainable transition: 'proponent' and 'opponent', with 'neutral' in the middle.

STEP 2. Zoom out to identify additional actors

Ask the participants to write down the names of people and organisations from the project's surrounding context on yellow Post-it notes, stating who will benefit from the project objective and for whom it will cause problems (e.g., because they might lose their jobs) and who will not see any significant consequences. This takes a maximum of five minutes.

STEP 3. Place all actors in the matrix

Take the set of stickers from one of the participants and ask him or her in which cells the individual Post-it notes should be placed. Then ask the other participants whether they agree with this placement (and discuss it if not) and whether they have similar stickers that can be placed on top of the Post-it notes that have already been placed (and do so if there are any). Then continue with a second participant, sticking their Post-it notes on the matrix as indicated. When everyone's notes are placed within the matrix, reflect jointly on the question whether this overview is complete or not. Authorities and national institutions are often left unmentioned, because people think that in practice, they do not have much to do with them. Ask why the topmost of the three rows is so poorly populated: might it not be possible for nationally implemented policies to be relevant in sustainable development? This expands the horizons from the day-to-day project work to the entire system and to the changes that are taking place within it.

TABLE V.1 Matrix for actor analysis

	Positive interest (proponent)	Neutral (bridging)	Negative interest (opponent)
Authorities			
Institutions			
Individual, niche			

STEP 4. Reflect on the involvement of actors in the current process

Now ask the participants to put the system level of sustainable transitions and powerful actors behind them, and switch their focus to the project itself. Which of the actors that are now in the matrix:

- are already closely involved with the project?
- could be a source of hindrance to the project during its execution?
- could be a source of hindrance to the project after it is completed (thereby forming an obstacle to sustainable implementation)?

The facilitator circles these actors using variously coloured marker pens (e. g. green for A, red for B, blue for C).

STEP 5. Reflect on the relationships of actors

Ask the participants to think about the relationships between these highlighted actors. What do we know about:

- the direction in which the money flows? – financial power and dependency
- the direction of hierarchical control? – formal power and dependency
- the direction in which information or knowledge flows? – the knowledge network, in which power and dependency can also play a role

Draw the appropriate arrows between the actors.

This last step completes the output of the actor analysis.

STEP 6. Formulate intervention strategies based on the actor analysis

The project team uses this inventory to decide which actors, and in particular, which people should be invited to participate in the project. Various forms of participation can be distinguished: in the project team, in network meetings, in regular workshops, as a speaker or a sponsor for important events such as openings, and so forth. The process manager or facilitator should record the argumentation lines since these can be useful later on, in writing reports and project evaluations.

In engaging with this step, the project team and the process manager divide the tasks of approaching these prospective new project participants for an exploratory interview amongst themselves. These discussions with potential participants can be used for testing assumptions: are the actors' positions with regard to the project and system innovation as anticipated? The interviews can also inspire opponents to shift to a neutral position or even become proponents. The discussions may also identify new, relevant actors, who also should be asked to participate within the project.

Put network information as a new fixed item on the agenda of subsequent meetings of the project team. Use this to keep the network up-to-date and be sure you all stay alert for new prime movers.

Further reading

De Cock Buning, T., B.J. Regeer and J.F.G. Bunders (2008). *Biotechnology and Food. Towards a Societal Agenda in 10 Steps*. Den Haag: COS, RMNO.

Mierlo, B. van, B.J. Regeer et al. (2010) *Reflexive Monitoring in Action. A Guide for Monitoring System Innovation Projects.* Wageningen/Amsterdam: Communicatie en Innovatiestudies, WUR; Athena Instituut, VU.

VI. Causal Analysis

Purpose of the tool

In your capacity as process manager, you may sometimes feel that the Connected Value Development is stagnating. A reason for this stagnation may be that the project participants have no clear guiding idea, and that they have a limited picture of the factors at the system level (and their interrelationships) that are holding back the project. This insight into what factors are influencing the Connected Value Development process is needed for building on the project description: what should be done? What items are we going to tackle and in what order? What exactly are the key items and the peripheral issues? And will this contribute to the desired system innovation, or will it not?

A causal analysis provides genuine understanding of factors that are hampering the project, which makes possible carefully considered interventions. In the causal analysis, 'why' questions are used to gather reflective answers systematically, thereby allowing the causes of problems or stagnating processes to be determined at increasingly deep levels. The answers can then be merged to produce a coherent scheme of cause-and-effect relationships: the causal tree.

An extended version of this tool was first published in Van Mierlo, Regeer et al. (2010) *Reflexive Monitoring in Action. A Guide for Monitoring System Innovation Projects.* Wageningen/Amsterdam: Communicatie en Innovatiestudies, WUR; Athena Instituut, VU.

How it works

Causal analysis can be especially useful when it comes to learning together and sharing insights when the causal analysis is done within a team or together with the project participants.

STEP 1. Collect initial ideas about the central problem

Write the central problem that is threatening the project's ambitions at the top of a large sheet. For example, "Project X is threatening to misfire". The participants are given a stack of Post-it notes. For the sake of simplicity, we will call the participants Peter (P), Marie (M), David (D) and Nicola (N). Ask them to stick their blank Post-it notes on their own sheet of paper as shown in figure VI.1. The participants then get five minutes to write down the causes and underlying causes of the central problem that was formulated, in the form of keywords on the individual Post-it notes.

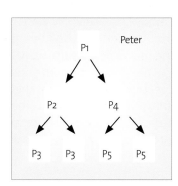
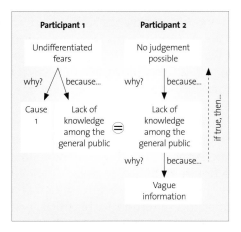

FIGURE VI.1 *Participant Peter sticks the blank Post-it notes on a sheet of paper and numbers them with his initial (P) and sequential numbers 1 through 5. This shows that P2 and P4 are the lower-level causes of P1. The Post-it notes labelled P3 are the underlying causes of P2, and so forth.*

STEP 2. Discuss the weight of each cause

Collect the Post-it notes with the top-level causes (i.e. the ones labelled P1, M1, N1 and D1) and stick them next to each other on a flip chart as primary causes, under the central problem. Ask the group whether these are indeed, in their opinion, the direct causes of the main problem. Some statements on the Post-it notes will look similar and can be merged. The more participants with different viewpoints take part in the workshop, the more complete this top series will be. It is also imaginable that Nicola places a cause at level 2 (N2), i.e. one layer lower, whereas Peter placed that same cause at level 1 (P1). She is therefore establishing the existence of an intermediate cause between the general problem and cause P1. When this happens, the facilitator takes the lower argumentation series, in this case Nicola's, by shifting P1 downwards to the position of N2, sticking the proposed cause N1 at the place thus made free, just under the central problem.

Now work out the detail of the second layer of deeper-lying causes. Cause M1 (from Marie) has two underlying causes (M2 and M4). The same applies to David's Post-it notes (D). Sometimes, the Post-it notes of two participants will be pretty much the same: synonymous or duplicates. If N4 and D4 say the same thing, they are a node. This means that the initial causes N1 and D1 both derive from the same underlying cause N4/D4. Keep an eye out for these kind of duplicates, since they create interconnections between the participants' main categories. You can use these connections to link the four individually-completed sheets into a network (see figure VI.2).

Repeat this method for the third level by sticking Post-it notes such as P3 under P2. Ask if anyone has similar keywords on their Post-it notes that could once again create nodes.

STEP 3. Discuss the connections between the causes

The causal tree is completed when all the Post-it notes are transferred from the individual sheets to the flip chart and linked with each other through cause-and-effect lines. The process of transferring the Post-it notes from one sheet to the other often reveals connections that nobody had originally thought of. Add these connections during the discussions, for example, by way of a new Post-it for an intermediate step. The causal analysis is not, after all, an end in itself, but rather a means to an end: understanding the causes of all the thresholds and problems that may hamper realisation of the projects' ambitions.

Invite the project group to challenge the robustness and validity of the causal tree. The construction of the causal analysis must be internally logical and consistent with factual or scientific knowledge. In addition, the logic of the usage must also be consistent with the visions of all people who have provided input. Test the logic of the resulting diagram by running through the steps top-down, using the criterion of whether it is "logical that the next step in the diagram shows a lower-level cause." If so, is it also true that it can be seen bottom-up as "logical that the higher step can be understood as a consequence of the lower-level step"? Be ready to modify the causal tree as new insights emerge.

Also listen carefully to the stories behind the keywords that are on the Post-it notes. It is important that the participants recognise and embrace the broad lines of the causal tree. The keywords must therefore fit in well with the discussions during the causal analysis process, not only in order to avoid manipulation, but even the appearance of manipulation. A good feel for language is very important.

STEP 4. Reflect on the completed causal tree
Once the causal tree is completed, ask the project team or the wider network to reflect on it. This will boost their creativity and inspiration. One question that might be asked is: "What is still missing, and which additional lines could still be drawn?" Then give each participant three stickers and ask them to place them on the three key issues. To put it another way, "Which issues need to be addressed?" Look to see which issues have been given most stickers (high priority) and which have only a few stickers (low priority). Ask why that is, and reflect on the explanations given. Finally,

choose the topic that has received the most stickers and discuss the following three questions:
- What possible solutions could be considered?
- Who might resolve or help resolve this issue? In other words, in terms of the actors (refer to the actor analysis), whose move is next?
- How can we assist that actor, so that the existing system will leave room for our innovative project?

The following hints may help improve the readability of the causal analysis diagram:
- Give multi-step reasoning priority over 'flashes of inspiration' that skip one or more steps, unless there are reasons why the two routes differ. Argumentation lines involving multiple steps will ultimately make the same causal connection, but generate more detailed content. This recommendation also helps keep the diagram simple.
- Use straight lines where possible, without bends and curves.
- Arrange all clusters of argumentation in such a way that you minimise the number of intersecting lines. PowerPoint has the 'connectors' tool to do this, allowing you to shift the blocks (the Post-it notes) any way you choose without breaking any of the lines. If the lines end up crossing each other, try to keep the angles at which they cross each other consistent throughout the diagram.

Further reading

De Cock Buning, T., B.J. Regeer J.F.G. Bunders (2008). *Biotechnology and Food. Towards a Societal Agenda in 10 Steps*. Den Haag: COS, RMNO.

Mierlo, B. van, B.J. Regeer et al. (2010) *Reflexive Monitoring in Action. A Guide for Monitoring System Innovation Projects.* Wageningen/Amsterdam: Communicatie en Innovatiestudies, WUR; Athena Instituut, VU.

VII. Timeline Workshop

Purpose of the tool

The process manager may find it valuable to reflect, along with the participants, on the challenges, successes, and learning experiences of the project. Joint reflection on the Connected Value Development process helps to get insight in the learning pathway, thereby making success and fail factors explicit. This information may be used to improve and refine the remaining phases of the project

The timeline method provides a working format for explicitly expressing these challenges, successes, and learning experiences, together with the project participants.

Using the tool

The timeline and the tool in the next section, the eye-opener workshop, are extensions of each other. The biggest difference is that the timeline is done with project participants and the eye-opener workshop is done with

An extended version of this tool was published in Van Mierlo, Regeer et al. (2010) *Reflexive Monitoring in Action. A Guide for Monitoring System Innovation Projects.* Wageningen/Amsterdam: Communicatie en Innovatiestudies, WUR; Athena Instituut, VU. It was first developed and described by Wielinga and others in the Netwerken in de Veehouderij (Networks in Animal Husbandry) programme (Wielinga et al., 2007).

outsiders. The eye-opener workshop can build on the results of reflecting on the timeline.

The timeline workshop is suitable for getting project members to reflect jointly on project events. Depending on the duration of the project and the number of participants, a timeline workshop will take about two to four hours. The timeline workshop can be directed by a facilitator or by the process manager.

STEP 1. Make a draft timeline of crucial events

As part of the preparation, the facilitator collects information about all the project events. This can be done, for example, by analysing project documents and holding interviews. Even if you have been involved intensively for a longer period of time as process facilitator, you will have to examine all the data again to identify important events within the process in order to construct a timeline. You can also ask the project manager to put together the timeline.

STEP 2. Present the draft time-line to the team

During the workshop, you, as facilitator or process manager, must list the important project events in chronological order. For this purpose a sheet of paper is put up on the wall showing a timeline, with various events marked on it. Do not interpret and analyse the events at this point, but tell them as a straight story, almost in a childlike style: "….and then…, and then…" Ask the participants to make associative notes as they listen. During this phase you should let the project members speak only in order to correct the story or to complete it. Once you have listed all project events, with the additions made by the team, ask the project members whether the story is correct and complete.

STEP 3. Organise reflection of the crucial moments on the time line

After the team has approved the timeline, participants get 15 to 30 minutes for themselves to interpret the events. During this time, the participants should determine which moments were key moments, and what were the highs and the lows, of the project. The participants then analyse their initial intuitive assessment for themselves. Why was this a high point? Why were there frictions at that point? These short reflections are written as keywords on Post-it notes.

STEP 4. Share the reflections with the whole team

The individual interpretations of each participant are shared within the group. The facilitator (preferably not the person who told the story of the timeline) asks the participants to select the three key comments from their Post-it notes. After the first participant has shared and explained his or her important remarks, the facilitator asks whether others have also put comments about the same event in their top three. The Post-it notes are stuck onto the timeline at the appropriate point. Events that appear to have been interpreted differently are discussed for longer. Discussing these differences of interpretation often yields insights into conflicts that had never been expressed explicitly. Finally, any remaining Post-it notes – the ones remaining after every participant's top three notes have been discussed – can also be placed on the timeline.

The way the workshop is concluded depends on its objective and placement within the project. Possible endings are:

- making choices about follow-on steps, based on what has been discussed;
- creating a new version of the dynamic learning agenda (see Tool III);
- jointly formulating a project narrative that participants can pass on to others;
- writing a project narrative as an evaluation, listing the key highs and lows, for use in a final report.

The results of the timeline workshop can also be used as input for an eye-opener workshop.

Further reading

Mierlo, B. van, B.J. Regeer et al. (2010) *Reflexive Monitoring in Action. A Guide for Monitoring System Innovation Projects.* Wageningen/Amsterdam: Communicatie en Innovatiestudies, WUR; Athena Instituut, VU.

Wielinga, E. et al. (2007) *Netwerken met vrije actoren: stimuleren van duurzame innovaties met netwerken in de veehouderij*, Lelystad: Wagening UR.

VIII. Eye-opener Workshop

Purpose of the tool

To stimulate learning between innovation projects it is important for a facilitator or project manager to convey the lessons learned during the Connected Value Development process to others, such as clients, fellow project managers and colleagues. Because these 'outsiders' are not familiar with the experiences acquired through the project, some of the more generic insights that participants may have gained will appear self-evident to them. For example, it is fairly obvious that mutual trust has to be created. But why it this so difficult and how it can nevertheless be achieved? These are insights that are worth getting across.

The eye-opener workshop is a tool for turning project outsiders into project insiders. During the eye-opener workshop, the experiences and results of the project are narrated in detail. After this narrative, the participants reflect on the events mentioned, each from their own perspective. This stimulates them to extract the lessons derived from their experience in such a way as to make them significant and relevant for their own situations. It is therefore not the facilitator or project manager who determines which lessons are relevant but rather, the (potential) knowledge recipient.

An extended version of this tool was first published in Van Mierlo, Regeer et al. (2010) *Reflexive Monitoring in Action. A Guide for Monitoring System Innovation Projects.* Wageningen/Amsterdam: Communicatie en Innovatiestudies, WUR; Athena Instituut, VU.

An eye-opener workshop takes at least three hours and is done with a small group of between three and eight participants.

Using the tool

The eye-opener workshop and the previously mentioned timeline workshop complement each other. The biggest difference is that the timeline is done with project participants, whereas the eye-opener workshop is done with outsiders. The eye-opener workshop can build on the results of reflecting on the timeline.

The eye-opener workshop is an appropriate tool for enabling outsiders to learn from the experiences of a Connected Value Development process. The aim is to extract insights from the project experiences that the workshop participants can benefit from in their own situations. The working format is based on the idea that the facilitator or project manager cannot determine what is relevant for others: this has to be done by the (potential) recipients of the knowledge themselves. The workshop itself (after the preparation and introduction, step 1 and 2) takes at least three hours and can be subdivided into three parts. In the first part, the project narrative is told (step 3). During the second part, reflections on the narrative are shared (step 4 to 5). Finally, the participants can react on how they can make use of the insights in their own contexts (step 6).

The eye-opener workshop can be used in a variety of situations:
- a comparable system innovation project that has just been started up needs hints and ideas;
- a programme that wants to develop generic lessons based on project experiences;
- a specific target group wants to identify relevant lessons.

Participants will learn from the eye-opener workshop themselves, and results can be used for wider communication to people who were not involved in the project but would like to learn from it.

STEP 1. Reconstruct a project narrative

The facilitator can reconstruct a project narrative, alone or together with the members of the project team. This narrative can be based on the timeline used during the timeline workshop, or it can consist of the key substantive and technical results Connected Value Development process. Put this narrative into words yourself, or ask someone else familiar with the project, ,for example, a scientist who was involved with research for the project. You may also use audiovisual material if there is any available (see Tool IX). Choose a point of focus for the story, depending on the needs of the workshop participants and on the goal of the workshop. The focus may be on the key moments, the highs and lows, or on specific actual results, for example.

STEP 2. Explanations and Introductions

Explain the workshop programme at the beginning. After having done so, ask the participants to introduce themselves, state their learning objectives, and give an indication of how familiar they are with the project being discussed.

STEP 3. Provide the project narrative

Hand out the project narrative on paper, but make sure to tell the story verbally as well. If it is in the form of a timeline, hang it on the wall, with important key events marked on it. In contrast to the timeline workshop, you can put a bit of emotion into telling the story this time, in order to gain the participants' interested and empathy. Telling the story takes half an hour to forty-five minutes. Ask the participants to make as many notes as possible on the hand-out as they listen: associations, ideas, eye-openers, questions, feelings, and so forth.

STEP 4. Let participants reflect

Give the participants fifteen minutes to put their own reflections in order. Get them to write these reflections (at least ten of them) on Post-it notes in the form of short phrases, keywords, or questions.

STEP 5. Discuss participant input

Ask the participants to choose their most important eye-openers and share them with the others taking part in the workshop. Thereafter, the other Post-it notes are discussed, for example chronologically, per person or per theme, depending on what seems most sensible. Finally, ask the participants what relevant information they think may still be missing. What further knowledge do they need in order to be able to answer questions relating to their own field of work? Discuss how this additional information can be obtained. Step 5 takes between one and one-and-a-half hours.

STEP 6. Reflect on relevance

Get the participants to think about which eye-openers are relevant to their own situations, and why. Ask them to express these eye-openers as 'lessons for the future'. Then ask them what changes they will make to their current situation as a result of the lessons from the workshop: their individual agendas for action. The participants then get fifteen minutes to think about these lessons, develop their action agendas, and make notes. Finally, each participant gets up to five minutes to share aspects, lessons, agendas, and notes that they have made.

Further reading

Mierlo, B. van, B.J. Regeer et al. (2010) *Reflexive Monitoring in Action. A Guide for Monitoring System Innovation Projects.* Wageningen/Amsterdam: Communicatie en Innovatiestudies, WUR; Athena Instituut, VU.

IX. Audiovisual Learning History

Purpose of the tool

Documenting the learning experiences of a project in an accessible and attractive way is quite a challenge for a facilitator or project manager. The project results are often described in conceptual terms (e.g., in scientific publications) or in management terms (in reports and memoranda). The 'personal' history of the project, however, can get lost in this process. The challenges that the project participants encountered along the way, the choices that they made and the lessons they learned – such aspects are not explicated enough in conceptual and management texts. However, recording these narratives of experiences is crucial if project members are to learn from their own experiences and from those of others. Moreover, participants in comparable projects can also benefit from this record of experience and knowledge.

The audiovisual learning history fulfils this need. Participants can use this tool to put their learning experiences into words and record their knowledge and experience on video. The audiovisual learning history is different from other tools because it is audiovisual in nature. It creates an accessible and attractive product that not only gives the viewer insights into the abstract learning experiences within the project, but also into the struggles

---

An extended version of this tool was first published in Van Mierlo, Regeer et al. (2010) *Reflexive Monitoring in Action. A Guide for Monitoring System Innovation Projects.* Wageningen/Amsterdam: Communicatie en Innovatiestudies, WUR; Athena Instituut, VU.

and questions faced by the project team members. The visible presence of the person who has gone through the learning experience can let them act as a source of inspiration or role model for the viewer.

Using the tool

In an Audiovisual Learning History (AVLH) project participants describe the key moments of the project in their own words. These snapshot descriptions have to remain as close as possible to the project context and experiences, so that outsiders will be able to re-experience the moments. The development of an (Audiovisual) Learning History consists of three phases. In the first phase (steps 1 through 4), the narratives and experiences of the project participants are filmed. These images are condensed into short fragments in the second phase (steps 5 and 6). In the final phase (steps 7 and 8), the video material is released. All the steps are described below in terms of recommendations to the facilitator.

STEP 1. Audiovisual Learning History (AVLH) rather than just a written report

There may be a need within a project for the learning experiences to be recorded in another way than merely in written reports, because those so often disappear into drawers. Another reason might be that project participants believe that what they are doing is so special that it should be preserved for posterity, i.e., that it should be recorded. This could, for example, relate to the struggles that the mixed group of KENGi actors has had while learning to work together. In situations such as this, the facilitator can suggest using the AVLH as a tool.

STEP 2. Gathering material

There are various ways of gathering material. You can choose project participants as your interview respondents because they are important for the specific matter of the learning history. Selection of the interviewees should take into account the extent to which each person was involved, the extent to which they know about the key moments of the project, whether they talked freely or were more reticent, and how they may appear on camera. You may also choose to have the interviews and recordings fit in with the activities that are already taking place, such as group discussions. In the latter case we would recommend doing the filming outside the workshop context, because group processes are very difficult to capture.

STEP 3. Discuss the project with the interviewee

When discussing the interview before it takes place, look back over the project together with your interviewee. Determine together what the key moments were, and what the most interesting way of describing them might be. Make clear that the descriptions given in the videoed interview must stay close to the experiences of the interviewee, and that the context of the problem also needs to be expressed explicitly. Explain this by using examples from the earlier discussions. If you are not taking on the interviewer role yourself, make sure that the preliminary conversation is extensive and detailed. This helps make the real context of the learning experience clearer.

STEP 4. Record the key moments

Record the descriptions of the key moments. Ideally, a second person should operate the camera and act as the director. After the initial discussion, get this second person to take the initiative and find a suitable place for recording. Pay sufficient attention to finding a suitable location which would help getting the learning experiences across and prevent the filming from being interrupted. While recordings are done, the other person acts as director and will stop recordings if image or sound quality are not good enough.

Ask participants who are being interviewed to describe the most crucial moments again in their own words, in a way that will be understood by a viewer who has no prior knowledge. Ask for descriptions of actions: what happened, how did they react, and how did they feel? When only the interviewee is in the picture, it is important that the interviewer not be heard in the recordings, not even making encouraging sounds.

STEP 5. Select usable material

Select usable video material. Two important selection criteria are:

a. the statements must be interesting and relevant, and
b. the technical quality of the picture, and more importantly, of the sound, must be good enough.

STEP 6. Edit the recordings

Use an editor to assemble the recordings, so that a healthy number of short film clips varying from 20 to 90 seconds are produced, expressing the key moments and learning experiences of the project participants. Any video editing programme can be used. Present these fragments to the interviewees for their approval. If they have any comments, alter the selection of clips.

STEP 7. Putting together the material

The material can now be used in two ways.

The first is to merge the clips into a single narrative showing all perspectives. This is a kind of "the making of" film, guiding the viewer along the relevant themes.

The other way of getting the experience/knowledge across to outsiders is to publish the short clips in a web environment. A good search engine will then let users browse through the material on their own or during a group session, discovering the experiences that are relevant to them. A skilled web developer or system builder is indispensable when putting together a suitable, dynamic web environment.

STEP 8. Using the material in learning sessions

The video clips only become meaningful when used sensibly. A suitable context might be a workshop focused on learning within projects. During these internal learning sessions, film fragments can be used to interpret various insights and perspectives of the project participants, to compare the present situation with a past situation, and to intensify a specific learning experience. Show the film fragments during the workshop session by using a timeline, or classify the segments by theme. Then ask the participants to jointly reflect on the images and to formulate eye-openers that are relevant for them.

Another context in which the audiovisual learning histories can be used is during workshops that aim to stimulate learning between projects or programmes (e.g. an Eye-opener Workshop, Tool VIII). In these workshop settings, film fragments of a specific project are shown to people participating in a comparable project. These film fragments force the participants to compare the experiences mentioned in the clips with their own context, which may bring up relevant themes to discuss within their own project team. In addition, the project participants may identify themselves with the people on screen: on the one hand, they feel acknowledged and recognise the problems they encountered, which they from that dare to term 'a problem'. On the other hand, they can see and experience how others view that specific problem, and how they solved it.

Ask the project manager what challenges or questions are relevant. Make a selection of film fragments with these criteria in mind. Show the film fragments using a classification of themes. Ask the participants to write down the statements and experiences that were touched by on Post-it notes. Let the participants share these statements and determine together the most relevant or appealing statement. Organise a joint discussion on the question: how should we resolve this problem? The clips can be used as a starting point. The facilitator asks participants how they can bring it to their own context and project situation.

Further Reading

Liesveld, R., M. van Amstel-van Saane, B.J. Regeer, J.F.G. Bunders, J. (2010) *Learning Within Innovation Projects: The Development of an Audiovisual Learning History*. Proceedings of the International Conference on Education and New Learning Technologies.

Mierlo, B. van, B.J. Regeer et al. (2010) *Reflexive Monitoring in Action. A Guide for Monitoring System Innovation Projects.* Wageningen/Amsterdam: Communicatie en Innovatiestudies, WUR; Athena Instituut, VU.

X. Value Creation Model

Purpose of the tool

People involved in a creative process often come up with the best ideas. To embed these great ideas in a realistic value proposition that really has a competitive advantage, it is important to look at all the necessary requirements. The value creation model is a tool for describing the relationships between the factors that influence the success of a project or innovation.

The value creation model is based on a model described by Poppe et al. (2009).[11] It consists of four mutual connected components. The distinctiveness of an innovation or the Unique Selling Point (USP) will eventually lead to envisioned results. These tangible results make it possible to do specific investments, which form the basis of the USP. From these investments, competences are derived, which are needed and must be used to continue the creation of the distinctiveness. The USP will again lead to results that are used as input for a new value circle.

This tool can help by embedding all the co-created ideas and aspects into a single conceptual model and in understanding the relationships between these aspects.

How it works

With the value creation model the following questions are posed and must be answered;

- what is the USP, or in other words the distinctiveness of the innovation
- what results can realistically be created based on this USP?
- which investments have been made or need to be made?
- which competences were derived from the investments and used or needed to create distinctiveness?

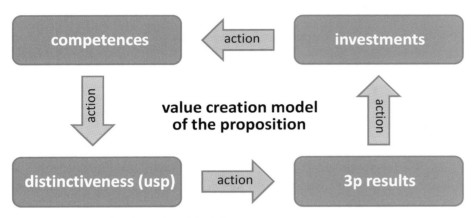

FIGURE X.1 Value Creation Model

By making this value creation model with your multi-stakeholder project team one gets a much better understanding of the relationships between these factors. It requires a rational approach and urges participants to re-think their proposition and ground their creativity in a more straight-forward manner. The tool is important in terms of agenda-setting. One may, for instance, come to the conclusion that one perceived USP does not directly lead to any results, and another USP may be understood to require competences that are not available in the current team or project. Or a USP may only lead to results in two out of the three P's. In all these cases, the value creation model presents the team with the issues that it must work on.

Beyond describing the four factors of the 3P value proposition, the model also requires the team to formulate the activities that are crucial for linking a factor to another. This gives the team a better understanding about what it really must do in order to make this value creation model work in practice.

An example of a value creation model of a TransForum project

This project has established a link between poultry farmers and a chicken coop constructor, the coop builder and research institutes, the coop builder and animal welfare organisations, and the various links in the chain: from coop builder, poultry farmer, egg dealer, and retailer, up to and including the consumer. The parties have jointly developed a viable commercial model for the Rondeel® chicken husbandry system, under which eggs are produced sustainably and responsibly. Rondeel® has acquired its licence to grow by developing its 3P value proposition and the design for its design chicken-husbandry system in cooperation with these stakeholders. This has led to a concept with three Unique Selling Points: the eggs are produced in the most animal-friendly manner, the production scores very well in terms of environmental efficiency, and the production is completely transparent (people can actually visit the housing system). Because of these USPs, Rondeel® was able to become a preferred supplier to Albert Heijn supermarkets under the 'Pure and Fair' brand. They were also rewarded with the maximum score of the Better Living certificate and the environmental 'Milieukeur' certificate. This required significant investments. In order to make consumers aware of the advantages of the Rondeel® egg, a visitor centre is currently being set up, where visitors can see how the chickens live and how the eggs are produced. The Rondeel® eggs are sustainably packed in the Rondeel® itself and transported directly to the supermarket, making for a simpler and hence less expensive logistics process. This required new competencies of the farmers: instead of being a producer of eggs, they had to become real entrepreneurs with a keen eye for consumer needs and preferences as well as market developments.

Further Reading

Poppe, K.J., K. de Bont, P. Luttik, M. Pleijte, H. Schepers, T. Vogelzang en H. de Vries *(2009) Kennissysteem en belangenbehartiging in de agrosector; Een toekomstverkennin*g. Den Haag:, LEI, 2009, Rapport 2009-071

Van Altvorst, A.C., R. Eweg, H.C. van Latesteijn, S.E. Mager & L. Spaans (2010) *Sustainable Agricultural Entrepreneurship: The Metropolitan Environment as Catalyst of New Agricultural Innovations. The Six Guises of Successful Agricultural Entrepreneurship Illustrated Through Nine Projects*. TransForum, Zoetermeer, November 2011 (in Dutch, English version in Press).

XI. Sustainability Scan

Purpose of the tool

'Sustainability' is a very broad concept relating to the ecological, social, and economic consequences of our actions. Absolute sustainability does not exist, or is at least very hard to define. A more workable concept is 'sustainable development', which implies that we are able to define more sustainable pathways and thus are able to measure a more sustainable performance. Sustainable development includes nature and environmental aspects (planet), social aspects (people), and economic aspects (profit). It refers to an on-going process of finding a balance between these aspects.

Measuring sustainability performance is thus complex, because an initiative does not necessarily result in improvements in all aspects of sustainability. There are many effects involved at different locations and with different timeframes. Blonk Environmental Consultancy has developed a specific evaluation method for the TransForum initiatives, where impacts are divided into three levels: local (in supply chain and community), global, and system impacts. This tool will help make the project's sustainability performance more tangible and easier to communicate. This is often crucial when trying to align with the perspectives of other stakeholders.

How it works

By using the tool the ultimate impacts of an initiative can be determined for each level: local (in supply chain and community), global and system impacts. To determine the sustainability performance of the initiative, it is compared on several values (see table XI.1) against a reference situation without the initiative, which is the baseline situation. The reference situation is not the current situation; it is a situation that would arise over the coming 5 to 10 years, the timeframe within which most initiatives become operational and lead to a physical change in production and consumption. To assess the sustainability performance of initiatives Blonk used a qualitative method with five scoring categories:

- Positive: when compared to the baseline, the initiative performs better against a sustainability indicator.
- Neutral: when compared to the baseline, the initiative performs neither better nor worse against a sustainability indicator.
- Negative: when compared to the baseline, the initiative performs worse against a sustainability indicator.
- Not relevant: when compared to the baseline, the sustainability issue/ indicator is not relevant to the initiative being evaluated.
- No evaluation possible (yet): the indicator is relevant to the evaluation; however essential information on the initiative or on the specific impact mechanism is lacking.

Blonk uses a scoring method that can combine qualitative and quantitative evaluation results. This has several advantages. First, it gives equal attention to aspects that can be quantified and to those that can be ranked only qualitatively. It prevents undue attention to the quantitative results at expense of the qualitative results, which are less articulated but may be of equal or greater importance. A second advantage is that it makes it easy to include other qualitative evaluation categories, which add valuable information but often disappear in a more quantitative evaluation. The results can be presented in both a table and/or a doughnut diagram (see figure XI.1) with different colours for the scoring categories.

TABLE XI.1 Evaluation methods: Blonk environmental consultancy for sustainability scan

Level	Domain	Value	Evaluation Method
LOCAL	PEOPLE	Human Rights, Labour Conditions Animal Welfare & Health	Evaluation is based on the extent and level of applied standards compared with the baseline situation. Standards may be certification schemes, codes of conduct, supplier conditions, etc. Better means wider use or use of better standards than the baseline.
		Human Health (other than emissions), Animal Disease Risks	Evaluation is based on a qualitative risk assessment, drawing on what is known about the applied hardware and management of initiatives compared with the baseline. Better means that there are obvious characteristics of the initiative which make a difference to health risks. While it is mostly possible to determine whether these issues are relevant, it is often difficult to come to an assessment because of a lack of information.
		Development Involvement	Evaluation is based on the specific activities of the initiatives aiming to improve community development or involvement which are not common in the baseline. This means that there must be a plan available containing a vision, aims, activities and monitoring, which makes it plausible that a distinct contribution is made to these items.
	PLANET	Environmental Quality, Biodiversity, Landscape	Evaluation is based on specific characteristics and activities of the initiatives that contribute to maintaining or improving ecosystems and/or landscape quality above the baseline level. There must be either available measurements or indirect evidence-based literature on comparable initiatives, or a plan (specially for landscape) containing a vision, aims, activities and monitoring.
		Emissions affecting ecosystems and human health	Impacts of emissions are calculated using LCA impact categories or, when available, local valid environmental impact assessment models in relation to the sensitivity of surrounding ecosystems and communities. Indicators often have to be subdivided to evaluate local impacts.
		Environmental Quality, Biodiversity, Landscape	Evaluation is based on specific characteristics and activities of the initiatives that contribute to maintaining or improving ecosystems and/or landscape quality above the baseline level. There must be either available measurements or indirect evidence-based literature on comparable initiatives, or a plan (specially for landscape) containing a vision, aims, activities and monitoring.
	PROFIT	Balance Sheet, Investment, Economic Value Creation	The evaluation of economic indicators is based on quantitative and qualitative information (argumentation) available in the business plan or other relevant documentation that give basic information on the viability and profitability of the initiative.

TABLE XI.1 Evaluation methods: Blonk environmental consultancy for sustainability scan (cont.)

Level	Domain	Value	Evaluation Method
GLOBAL	Planet	Land use, Greenhouse gas effect, Depletion of fossil fuels, Depletion of phosphate	The evaluation is based on a life cycle assessment in which the initiative is compared with the baseline. Better means 10% lower impact than the baseline. Worse is 5% higher than the baseline. Thresholds are derived from an autonomous improvement trends.
SYSTEM	People	Health, Other welfare aspects, (Individual) Welfare and Prosperity of Community	Evaluation is based on a qualitative assessment of product characteristics compared with a baseline situation in which the functionality of the products is absent. Better means that there is obvious evidence of improvement. While it is mostly possible to determine whether these issues are relevant, it is often difficult to come to an assessment because of a lack of knowledge.
	Planet	Land use, Greenhouse gas effect, Depletion: fossil energy use, Depletion: phosphate rock	Evaluation is based on a life cycle assessment to calculate the impacts, combined with the expected price of the product. Better means 10% lower impact than the baseline. Worse is 5% higher than the baseline. Thresholds are based on an autonomous improvement trend.
	Profit	Financial budget, Time budget	Evaluation is based on the expected impact on the money or time budget across the whole life cycle of the product. Better means a lower time or cost expenditure.

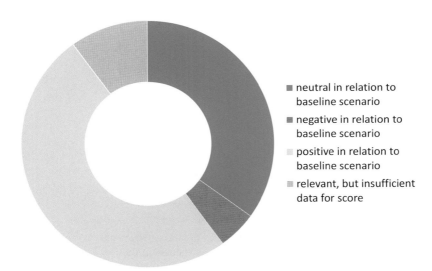

- neutral in relation to baseline scenario
- negative in relation to baseline scenario
- positive in relation to baseline scenario
- relevant, but insufficient data for score

FIGURE XI.1   Doughnut diagram – a quick impression of knowledge gaps (light grey) and positive sustainability performance (light blue)

Further reading

Blonk, H., Scholten, J. and Broekema, R. (2010). *Measuring the Sustainability Performance of Agro-Food Chain Initiatives – a Method for Estimating the Potential Sustainability Performance of the Initiatives in Which TransForum Participated.* Gouda: Blonk Milieuadvies & TransForum. www.blonkmilieuadvies.nl

Notes

Introduction

1. Meadows, D.H., D.L. Meadows, J. Randers, and W.W. Behrens (1972) *The Limits to Growth*. New York: Universe Books.
2. Douglas, M. and A. Wildavsky (1982) *Risk and Culture: An Essay on the Selection of Technical and Environmental Dangers.* Berkeley: University of California Press. And: Rotmans, J. (2005) *Societal Innovation: Between Dream and Reality Lies Complexity.* DRIFT Research Working Paper, 3 June 2005, University of Maastricht.
3. Schön, D. and M. Rein (1994) *Frame Reflection: Toward the Resolution of Intractable Policy Controversies.* New York: Basic Books.
4. Hisschemöller, M. and R. Hoppe (1996) Coping with Intractable Controversies: The case for Problem Structuring in Policy Design and Analysis. *Knowledge and Policy* 8(4):40-60.
5. Loorbach, D. (2007) *Transition Management: New Mode of Governance for Sustainable Development.* Utrecht: International Books.
6. Churchman, C. West (1967) Wicked Problems. *Management Science.* 14(4) December 1967. Guest Editorial.
7. See: Rittel, H.W.J. and M.M. Webber (1973) Dilemmas in a General Theory of Planning. *Policy Sciences* 4:155-169. And: Conklin, J. (2005) *Dialogue Mapping: Building Shared Understanding of Wicked Problems.* Chichester: Wiley.
8. The term 'institutional void' was coined by Maarten Hajer. See: M. Hajer (2003) Policy without Polity? Policy Analysis and the Institutional Void. *Policy Sciences* 36(2):175-195.
9. We have added 'licence to grow' to the three other 'licences' businesses have with society, as proposed by Casimir and Dutilh (2003). They are: the licence to produce, the licence to sell, and the licence to operate. See: G.J. Casimir

and C.E. Dutilh (2003) Sustainability: A Gender Studies Perspective. *International Journal of Consumer Studies* 27(4):316-325.

Part I The Guide

1. Connecting Values

1. Mintzberg, H. (1987) Crafting Strategy. In: *Harvard Business Review*, July-August, pp. 66-75

2. The Two Faces of Value

2. The term (also TBL, or 3BL) was coined by John Elkington (1998) in his book *Cannibals with Forks: the Triple Bottom Line of 21st Century Business*, Gabriola Island BC, Canada: New Society Publishers. Freer Spreckley (1981) first described the concept of the triple bottom line in *Social Audit - A Management Tool for Co-operative Working* Leeds: Beechwood College.
3. Hamilton, H. (2010) Why Sustainibility Needs Big Business, and Why That's Not Enough: the Story of the Sustainable Food Lab. *Fall 2010 Newsletter, Sustainable Food Laboratory.*
4. Barnes, C., H. Blake, D. Pinder (2009) *Creating and Delivering Your Value Proposition: Managing Customer Experience for Profit* London: Kogan Page.
5. Based on: D. Mahler, J. Barker et al. (2009). *"Green" Winners. The Performance of Sustainability-focused Companies During the Financial Crisis.* Chicago, A.T.Kearney.
    Manenti, P., R. Parker et al. (2009). *The Business Case for Environmental Excellence Is Real.* IDC &Atos Origin.
6. Giddens, A. (1979) *Central Problems in Social Theory. Action, Structure, and Contradiction in Social Analysis.* Berkeley: UC Press.
7. Holland, J. (1995) *Hidden Order – How Adaptation Builds Complexity.* Cambridge, Massachusetts: Perseus Books, Helix Books. Johnson, N.F. (2007) *Two's Company, Three is Complexity: A Simple Guide to the Science of All Sciences* Oxford: Oneworld.

3. Creating Innovation Space

8. Scharmer, C.A. (2009) *Theory U, Leading from the Future as It Emerges*. San Francisco: Berret-Koehler. (pp. 129-133)
9. Text based on: H.C. van Latesteijn and K. Andeweg (Eds.) (2010) *The Trans-Forum Model: Transforming Agro Innovation Toward Sustainable Development*. Dordrecht: Springer.
10. Collins, H.M. (1992) *Changing Order, Replication and Induction in Scientific Practice*. Chicago: The University of Chicago Press.
11. See for example: Larman, C. (2004) *Agile and Iterative Development: a Managers Guide*. Boston: Addison-Wesley.
12. Johnson, S.B. (2010) *Where Good Ideas Come from: The Natural History of Innovation*. New York: Penguin Books.
13. Austin, N. and T.J. Peters (1985) *A Passion for Excellence, The Leadership Difference*. Clayton: Warner Books.
14. Senge, P.M. (1990) *The Fifth Discipline: The Art and Practice of the Learning Organisation*. New York: Currency Doubleday. (p. 3)
15. Chesbrough, H. (2003) *Open Innovation: The New Imperative for Creating and Profiting from Technology*. Boston: Harvard Business School Press.
16. Peterson, Ch.H. and S.E. Mager (2010) From Motivating Assumptions to a Practical Innovation Model. In: H.C. van Latesteijn and K. Andeweg (Eds.), *The TransForum Model; Transforming Agro Innovations Towards Sustainability* Dordrecht: Springer (pp 97-129).
17. Minzberg, H. and J.A. Waters (1985) Of Strategies, Deliberate and Emergent. *Strategic Management Journal* 6(3): 257-272.
18. Ibid. p. 261
19. Kahane, A. (2004) *Solving Tough Problems*. San Francisco: Berrett-Koehler.
20. Kahane, A. (2010), Presentation During the First Global Summit on Metropolitan Agriculture, 29 September, Van Nelle Fabriek, Rotterdam
21. McGill, I. and L. Beaty (1995) *Action Learning: a Guide for Professional, Management and Educational Development*. 2nd ed., London: Kogan Page. (p. 21)
22. Broerse J.E.W. (1998) *Towards a New Development Strategy. How to Include Small-scale Farmers in the Biotechnological Innovation Process*. Delft: Eburon.
23. The deep learning cycle as described by Senge, P.M. (1994) Moving forward. In: P.M. Senge, A. Kleiner, C. Roberts, R.B. Ross and B.J. Smith (Eds.) *The Fifth*

Discipline Fieldbook. Strategies and Tools for Building a Learning Organization. New York: Doubleday (pp. 15-47).

24. Longhi C. and D. Keeble (2000) High-Tech Clusters and Evolutionary Trends in the 1990's. In: D. Keeble and F. Wilkinson (Eds.), *High-Technology Clusters, Networking and Collective Learning in Europe* (pp. 21-56), Aldershot UK: Ashgate.

25. Some of the examples in Stubborn Reality have been published before in: B.J. Regeer and J.F.G. Bunders (2009). *Knowledge Co-creation: Interaction between Science and Society. A Transdisciplinary Approach to Complex Societal Issues.* Den Haag: RMNO/COS.

Intermezzo 1

26. Peterson Ch.H. and S.E. Mager (2010) From Motivating Assumptions to a Practical Innovation Model. In: H.L. van Latesteijn and K. Andeweg (Eds.) *The TransForum Model: Transforming Agro Innovation Toward Sustainable Development.* Dordrecht: Springer (pp. 97-129).

4. Exploration & Alliance Building

27. Hoes, A.C. et al. (submitted) Adoption of New Land Use Facilities in a Normative Diverse Society: Exploring the New Mixed Farm Case. *Journal of Environmental Policy & Planning*

28. Hoes, A.C., V. Beekman, B.J. Regeer, J.F.G.Bunders, (2011) Unravelling the Dynamics of Adopting Novel Technologies: An Account of How the Closed Greenhouse Opened-up. In: *International Journal of Foresight and Innovation Policy* 7 (1)

29. This box is inspired by M.J.M. van Mansfeld, A.L.W. Wintjes, J.M. de Jonge, M. Pleijte, P.J.A.M. Smeets (2003) *Regiodialoog: Naar een systeeminnovatie in de praktijk.* Wageningen, Alterra.

30. In the Interactive Learning and Action approach of the Athena Institute, VU University Amsterdam, organising a 'support network' is one of the key principles for success. J.E.W. Broerse (1998) *Towards a New Development Strategy. How to Include Small-scale Farmers in the Biotechnological Innovation Process.* Delft, Eburon.

31. Laurentzen, M., R.P. Kranendonk et al. (2009) *The Making of Greenport Venlo – Eindrapportage Streamlining Greenport Venlo.* Wageningen, TransFor-

um, Alterra WUR, VU University Amsterdam, KnowHouse, provincie Limburg: 52.

32. Hoes, A.C., B.J. Regeer, J.F.G. Bunders (2008) TransFormers in Knowledge Production. Building Science-practice Collaborations. *Action Learning: Research and Practice, 5*(3), 207 - 220.

33. Caron-Flinterman, F. (2005) *A New Voice in Science. Patient Participation in Decision-making on Biomedical Research.* Zutphen.

34. Collins, H.M. and R.J. Evans (2002) The Third Wave of Science Studies: Studies of Expertise and Experience, *Social Studies of Sciences*, Vol. 32, No. 2, (April), p. 256.

35. Hoes, A.C., B.J. Regeer, J.F.G. Bunders (2008) Op. cit.

36. Distinguishing Debate from Dialogue: A Table, 1992 Public Conversations Project.

37. Mansfeld, van M.J.M., A.L.W. Wintjes, J.M. de Jonge, M. Pleijte, P.J.A.M. Smeets (2003) Op. cit.

38. Senge, P., O. Scharmer et al. (2005) *Presence: An Exploration of Profound Change in People, Organizations, and Society.* New York: Double Day.

39. Kahane, A. (2010) Presentation during the First Global Summit on Metropolitan Agriculture, 29 September, Van Nelle Fabriek, Rotterdam.
Scharmer, C.A. (2007) *Theory U, Leading from the Future as It Emerges.* San Francisco: Berret-Koehler. (pp. 129-133)

40. Wallace, D.F. 'Plain Old Untrendy Troubles and Emotions', *The Guardian*, 20 September 2008.

41. Bateson, G. (1972) *Steps to an Ecology of Mind: Collected Essays in Anthropology, Psychiatry, Evolution, and Epistemology.* Chicago: University of Chicago Press.

42. Argyris, C. (1977) Double-loop Learning in Organizations. *Harvard Business Review*, 55(5), pp. 115-125.

43. Schön, D. (1987) *Educating the Reflective Practitioner*, San Francisco: Jossey-Bass.

44. Qvortrup, L. (2004) The Mystery of Knowledge. *Cybernetics & Human Knowing*. 11(3) pp. 9 -29.

45. Regeer, B.J., A.C. Hoes, M. van Amstel-van Saane, F. Caron-Flinterman, J.F.G. Bunders (2009) Six Guiding Principles for Evaluating Mode-2 Strategies for Sustainable Development. *American Journal of Evaluation* 30(4), pp. 515-537.

46. Bunders, J.F.G. (Ed.) (1990) *Biotechnology for Small-scale Farmers in Developing Countries, Analysis and Assessment Procedures.* Amsterdam: VU University Press.
47. Bunders, J.F.G. and J.E.W. Broerse (1991) *Appropriate Biotechnology in Small-scale Agriculture: How to Orient Research and Development.* Wallingford: CAB International.

Intermezzo 2

48. Caron-Flinterman, F. (2005) *A New Voice in Science. Patient Participation in Decision-making on Biomedical Research.* Zutphen.
49. Hoes, A.C., B.J. Regeer, J.F.G. Bunders (2008) TransFormers in Knowledge Production. Building Science-practice Collaborations. *Action Learning: Research and Practice*, 5(3), pp. 207 - 220.
50. Hoes, A.C., B.J. Regeer, J.F.G. Bunders. *Facilitating Learning in Innovative Projects: Reflections on our Experiences with ILA-monitoring* Paper presented at the International Conference on Organizational Learning, Knowledge and Capabilities OLKC 2010 (Boston, 3-6 June 2010).

5. Co-creation & Experimentation

51. Prahalad, C.K. and V. Ramaswamy (2004) *The Future of Competition: Co-Creating Unique Value with Customers.* Boston, Mass.: Harvard Business School Press.
52. Ibid.
53. Klein, J. T., W. Grossenbacher-Mansuy et al. (2001) *Transdisciplinarity: Joint Problem Solving among Science, Technology, and Society. An Effective Way for Managing Complexity.* Basel: Birkhauser.
Regeer, B. J. and J. F. G. Bunders (2009) *Knowledge Co-creation: Interaction Between Science and Society. A Transdisciplinary Approach to Complex Societal Issues.* Den Haag: RMNO/COS.
Hirsch Hadorn, G., H. Hoffmann-Riem et al., (Eds.) (2008) *Handbook of Transdisciplinary Research.* Heidelberg: Springer.
Bunders, J.F.G. et al. (2010) How Can Transdisciplinairy Research Contribute to Knowledge Democracy. In: R.J. In 't Veld (Ed.) *Knowledge Democracy. Consequences for Science, Politics and Media.* Heidelberg: Springer (pp. 125-152).

54. Nowotny, H., P. Scott et al. (2001). *Re-thinking Science. Knowledge and the Public in an Age of Uncertainty.* Oxford: Polity Press.
55. Peterson, H.C., (2009) Transformational Supply Chains and the 'Wicked Problem' of Sustainability: Aligning Knowledge, Innovation, Entrepreneurship, and Leadership, *Journal on Chain and Network Science,* 9(2): 71-82.
56. Ibid. Peterson, H.C., (2009: 74).
57. Regeer, B.J. (2010) *Making the Invisible Visible. Analysing the Development of Strategies and Changes in Knowledge Production to Deal with Persistent Problems in Sustainable Development.* Oisterwijk: BoxPress, p. 201 referring to Chiva and Alegre, 2005, Cook and Brown, 1999, Currie and Kerrin, 2004.
58. E.g. see B.J. Regeer and J.F.G. Bunders (2003) The Epistemology of Transdisciplinary Research: From Knowledge Integration to Communities of Practice. *Interdisciplinary Environmental Review* 5(2): 98-118.
59. Tsoukas (2003: 410) cited in Regeer (2010) Op.cit.
60. Wenger, E. (1998) *Communities of Practice: Learning, Meaning, and Identity.* Cambridge: Cambridge University Press.
61. E.g. see R. McDermott and A., Douglas (2010) Harnessing your Staff's Informal Networks. *Harvard Business Review* 88.
62. Senge, P.M. (1990) *The Fifth Discipline: The Art and Practice of the Learning Organisation* New York: Double Day
63. Friedrich, T.L., W.B. Vessey, M.J. Schuelke, G.A. Ruark, M.D. Mumford (2009) A Framework for Understanding Collective Leadership: The Selective Utilization of Leader and Team Expertise Within Networks. *The Leadership Quartely* 20: 933-958.
64. Uhlbien, M., R. Marion, B. Mckelvey (2007) Complexity Leadership Theory: Shifting Leadership from the Industrial Age to the Knowledge Era. *The Leadership Quarterly* 18(4): 298-318. p. 299.
65. Ibid.
66. Termeer, C.J.A.M. (2006) *Vitale verschillen, over publiek leiderschap en maatschappelijke innovatie,* Wageningen: Wageningen Universiteit, Oratie 2006.
    Kersten, P., R. Kranendonk, B.J. Regeer (2006) *CoP Working in Greenport Venlo (NL) to Develop Sustainable Regional Development: From Conflict to Common Interest.* Paper presented at the International Conference Civil Society and Environmental Conflict: Public Participation and Regulation, Finnish Environment Institute (SYKE), Helsinki, Finland.

67. Imam, I., A. LaGoy, and B. Williams (2007). Introduction. In B. Williams and I. Imam (Eds.), *Systems Concepts in Evaluation. An Expert Anthology* (pp. 3-10). Point Reyes, CA: EdgePress/American Evaluation Association, p. 8.
68. Paragraph adapted from B.J. Regeer, A.C. Hoes, M. van Amstel-van Saane, F. Caron-Flinterman, J.F.G. Bunders (2009) Six Guiding Principles for Evaluating Mode-2 Strategies for Sustainable Development. *American Journal of Evaluation* 30(4), pp. 515-537.
69. Just like learning histories: see A. Kleiner and G. Roth (1996) *Field Manual for the Learning Historian.* Boston: MIT, Center for Organizational Learning, p. 20
70. Ibid, p. 14.
71. Kunneman, H. (2006) *Voorbij het dikke-ik. Bouwstenen voor een kritisch humanisme.* Humanistics University Press.
72. Paragraph adapted from B.J. Regeer et al. (2009) Op. cit.
73. Paragraph adapted from Ibid.

Intermezzo 3

74. Collins, H.M. and R.J. Evans (2002) The Third Wave of Science Studies: Studies of Expertise and Experience, *Social Studies of Sciences*, Vol. 32, No. 2, (April), p. 256.
75. Hoes, A.C., B.J. Regeer, J.F.G. Bunders (2008). TransFormers in Knowledge Production. Building Science-practice Collaborations. *Action Learning: Research and Practice*, 5(3), pp. 207 – 220, p. 211.

6. Embedding & Alignment

74. Hoes, A.C. et al. (submitted) Adoption of New Land Use Facilities in a Normative Diverse Society: Exploring the New Mixed Farm case. *Journal of Environmental Policy & Planning*
75. Wenger, E. (1998) *Communities of Practice: Learning, Meaning, and Identity.* Cambridge: Cambridge University Press, p. 179.
76. Grin, J., H. van de Graaf (1996) Implementation as Communicative Action. An Interpretive Understanding of Interactions Between Policy Actors and Target Groups, *Policy Sciences* 29 (4): 291-319, p. 304.
77. Hoes, A.C. et al. (submitted) Op.cit.

78. Dart, J.J. and R.J. Davies (2003) A Dialogical Story-based Evaluation Tool: The Most Significant Change Technique. *American Journal of Evaluation* 24 (2): 137-155.

79. Mierlo, B. van, B.J. Regeer et al. (2010) *Reflexive Monitoring in Action. A Guide for Monitoring System Innovation Projects.* Wageningen/Amsterdam: Communicatie en Innovatiestudies, WUR; Athena Instituut, VU.

Intermezzo 4

80. Nijhof, A and T. van Someren (2010) *Triple P Business Development in the Dutch Agro-Food Sector; 9 Cases of Strategic Innovation.* Assen: Van Gorcum.

7. Reflections

81. See also Broerse, J.E.W. and J.F.G. Bunders (2000) Requirements for Biotechnology Development: The Necessity for an Interactive and Participatory Innovation Process. *Int. J. Biotechnology*, Vol. 2, No. 4: 275-296, and, Zweekhorst, M.B.M. (2004). *Institutionalising an Interactive Approach to Technological Innovation. The Case of the Grameen Krishi Foundation.* Amsterdam: Vrije Universiteit.

82. Broerse, J.E.W. (1998) *Towards a New Development Strategy: How to Include Small-scale Farmers in the Biotechnological Innovation Proces.* Delft: Eburon.

The Bubbles

Changes in Sustainable Development Practices

1. Latesteijn, H. van and K. Andeweg (Eds.) (2011) *The TransForum Model: Transforming Agro Innovation Toward Sustainable Development.* Dordrecht: Springer Science+Business Media (p.13).

2. From the album *Graceland* (1986), Warner Bros. Records.

3. Conklin, J. (2005) *Dialogue Mapping: Building Shared Understanding of Wicked Problems.* Chichester: Wiley (p.1).

9. The Business Bubble

4. Ray Anderson, famous industrialist and sustainability advocate, quoted in: R. Todd (2006) The Sustainable Industrialist: Ray Anderson of Interface. *Inc. Magazine*, November 1.
5. Casimir, G.J. and C.E. Dutilh (2003) Sustainability: A Gender Studies Perspective. *Int. Journal of Consumer Studies*, 27(4): 316-325.
6. NWO (2010) *Milieuorganisaties geven impuls aan maatschappelijk verantwoord ondernemen.* (www.nwo.nl/nwohome.nsf/pages/NWOP_84JBFW). More examples can be found on the website 'Business and Sustainable Development', www.iisd.org/business/ngo/
7. Prahalad, C.K. and V. Ramaswamy (2004) *The Future of Competition: Co-Creating Unique Value with Customers.* Boston: Harvard Business School Press.
8. Ibid. p. 23.
9. Ramaswamy, V. and F. Gouillart (2010) *The Power of Co-creation: Build it with Them to Boost Growth, Productivity, and Profits.* New York and London: Free Press.
10. Nidumolu, R., C.K. Prahalad and M.R. Rangaswami (2009) Why Sustainability is Now the Key Driver of Innovation. *Harvard Business Review* (pp.57-64).
11. Ibid.
12. Prisma and Partners (2009) *Pearls in People Planet Profit, Interviews with Dutch Companies About Anchoring People and Planet Values.* Amsterdam: Athena Institute, VU University (pp.16-17)
13. Porter, M.E and M.R. Kramer (2011) The Big Idea: Creating Shared Value. How to Reinvent Capitalism and Unleash a Wave of Innovation and Growth. In: *Harvard Business Review* (January - February 2011)
14. Based on: Prahalad and Ramaswamy (2004:6) Op. cit.
15. Based on: Prahalad and Ramaswamy (2004) Op. cit. and Nidumolu et al. (2009) Op. cit.

Intermezzo 5

16. Hawken, P. (1994) *The Ecology of Commerce: A Declaration of Sustainability.* New York: HarperCollins.
17. Todd, R. (2006) The Sustainable Industrialist: Ray Anderson of Interface. In: *Inc. Magazine*, November 1.

10. The Science Bubble

18. Klein, J.T., W. Grossenbacher-Mansuy, R. Haberli, A. Bill, R.W. Scholtz and M. Welti (Eds.) (2001) *Transdisciplinarity: Joint Problem Solving Among Science, Technology, and Society. An Effective Way for Managing Complexity.* Basel: Birkhäuser. p.7

19. Regeer, B.J. and J.P.G. Bunders (2009). *Knowledge Co-creation: Interaction Between Science and Society. A Transdisciplinary Approach to Complex Societal Issues.* Den Haag: RMNO/COS. p.38

20. For an overview of developments in sustainability science, see: Clark, W.C. & N.M. Dickson (2003) Sustainability Science: The Emerging Research Program. *PNAS* 100: 8059–8061.

21. Ibid. p. 8059.

22. Ibid.

23. Kuhn, T.S. (1962) *The Structure of Scientific Revolutions.* Chicago: The University of Chicago Press.

24. Latour, B. and S. Woolgar (1979) *Laboratory Life: The Social Construction of Scientific Facts.* Beverly Hills, California and London: Sage Publications.

25. Latour, B. (1987) *Science in Action: How to Follow Scientists and Engineers through Society.* Cambridge, Mass.: Harvard University Press (p.15).

26. Ibid.

27. Van Rijnsoever, F. J. and L.K. Hessels (2011) Factors Associated with Disciplinary and Interdisciplinary Research Collaboration. *Research Policy,* 404, 63-472.

28. Leydesdorff, L. (2008). Caveats for the Use of Citation Analysis in Research and Journal Evaluation. *Journal of the American Society for Information Science and Technology,* 59(2), 278-287.

29. Weingart, P. (2005). Impact of Bibliometrics upon the Science System: Inadvertent Consequences? *Scientometrics,* 62(1), 117-131.

30. Schwarz, M. and R. Jansma, (Eds.) (1989). *De technologische cultuur.* Amsterdam: Uitgeverij De Balie.

31. Collins, H.M. and R. Evans (2002) The Third Wave of Science Studies: Studies of Expertise and Experience. *Social Studies of Science* 32(2):235-296.

32. Bunders, J.F.G. et al. (2010:134), How Can Transdiscipinairy Research Contribute to Knowledge Democracy. In: In 't Veld, R.J (ed.) *Knowledge Democracy, Consequences for Science, Politics and Media.* Heidelberg: Springer Verlag

33. Collins and Evans (2002) Op. cit.

34. Wynne, B. (1996) May the Sheep Safely Graze? A Reflexive View on the Expert-Lay Knowledge Divide. In: S. Lash (ed.) *Risk, Environment and Modernity: Towards a New Ecology*. London: Sage (pp. 44-83).
35. Polanyi, M. (1958) *Personal Knowledge: Towards a Post-critical Philosophy*. Chicago: University of Chicago Press.
36. Reber, A.S. (1967) Implicit Learning of Artificial Grammars. *Journal of Verbal Learning & Verbal Behavior* 6(6):855-863.
37. Nowotny, H., P. Scott et al. (2001) *Re-thinking Science. Knowledge and the Public in an Age of Uncertainty*. Oxford: Polity Press.

Intermezzo 6

38. Text based on: Hoes, A-C, Beekman, V., B.J. Regeer, J.F.G. Bunders (2011) Unravelling the Dynamics of Adopting Novel Technologies: An Account of How the Closed Greenhouse Opened-up. In: *International Journal of Foresight and Innovation Policy 7* (1).
39. Hoes, A.C., B.J. Regeer, J.F.G. Bunders (2008) TransFormers in Knowledge Production. Building Science-practice Collaborations. In: *Action Learning: Research and Practice,* 5(3), 207 - 220.

11. The Policy Bubble

40. Hendriks, C.M. and J. Grin (2007) Contextualizing Reflexive Governance: The Politics of Dutch Transitions to Sustainability. In: *Journal of Environmental Policy & Planning* 9(3-4):333-350.
41. Fisher, F. (2003) *Reframing Public Policy: Discursive Politics and Deliberative Practices*. Oxford: Oxford University Press.
42. Dryzek J.S. (2010) *Foundations and Frontiers of Deliberative Government*. Oxford: Oxford University Press.
43. Ibid.
44. Doyle, T. (2000) *Green Power: The Environment Movement in Australia*. Sydney: UNSW Press.

Intermezzo 7

45. Grin, J., H. van de Graaf et al. (2003) Een derde generatie milieubeleid: Een sociologisch perspectief en een beleidswetenschappelijk programma. *Beleidswetenschap* (1): 51-72.
46. Weale, A. (1992) *The New Politics of Pollution: Issues in Environmental Politics.* Manchester: Manchester University Press.
47. O'Neal, K. (1997) *Ecological Modernisation or Regulatory Convergence? Recent Trends in the Environmental Policies of the EU Member States.* Paper prepared for the Annual Meeting of the European Community Studies Association, Seattle, May 28 – June 1, 1997.

12. The Bubble of Societal Organisations

48. Casimir, G.J. and C.E. Dutilh (2003) Sustainability: A Gender Studies Perspective. *Int. Journal of Consumer Studies*, 27(4): 316-325.
49. Huijstee, M.M. van (2010) Business and NGOs in Interaction: A Quest for Corporate Social Responsibility. *Netherlands Geographical Studies* Vol. 393.
50. See: 'Limits to Collaboration [with NGOs]' at: www.iisd.org/business/ngo/limits.aspx
51. See: R. van Tulder, E.M. van Mil and R.A. Schilpzand (2004) *De Strategische stakeholderdialoog.* Rotterdam: Erasmus Universiteit.
52. Hajer, M. (2003) Policy without Polity? Policy Analysis and the Institutional Void. *Policy Sciences* 36(2):175-195.

Appendix: Tools

1. Brown, Juanita and David Isaacs (2005) *The World Café: Shaping Our Futures through Conversations that Matter.* San Francisco (CA): Berrett-Koehler Publishers.
2. Owen, H. (1997) *Open Space Technology, A User's Guide.* San Francisco (CA): Berrett-Koehler Publishers